Online Education FOR DUMMIES®

by Kevin Johnson and Susan Manning, EdD

Foreword by Jonathan Finkelstein

WILEY

Wiley Publishing, Inc.

Online Education For Dummies®

Published by
Wiley Publishing, Inc.
111 River St.
Hoboken, NJ 07030-5774
www.wiley.com

About the Authors

Kevin Johnson is the CEO of The Cutting Ed, Inc., a consulting company that specializes in helping clients envision education and training for the 21st century. He has more than 20 years' experience working in education and figuring out how to use technology to his advantage.

Kevin's start with technology began as a 14-year-old teaching himself to program. Completing his bachelor's degree at Eastern Illinois University and his master's at the University of Illinois, Kevin developed curriculum and taught in academic and corporate environments for the next 13 years. Due to his desire to save paper (not to mention not wanting to fight for the copy machine), he started providing lecture notes and other resources to students on CDs. As the Internet emerged, he began teaching Web development courses. It was a natural transition to move from burning CDs to placing course content on the Web. Before long, Kevin was interacting with his students electronically and his interest in online education began.

Kevin stays triple-busy pursuing his doctor of education degree in Instructional Technology and Distance Education. As you might guess, he is studying online!

Susan Manning is best known as a teacher's teacher. She develops faculty and prepares them to teach online. Susan teaches online courses for the University of Wisconsin-Stout and the University of Illinois' Illinois Online Network in online learning, instructional design, technology tools, the synchronous classroom, and group work online. She has taught hundreds of faculty, including international faculty from Saudi Arabia, Denmark, Vietnam, and Russia. Because Susan's teaching career began with adult students learning English as a second language, she continues to teach immigrants at Waubonsee Community College. These students remind her that basic human interaction and communication skills always trump technology.

Susan's online career began more than 10 years ago when she was asked to investigate the possibility of training literacy volunteers online. Knowing that she needed additional training and skills development, Susan became an online student and earned her certification as Master Online Teacher from the University of Illinois. Additionally, she holds a doctorate in Adult Education from Ball State University, a master's in College Student Personnel from Bowling Green State University, and a bachelor's degree in Communications from Truman State University.

Susan can be heard regularly on The LearningTimes GreenRoom podcast www.ltgreenroom.org, a series she co-hosts with friend Dan Balzer as they examine issues and topics related to learning.

Dedication

We would like to dedicate our first book to our families. We didn't get this far without good guidance from our parents and couldn't have worked through the development of this book without awesome support from our husbands and children.

Authors' Acknowledgments

We didn't write this alone! We first want to say thanks to the entire editorial staff at Wiley for making us sound so smart, especially Georgette Beatty, Erin Calligan Mooney, and Christy Pingleton. Georgette Beatty, you really should go into teaching because you have the patience and presence of a true educator. This was a wonderful learning experience for us. We also had help, encouragement, and insights from the following people (listed alphabetically):

Dan Balzer, a great friend with international appeal. Because he has lived in various corners of the globe, Dan was a natural to give us insights and ideas regarding international students and online education.

Eileen Cable, our technical reviewer, for her tireless review of our work. A librarian by trade, we bet she wanted to hide in the stacks with some of the chapters!

Virginia Fleming from Pennsylvania Leadership Charter School, who read and checked our information for accuracy and let us play with her in the virtual classroom so we could capture that wonderful screenshot in Chapter 16.

Christie Gilson, friend and Assistant Professor in the Education Department at Moravian College. We thank her for reading and providing input on accessibility issues specific to online education.

Kay Johnson and the others from Florida Virtual School who read for us and provided us insights concerning K-12 online education.

Diane Stegmeyer, Susan's friend and neighbor, who patiently stepped us through the admissions and registration processes from a variety of perspectives.

Joan Vandervelde, Online Professional Development at University of Wisconsin-Stout, who graciously read for us and provided insights for the K-12 portions.

Thanks to the following agencies and organizations that helped us with screenshots: Angel Course Management System, ASCD, Desire2Learn, EBSCO, Elluminate, Florida Virtual School, Nova Southeastern University, Pennsylvania Leadership Charter School, Skype, University of Illinois Global Campus, and University of Wisconsin-Stout.

Publisher's Acknowledgments

We're proud of this book; please send us your comments at http://dummies.custhelp.com. For other comments, please contact our Customer Care Department within the U.S. at 877-762-2974, outside the U.S. at 317-572-3993, or fax 317-572-4002. Some of the people who helped bring this book to market include the following:

Acquisitions, Editorial, and Media Development

Senior Project Editor: Georgette Beatty

Acquisitions Editor: Tracy Boggier

Copy Editor: Christine Pingleton

Assistant Editor: Erin Calligan Mooney

Editorial Program Coordinator: Joe Niesen

Technical Editor: Eileen Cable

Editorial Manager: Michelle Hacker

Editorial Assistant: Jennette ElNaggar

Cover Photo: iStock

Cartoons: Rich Tennant (www.the5thwave.com)

Composition Services

Project Coordinator: Katherine Crocker

Layout and Graphics: Ashley Chamberlain, Timothy Detrick, Joyce Haughey, Melissa K. Jester, Christine Williams

Proofreader: Evelyn C. Gibson

Indexer: Valerie Haynes Perry

Special Help
Victoria M. Adang

Publishing and Editorial for Consumer Dummies

    Diane Graves Steele, Vice President and Publisher, Consumer Dummies

    Kristin Ferguson-Wagstaffe, Product Development Director, Consumer Dummies

    Ensley Eikenburg, Associate Publisher, Travel

    Kelly Regan, Editorial Director, Travel

Publishing for Technology Dummies

    Andy Cummings, Vice President and Publisher, Dummies Technology/General User

Composition Services

    Debbie Stailey, Director of Composition Services

Contents at a Glance

Table of Contents

Foreword

We are all already learners. We learn in all kinds of ways, and we learn every day in ways large and small. Whether we are in conversation with colleagues, friends, or family; reading or watching the news; attending a seminar or meeting; or stopping to ask someone for directions; we are absorbing and processing new information.

And if you are one of the many people who access the Web as part of your regular routine to search, shop, socialize, or send messages, you're already learning online.

The leap from here to the more formal world of online education — engaging in online classes, pursuing a degree online, or continuing one's education in a virtual classroom — is not very large, but it does help to understand the landscape; to be prepared mentally, emotionally, and technologically; and to make some good decisions.

In the course of my day facilitating online learning programs, one element always emerges as a key indicator of the success of the online experience: the motivation of the learner. As learners, we need to understand why we're engaging in the process, why it matters to us, and what outcomes we hope for and expect. If you are reading this, you are probably already quite motivated. You are taking steps to continue your formal education and to enhance your life in ways that matter most to you.

The other main ingredient of successful online learning experiences is a humanely designed, appropriately stimulating, instructionally sound, and well-supported online program offering. It's not always obvious when peering in from the outside whether you have found such a program, which is why some guidance from the likes of the professionals who wrote *Online Education For Dummies* is so handy.

When I first started helping others move their instruction and learning online, I often was greeted with doubts that Web-based learning could be "as good as" face-to-face experiences. I don't know about you, but not every in-person class I took deserved a trophy. Thankfully, there is now ample evidence — much of it in the form of success stories from alumni — that online learning experiences can be even better than offline equivalents. With strong learner motivation and good design, facilitation, and support, any learning program can be great.

Everyone has his or her own learning style. My own personal preference when it comes to learning online is for approaches that feature knowledgeable, authentic, and supportive guides who accompany the learner through new or unfamiliar terrain. That is exactly what you have in *Online Education For Dummies*. Enjoy your journey.

Jonathan Finkelstein
Founder, LearningTimes.net
Author, *Learning in Real Time*

Introduction

- -

*A*ccording to a report published by the Alfred P. Sloan Foundation in 2008, nearly one in five college students experienced some sort of Web-based instruction. That's a lot of students learning online! And, considering that college is no longer limited to advantaged 18- to 22-year-olds, that means a lot of those online students may be older and less familiar with the tools that come with the territory. That's why we've written this book — for the many learners who find themselves in school, online, and confused.

The ups and downs of the global economy have sent more learners back to school to retool or add credentials to their resume. However, balancing work, family, civic commitments, and school is an arduous task at best. Online education allows learners to address their professional development needs at a time and in a manner that may be more flexible with their lifestyles. This may be part of the reason that online enrollments have mushroomed over the past few years.

Five years ago when we tried to explain to people that we taught college courses online, we were met with, "How does that work?" Today, we hear stories of family members or colleagues taking courses online, but many questions still remain. There's a bit of controversy, too, in that students may not have a choice but to take a course online, and too often they are left to flounder with inadequate guidance from advisors and faculty.

Regardless of age or experience, students who know what they want and are willing to work hard are the ultimate winners in the world of education. *Online Education For Dummies* helps students become winners in the online classroom by explaining just how it works. We take you from the decision-making process of determining whether this venue is right for you, through applying and enrolling, to the skills you need to succeed.

About This Book

Online Education For Dummies is not a highly academic book written for scholars. It's a book for everyday students who find themselves faced with online possibilities. You can trust this book when you need to quickly understand something about online education. Consider these examples:

✔ If you're a working professional who needs to earn an additional degree or certification for career advancement, we can show you how to put together your application materials and get started in a program.

✔ If you want to go to school full-time but don't have the funding, we can tell you who to talk to regarding financial aid.

✔ If you want to take online courses but are unfamiliar with the technology involved, we can walk you through the kinds of tools you'll use to support classroom discussion and submit your assignments.

✔ If you're a high school student thinking about non-traditional schooling, we can give you the information you need. We also cover students with disabilities and international students.

Depending on who you are and what you need in terms of online education, you can easily skip around this book to find exactly what you need. (But don't worry — we won't complain if you want to read it from cover to cover!)

Conventions Used in This Book

We use several standard conventions throughout this book:

✔ New terms are *italicized*. We try to use as little jargon as possible, but because online education utilizes some slightly new vocabulary, some terms are unavoidable. Italicized words are followed by definitions in layman's terms. (We also italicize any words we want to emphasize.)

✔ Key words in bulleted and numbered lists are **bold**, so you know what's most important.

✔ You'll see a lot of Web addresses in `monofont`; how could you not when we're talking about *online* education? Also keep in mind that when this book was printed, some Web addresses may have needed to break across two lines of text. If that happened, rest assured that we haven't put in any extra characters (such as hyphens) to indicate the break. So, when using one of these Web addresses, just type in exactly what you see in this book, pretending the line break doesn't exist.

✔ We've alternated the use of gender-related pronouns throughout the book (with no preferential treatment intended). That's because teachers and students come in both varieties!

What You're Not to Read

Of course, our egos hope that you read and digest every word. But, the realists in us know that you're busy and might want to read only the essential material. So, if you need to skip a few things due to time, here are a few suggestions:

✔ Sidebars (in shaded gray boxes) contain information that is interesting but not critical to understanding online education. You can skip these boxes, especially if you understand the context of the surrounding material.

✔ We use the Technical Stuff icon for any topic that may require a little more explanation as to what it is and how it works. However, providing an understanding of technical details isn't the purpose of this book. Therefore, paragraphs marked with this icon can be skimmed over quickly or skipped entirely if you prefer.

Foolish Assumptions

As a way of helping us focus on what to write, we made several assumptions about you, dear reader, when writing this book:

✔ **You know how to use a computer for the basics.** We hope this is true about you. If it isn't true, perhaps you'll want to skim Chapter 3 and then decide whether online education is really for you.

✔ **You're considering going back to school and are leisurely looking at alternatives.** Maybe you're curious about how online education works and want to get a sense before you select a school or program. In that case, you have plenty of time and may read the book cover to cover.

✔ **You know what you want to study.** We know that not everybody knows exactly what they want to study or what career they want to have upon graduation. We've done our best to speak to those who want to participate in a full-fledged online program as well as those who want to explore options and possibly only take one or two classes total.

✔ **You're faced with an online course, have no idea what you're in for, and need the information quickly!** This is where the majority of online students find themselves the first time. If you're already enrolled, you may want to jump right to Part III and learn what you need to excel.

✔ **You're an online instructor (or thinking about becoming one) and are curious about the various ways in which online courses are structured and how students and staff interact in cyberspace.** This book can help you see online education from the student's perspective, and it may inspire you to try a new idea or two. Heck, it may even inspire you to consider taking an online course as a way of growing professionally.

✔ **You're an online instructor and you need your students to be better prepared for taking online courses.** Perhaps your students are coming to your virtual classroom unprepared, with false expectations about online learning. In this case, consider recommending this book to your school bookstore to help your future students get settled into your online course quicker.

How This Book Is Organized

Online Education For Dummies is organized in five parts. The parts are organized so that you can start by looking at the big picture of online education, and then walk through the decision-making and application processes, get into courses and succeed, and ultimately move out of the educational realm to apply your newfound skills and knowledge.

Part I: Introducing a Different Kind of Classroom

In this part we give you the basic landscape of online education. In particular, we discuss what you may need to consider about online education to see whether this is truly a fit for you. In addition, we give you an overview of the technological competencies you should have before taking an online course.

Part II: Preparing to Be a Student

If you haven't gone to school in the past ten years, you're in for a surprise! Almost everything is online, from course catalogs to applications to live advisors. This part walks you through the processes you need to follow to select an appropriate program or course, apply, register, and enroll.

Part III: The Virtual Classroom: Being an A+ Student

This part is where we talk about the specifics of how online courses work. Drawing from years of helping new students get acclimated to online courses, we take you through the common activities and processes you need to know as an online student. This includes communication skills, identifying important documents and resources in a course, and understanding your role and tasks as a student. Even if you've taken an online course previously, you may be surprised at the details we address.

Part IV: Special Considerations in Online Education

One of the truisms about online education is that it offers more educational possibilities for students who may not have access to a more traditional educational system. This includes younger students (those in kindergarten through high school), international students outside the United States, and students with disabilities. Online classrooms are diverse, and we address special needs in this part of the book.

Part V: The Part of Tens

Every *For Dummies* book concludes with a short summary of key information and tips. In our Part of Tens, we have included ten myths about online education and ten top online schools.

Icons Used in This Book

As is customary in any *For Dummies* book, we've used a few standard icons. Here's what the symbols mean and how you should interpret them.

Any information marked with this icon is worth remembering and taking away from this book.

We use this icon when we feel the need to provide more background information on a topic — material that's interesting, but not essential to your understanding.

We use this icon to mark strategies and techniques we've learned from being online students ourselves or from our former students.

This icon denotes things you should be cautious of. Taking note of this info can help you avoid unnecessary headaches.

Where to Go from Here

We understand that your situation is specific to you and that you may not necessarily need the same information as other readers. Feel free to look over the table of contents and decide what chapter might best meet your needs. Our recommendation is that if you're brand new to the idea of online education, flip to Chapter 1 for an introduction and move through the book sequentially. If you're already taking an online course, head to Part III for pointers on succeeding in your class.

We truly hope that you not only enjoy reading the book, but that it also helps you make some very important decisions, provides you with the right questions to ask on your academic journey, and better prepares you for your online adventures.

As educators, we encourage our students to provide us with feedback on how we're doing. We encourage you to do the same. Please submit suggestions to authors@thecuttinged.com. Your suggestions could help us update future versions of the book to ensure that future readers are even better prepared for taking online classes.

We wish you luck in your online journey and prosperity in your future careers and academic adventures.

Part I
Introducing a Different Kind of Classroom

The 5th Wave   By Rich Tennant

"It was the hardware requirement for my online bartending class."

In this part . . .

*1*f you're considering the possibility of taking an online course but really have no idea what that means, we can help. In this part, we give you the basic landscape of online education. We explain the different kinds of online courses out there and introduce you to some of the benefits of online education. We also address the dark side and a couple of the potential pitfalls of online education.

Because it's natural to question whether online education is right for you, we describe the kinds of personal qualities and attitudes that online students need to succeed. Finally, we overview the kinds of technological competencies you should have before taking an online course. By the time you finish this part, you'll know where you fit in the world of online education!

Chapter 1

Heading Online for Your Education

. . . .

In This Chapter

▶ Seeing what online education is all about

▶ Walking through the process of becoming an online student

▶ Finding out what it takes to succeed in online classes

▶ Looking at special populations that may benefit from online courses

. . . .

*H*ello, and welcome to the world of online education. We are very excited that you picked up this book to help you understand online education and what it takes to succeed in the online classroom. In this book, we explore the ins and outs of online education. We share personal stories from both instructor and student perspectives as a way of helping you understand what is expected of students and the sometimes false expectations of new online students.

You may have some specific questions about online education. For example:

✔ What is online education, and how does it differ from the traditional face-to-face classroom?

✔ What institutions offer online programs/courses and how do I find them?

✔ What type of computer and technological skills do I need to take an online class?

✔ What kind of work will I be expected to do, how will I complete that work, and how will I be graded?

✔ What resources are available if I need help?

Our hope is that we have created a resource that answers these questions and more in order to help you succeed as an online student. In this chapter, you begin your journey into the virtual world of online education.

Examining the Characteristics and Advantages of Online Education

Online education is about connecting the student to educational materials by way of the Internet. Online education combines a student (you), a curriculum (determined by the school or instructor), and an Internet connection. In this section, we introduce a few traits and advantages of online education; we cover both topics in more detail in Chapter 2.

The nature of online education

The information for an online course and the way in which you prove that you are learning may vary widely. A few common formats include

- ✔ **Reading material, engaging in online discussions with your classmates, and then submitting papers or projects at the end of the term.** This is probably the most common design. You complete the work when it's convenient for you, but within the guidelines established by the instructor. For instance, if he says you need to post discussions by Monday at midnight, you can work through the weekend and get your ideas on the board before you begin your work week. These courses are often facilitated by an instructor (they're referred to as *instructor-led*) who not only shares his expertise in the field, but helps guide you through the entire online learning process.

- ✔ **Reading material and then taking a test.** This is our least favorite method, and many students find it horribly dull. However, for some subjects, you can zip through the basic background information quickly and move on. You typically have very little interaction with your peers. As a matter of fact, in some *self-paced* courses, you have no interaction with peers and little interaction with the instructor.

- ✔ **Reading materials, logging into a real-time Web conference, and listening to the instructor or interacting with peers.** You take a test or submit papers later to demonstrate your understanding. This synchronous (real-time) method of online education is becoming more popular, but it requires you to adjust your schedule to accommodate the class, just as you would a traditional class. These courses are also instructor-led, but sometimes include peer presentations as well.

In Chapter 2 we provide more examples of how the nature of online education is unique. However, we want to emphasize an attitudinal shift in online education: The learner (you!) must assume responsibility for learning the material. There's no cyber-prof in the room to nag you or tell you when it's time to log in. Of course, wonderfully encouraging and compassionate faculty want to see you succeed and communicate with you regularly to keep you engaged, but the nature of online education requires the student to take charge and complete the work.

So what kind of student thrives in this kind of educational landscape?

- **A student who needs flexibility in when courses are offered:** If you don't have a free moment until 11 p.m. because of competing life demands, but you really want to learn, an online course you can complete at 1 a.m. may work. (We hope you get to sleep in until later in the morning!)

- **A student who comfortably sets his own agenda and manages his time well:** If you're good at crafting a plan and sticking to it, online education may be for you. While the instructor may provide a schedule and deadlines for assignments, you have to work them into your lifestyle.

- **A student with strong reading and writing skills:** Because much of what you need to know comes through textbooks or Web pages, you need to be a decent reader prior to taking an online course. In addition, the way you show that you know the material requires writing summaries and short essays. Clear, concise written communication skills earn students A's.

- **A student who's comfortable with technology:** Later in this chapter we say more about this topic, but the bottom line is that an online course requires familiarity with your computer. This isn't the place to learn *about* the computer.

A few pros of online education

Online courses have been steadily growing in popularity for the last few years. Here are just a few reasons why online education is so popular:

- **You can work around your schedule.** Who isn't triple-scheduled these days with demands of work, family, and community? Few of us have large blocks of time available for classes, but we may have an hour here or there. With an online course, you can log in and work when it fits into your schedule. You may find that studying for an hour first thing in the morning or over your lunch break is just what you need to get you back into the academic groove.

- **You can save time and money by not having to commute to school.** Even if your local college is 5 miles from your home, the process of packing up your gear, getting to the school, finding parking, and walking to the classroom takes thirty minutes. Save the gas money and time, and study from home!

✓ **In some cases, courses are accelerated and you complete the degree or program sooner.** A mixed blessing, many online programs have accelerated a traditional semester-long course into eight weeks. While you may only take one course at a time (two per semester), these courses move fast! The good news is that these kinds of programs typically run year-round and get students through degrees and certificate programs faster than they would otherwise. (Flip to Chapter 4 for more information on accelerated classes.)

✓ **Some of the pettiness and bias in traditional classes gets left behind in the online world.** No one knows whether you are shy, speak with a lisp, or have multiple tattoos when you're an online student. What others care about are your ideas and how you communicate these ideas about the course material. Many students find this liberating.

Knowing the Technology and Computer Skills You Need to Succeed

Many non-traditional or adult students shy away from online education because they're afraid their computer skills aren't good enough or they worry that they need a state-of-the-art computer. Don't let these thoughts scare you away from reaching your academic goals. Most institutions provide technological support and detailed lists of hardware, software, and competency requirements. Family, friends, and your local library also can serve as great backups when technology breaks or your Internet access is lost.

Don't get us wrong though: A few minimum requirements must be met to adequately learn online. Chapter 3 describes the technology you need and all the skills necessary to be an online student. In short, students taking online courses should have access to the following basic hardware and software:

✓ A computer with monitor, keyboard, and mouse

✓ Access to a reliable Internet connection

✓ A Web browser (for example, Internet Explorer, FireFox, or Safari)

✓ A printer

✓ Speakers, microphone, or a headset with microphone (optional, but may be required by some programs)

✓ Word-processing software

✓ Presentation software such as PowerPoint or Keynote

Additionally, you should be able to handle the following basic tasks before taking an online course:

- Opening your Internet browser and navigating to a given Web-site address (URL)

- Sending and receiving e-mails with attachments

- Opening a word-processing application and formatting, saving, and retrieving documents

- Reading and scrolling Web pages efficiently

- Typing quickly and accurately

- Organizing folders on your computer's hard drive or an external flash drive

- Downloading and installing software

- Running virus protection software

Seeing How to Go About Becoming an Online Student

After you have an idea of what may be involved in online education, as well as the technological competencies you need, you can turn your attention to finding the right program and school and getting your seat in the class. You also need to know the process for applying to a school and how you can get ready for class. We introduce the basics in this section.

Finding available courses

We assume you know what you want to study — for instance, you know whether you want art history or business administration. That said, do you want to take a course or two, or do you need a degree or certificate? We ask this question because it influences how you go about finding an online course. Setting your sights on a degree means investing more time and money in the learning process. If you're like most people, the stakes seem a little higher when money is mentioned, and you want to make the best decision.

Here are a few possibilities, and you may want to explore all three:

- **If all you need is a course or two in one area, check with your local two-year school.** Many two-year colleges offer online courses at a fraction of the cost of traditional four-year institutions.

✔ **If you're looking for a graduate-level course in your professional area, go back to where you earned your undergraduate degree and see whether they offer online courses.** You already have a relationship with the institution, and you may find the application and admission processes are streamlined.

✔ **Use a standard search engine to explore the possibilities through major online institutions.** We list ten top online schools in Chapter 20. Chances are very good that one of them can serve your needs. Just be prepared to receive solicitations the minute you submit a Web-based form asking for more information!

Jump to Chapter 4 for a more detailed explanation of the process of finding the courses and programs available online.

Evaluating schools

Regardless of whether you want one course or a degree program, you must select a school that is respected and accredited. Don't sink your money into a diploma mill that teaches nothing and wastes your time. In Chapter 5 we detail how to determine a school's accreditation, but we can tell you up front that *it should be obvious.* When you visit the Web site for the school or review its printed material, you should see accreditation credentials listed.

After accreditation, you may want to consider other factors when you evaluate online schools (see Chapter 5 for more details and lists of questions to ask academic advisors, instructors, and other students):

✔ **General style of the courses:** Are these self-paced courses where you read and take tests, or do they engage the learner in discussions and active participation? You need to find a course that meets your expectations of what learning should be ideally. Also, consider whether you will work on your own schedule or whether your courses are scheduled with real-time meetings conducted via Web conferencing.

✔ **Class size:** How many students does the school squeeze into the virtual classroom? If you're one of 20, that's a great ratio. If you're one of 50, expect the instructor to be harried and the quality of your interaction to be markedly different.

✔ **Completion and retention rates:** This is a very telling statistic. How many students actually complete the courses or degrees? If only 20 percent of starters get to the finish line, the courses may be poorly designed, too difficult, too boring . . . you get the picture. This is an area worth exploring with a counselor or advisor.

✔ **Faculty background and training:** Who teaches at this school? What kinds of credentials do they possess, including technology training? Surprisingly, you don't need to consider whether the faculty are full-time or part-time, because many online faculty are actually subject-matter experts with impressive professional credentials in their disciplines. The most critical issue is whether they know what they're doing when teaching online.

✔ **Student support services available:** Who is going to help you get registered, select the right courses in the right sequence, figure out the technology, and so on? What if you need accommodation for a disability? Quality schools and programs address these student services from the beginning; you know you have a whole team behind you.

Applying to school and getting the money you need

If you're an adult learner, you may remember the lengthy college application process where you filled in forms, wrote an essay, took exams, and so on. Your high school guidance counselor probably walked you through the steps. Some of that process is the same online, just Web-based. Other processes are slightly different. For example, you may not need entrance exams like ACTs and SATs. Transcripts can be sent electronically.

Chapter 6 provides an overview of the whole process. It may surprise you that applying to an online school and then following through with registration still involves a guidance counselor of sorts. In the digital world, this usually involves continual communication with a representative from the school. For example, if you need to know more about a program, you may be asked to fill in a Web-based form. That form generates a phone call, and you quickly have a personal counselor or advisor working with you.

Not only do you have to think about the application process, but you also have to consider the cost of classes. College isn't cheap. However, just as you may consider financial aid for traditional courses, you should explore this area for online programs (see Chapter 6). Your financial options may include

✔ **Scholarships based on academics, demographics, or some other criterion.** These do not have to be paid back.

✔ **Grants awarded by the federal government based on financial need.** To qualify, you must first complete the same financial aid paperwork as all other students, available at `www.fafsa.ed.gov/`

✔ **Loans, either through the government or private lenders.** When you need to pay these back and at what interest rate depends on the lender.

Are online courses less expensive than traditional on-ground courses? Yes, probably. Tuition may be the same, but you save money by not having to pay transportation costs. Other expenses, such as child care, may or may not affect you. For example, one parent may be able to study while children nap or do their own homework; another may need childcare to keep a busy toddler occupied so he can focus on schoolwork.

If you study more than part-time at a regionally accredited institution that receives federal financial aid, you may be eligible for assistance. You have to be part of a degree or certificate program, however. Check with the school for the details of what may be available, as well as its process. This is where selecting a school with a full suite of student services pays off, literally.

Getting accepted and getting ready for class

After you've applied to an institution, your application and supplemental materials (transcripts, letters of reference, and personal statements) are reviewed by the institution. Of course, being the smarty that you are, you're accepted. You receive notice of your acceptance via e-mail; however, some institutions follow up with a more formal acceptance letter via standard U.S. mail. If for any reason you're not accepted, don't panic. Would-be students may not be accepted for any of several reasons, many of which are merely administrative. In Chapter 7 we discuss in more detail what to do once you're accepted and strategies for moving forward if your application is rejected.

Once you are accepted, you must enroll in courses. This process is also completed using the Web. Most institutions, even those teaching face-to-face, require students to log on to a Web site where they access the institution's course catalog and register for desired classes. These sites also provide you with a list of the required textbooks chosen for each class. If you don't know which class or classes you should take first or in what order you should take them, contact your academic advisor to work out these details.

Imagine that you're in between registering and actually starting class. What's left to do? Get oriented! Any decent school will provide you with an orientation experience. This may be a series of prerecorded tutorials to guide you through common technology processes. Or, it may be an invitation to attend a live Webinar to see and experience the same. Orientation in its simplest form may consist of you receiving a document with printed procedures. See Chapter 7 for full details.

Being a Star Student

After you register for classes, it's time to begin learning. This can be a little nerve-wracking, especially if you haven't been in school for awhile. However, like most things in life, a little preparation goes a long way. We help you with the basics in this section.

Making your way around your classroom

To really succeed in the online classroom, it helps to be prepared and take the necessary time to become familiar with your classroom. In many cases, institutions will even open your virtual classroom one or two days before classes officially begin. Be sure to take advantage of this opportunity by logging into your course and becoming familiar with the following aspects:

- ✔ General course structure
- ✔ Instructor announcements
- ✔ Instructor contact information
- ✔ Syllabus
- ✔ Calendar
- ✔ Course policies (including grading)

Flip to Chapter 8 for plenty of help with navigating your classroom.

Meeting the instructor, fellow students, and other important folks

You may think you're alone on your academic journey just because you're not physically in the same room or building as your instructor and classmates. Nothing could be further from the truth. As a matter of fact, some of our students have shared with us that they feel more connected to their online peers than they feel about the people they work with on a daily basis.

When taking online courses, you have a plethora of academic and technical support. Not only do you have your instructor and peers, but most institutions also connect you with academic advisors, technical support staff, guest speakers, and more. Check out Chapter 9 for more information on meeting all the people in and around your classroom.

If you ever do feel alone, don't hesitate to reach out. One way to stay connected to peers is to form a virtual study group that meets synchronously each week to discuss course content and upcoming assignments. You can do this through several free online tools like Google Chat or Skype.

Communicating with clarity

Though you may have opportunities to communicate with your instructors and peers via voice and/or video, most communication occurs in text. Therefore, communicating clearly, concisely, and respectfully in writing is important.

Online courses utilize two standards of writing: formal and casual. Being able to follow the instructor's cue and write according to the standard of each particular course is important. For the most part, though, initial discussion posts and assignments use formal writing skills, whereas responses to peers, questions, and cyber-lounge posts are much more conversational.

Chapter 10 has full details on how to communicate clearly online.

Strengthening your study habits

With freedom comes responsibility. This statement couldn't be more true when it comes to developing good online study habits. As an online student, you have more freedom to choose the days and times that you study and complete assignments. This may sound great until family and friends want to go see the latest action film or your child begs you to read his favorite book for the 400th time. Developing a strict schedule for studying is important in order to keep up with readings and assignments.

Not only is it helpful to have a set schedule for studying, but you also need to establish efficient and effective study skills to maximize productivity. Looking for patterns within your course schedule, bookmarking important sites such as the library, and writing initial posts offline are all things you can do to use your time more efficiently. Flip to Chapter 11 for information on developing good study habits for online classes.

Working well in a group

Yep, you read correctly: group work. The fact that your instructor and peers aren't in your geographical location doesn't get you out of completing group assignments. Research shows that working in groups is tremendously beneficial, and being able to do it in an online setting takes skills, patience, and a lot of communication.

As with any group-based task, there are a few things you can do to help make group work more efficient and effective (as you find out in Chapter 12):

✔ Communicate as soon as possible and as often as possible.

✔ Summarize the project, and break it into manageable tasks.

✔ Delegate tasks to group members.

✔ Establish roles.

✔ Document progress.

Most conflicts among group members are about one or more members of the group not doing their share. Documenting progress, or lack thereof, and keeping your instructor in the loop helps keep each member accountable and helps your instructor better facilitate conflict resolution when necessary.

Understanding online manners and ethics

One problem with communicating mostly by text is that anyone can misinterpret what is written. Therefore, you should keep humor to a minimum and avoid posting questionable content. You also need to recognize when and where to address individuals when problems do arise, including your instructor. For example, have you ever been in a face-to-face course when someone inappropriately questioned an instructor? In most cases the instructor wins, and the student ends up looking like a fool. The same is true in the online environment. If you need to question your instructor or another peer, post the question or concern privately and respectfully. In return, your instructor should also communicate concerns privately, along with other personal information such as your grade and assignment comments.

Part of being respectful and honest is posting original content and giving credit where credit is due when posting someone else's work. You should cite sources in formal assignments and in everything you post, e-mail, or present. If the idea isn't yours, cite it! If you have a question as to whether or not to cite something, or you're unfamiliar with the proper way to cite sources, ask your instructor or a librarian. We discuss this topic and others related to ethical behavior in Chapter 13.

Institutions often provide instructors with tools to check assignments for originality. These tools include comparing your assignments to a database of other assignments, Web content, and dissertations. Know your institution's guidelines for quoting/citing sources and developing original work. Some schools consider repurposing an assignment from one class for another plagiarism. The penalties for plagiarism can be quite severe, including removal from a program. Again, if you have a question about whether or not you can do something, ask. Don't assume.

Completing and turning in assignments

Some people believe that when you take an online class you simply read something and then take a test. This is partially true, but not as prevalent as you may think. Online instructors use a variety of assessment techniques to determine your level of understanding. As an online student, you may be asked to answer questions about the readings, write an essay that analyzes and evaluates research, give an oral presentation, or create a project to share with the class. All of these are formal assessment techniques that require you to create something in a scholarly manner with proper citation and style formatting, depending on your instructor's directions.

How you submit each type of assignment can also differ. You may be asked to post your assignment in a public discussion forum for others to read and respond to. Alternately, you may be asked to submit your work via a private, virtual drop-box that only the instructor has access to. Other types of submission methods exist, too. The method for submission depends on the assignment, the purpose of the assignment, and your instructor's preference. Most online classes use a variety of submission methods.

We discuss how to finish and submit different types of assignments in detail in Chapter 14.

Transitioning after you're done with school

Many students go to school to either start a new career or to get a promotion at their current job upon graduating. Reminding yourself why you're going to school and tracking your progress can help you stay on track and prepare for that transition. Some degree programs require students to develop and maintain an electronic portfolio, also known as an ePortfolio. Think of this as an electronic resume that allows invited visitors to see your academic/work history, example assignments, and other pertinent information. Find out more about this and other topics related to transitioning in Chapter 15.

Looking at a Few Special Situations in Online Education

Online education opens access for learners who struggle in other contexts. In this section, we show how certain groups of students can be served through online courses. We begin with a discussion of where the youngest group, homeschooled and high school students, fit in, and then move to international students and those with disabilities.

Students in kindergarten through high school

Sometimes young learners want or need a different structure for learning than traditional schools offer. This includes kids who fall into these broad categories (among others):

- ✔ **Child actors and athletes who need to travel:** Whereas these kids used to have private tutors, now they can stay on top of coursework by enrolling in online schools.

- ✔ **Kids who live in areas where the schools can't offer advanced or specialized courses:** This describes a good number of rural communities. Online courses can fill in the gaps.

- ✔ **Learners hoping to avoid some of the high school influences of drugs or gangs:** Online students can focus on the academics.

- ✔ **Students who fail a class and jeopardize graduating on time:** The process of making up coursework used to mean summer school; now it includes online courses.

In many cases, states support online education for kids in kindergarten through high school via charter schools. Students within the state can take online courses to supplement or augment traditional curricula. Or, they may choose to forego traditional education altogether and take online courses exclusively. In Chapter 16, we discuss online education for kids of all ages, including how it differs from online education for adults, the variety of online schools available for kids, and the K-12 enrollment process.

Students from abroad

The Internet blurs geopolitical borders by allowing people to communicate with anyone around the globe. This benefits students from every country in the world as they enroll in online courses offered through schools based in the United States. The resulting international diversity enriches the academic experience for everyone involved.

Why would someone in another country want to take an online course from the United States? Here are just a few reasons:

- ✔ The United States has a reputation for excellence in higher education, but studying here is very expensive. Online education erases one of the expenses by removing the hassle of relocating to the United States.

✔ International students, like their U.S. counterparts, can balance work and family with school easier if they stay in their home countries with their established support systems (family, babysitters, church, and so forth). Earning the same degree online often means higher wages and improved lifestyles for international students, without the resulting costs of moving.

✔ Finally, international students don't have to apply for student visas if they study online. No political issues are involved!

One possible downside to studying online as an international student at an online school based in the United States may be the issue of English. Because online courses demand strong reading and writing skills, students whose first language isn't English may struggle with courses from a U.S.-based school.

We talk about online education for students outside the United States in detail in Chapter 17.

Students with disabilities

Online classes provide a great alternative educational opportunity for students with disabilities. People with physical disabilities can avoid the hassle of getting to campus and navigating the physical classroom. For students with learning disabilities, technology can assist in activities such as prolonging test times and spell-checking documents. However, depending on a person's specific impairment and the institution's knowledge regarding the creation of accessible content, online education may still present some difficulties.

State and federal laws continue to be created that require public institutions to develop all materials in an accessible manner. However, not all those responsible for creating online courses are aware of these regulations or trained on how to implement the guidelines. Therefore, Web sites, course management systems, and course content can sometimes lack design structures that meet accessibility standards. In Chapter 18, we provide a list of questions you can ask to help determine whether an institution is prepared to accommodate your learning needs.

The law provides students with disabilities rights to equal access to information in a comparable format to their peers who are without a disability. However, with this right comes responsibility. In order to receive appropriate and reasonable accommodations, students must voluntarily disclose and document their impairment before accommodations will be made. Accommodations are based on each individual's needs and are usually determined with the help of the institutions' disability services department staff. Find out more about this process in Chapter 18.

Chapter 2

The Traits and Benefits of Online Education

In This Chapter

▶ Comparing online education to its traditional counterpart

▶ Looking at who's learning online

▶ Watching out for a few potential disadvantages

▶ Considering the traits you need to succeed

Ask almost anyone in the civilized world to describe school, and they will probably tell you about a physical place — a shelter with a roof, desks, and chairs — along with people who assume specific roles like teacher or student. The teacher decides what is to be taught, passes on the information to students, and awards scores to indicate their progress. The students sit attentively, do the work prescribed by the teacher, and perform tasks or take tests that measure how much they've achieved. That's the old-fashioned model of a school, one that is familiar to most people. Even a one-room Amish schoolhouse fits that description.

Online education is nothing like that! In this chapter, we sort through what makes the online experience different from traditional education. Looking at who is learning online and what they're getting from the experience, along with doing some honest self-assessment, may help you determine whether this type of education is right for you.

What Makes Online Education Different from Traditional Education?

You may find it hard to remember life without the Internet, but it hasn't been that long since the only choices for learning were attending a traditional school or taking correspondence classes by mail. In response to an increasing demand for alternatives, some colleges began offering classes in the evenings or on weekends to accommodate working adults, but their format remained similar to the one we'd known for a century. All that changed when the Internet became available to everyone! In this section, we compare the traditional school setting to the world of online education.

Connecting to coursework and people via the Internet

Online education is about connecting the student to educational materials by way of the Internet. As we show you throughout this book, online education can happen in a variety of forms and fashions, but the underlying use of the Internet and its technologies are fundamental. Lessons, communication, and assessment (grading) all happen by way of the World Wide Web. In the following sections, we describe the two major models for this communication and assessment: instructor-led and self-paced.

You're not alone: Instructor-led and -facilitated courses

The most common model of online education is instructor-led or instructor-facilitated. That means there is an instructor who determines the content and pace of the instruction. In a sense, this is really no different from a traditional classroom experience. In a quality online course, you interact frequently with that instructor, either privately through e-mail or publicly in discussion areas, just as you would have open discussions in a traditional classroom or private conversations on the side. We talk more specifically about how online discussion works in Chapter 10.

Sometimes online teachers are known as facilitators. In contrast to what you may think of as traditional education with a professor lecturing and students soaking up the information, a facilitator provides resources for students to consider, and then facilitates their understanding through a series of discussions or activities. Although facilitation happens in traditional classrooms too, it takes on a special significance in online education. Typically, instructor-led courses require students to interact with one another and everyone follows the same schedule, so they're always aware that others are taking the course with them. We explain more about who you're likely to find in your online classroom in Chapter 9.

In most cases, instructors are present in the online environment just as they are in a traditional one. However, what they do with their time in the environment might be a little different than what you would expect an instructor to do in a traditional classroom. Instead of lecturing, the instructor might post a series of narrated slides she created. Or, she might draw out additional responses in discussion instead of telling the class the answers.

Okay, sometimes you're alone: Self-paced courses

Another prevalent model of online education is self-paced. That means computer-based instruction is delivered to you without an instructor attached. You access the lessons, follow the instructions, and return the required products, for example, a completed test on the material demonstrating your understanding. A computer scores the test. You work through this at your own pace with no intervention or guidance from a teacher, and you have no way of knowing whether other students are even in the class with you. You could be the only student or one of a thousand.

In the business world, self-paced learning is the most common form of online education. A lot of corporate training is delivered through Web-based programs that look similar to PowerPoint slides, sometimes with audio or video attached. At the end of the presentation, you typically find a self-test worked into the program. As the student, you make the decisions and control the pace of the instruction with a simple click of the mouse.

Here's an example: At one time, state employees were required to complete ethics training that was delivered online. Some employees completed the training in 20 minutes whereas others needed two hours, depending on how fast they read and how comfortable they were with technology. The program summarized basic information about state laws regarding campaigning, accepting gifts, and so on. Then the employees were instructed to consider different scenarios and select the most ethical responses. The results were stored, and each employee received a compliance certificate.

Can you imagine the cost of calling together all employees to complete the same training in classrooms? Not only would time be lost on the job, but facilities would need to be considered, and travel time could possibly be involved. The self-paced model was much less costly.

The roots of distance education

You may be curious as to the origins of distance education. Online education is just an extension of what began in 1728 when Caleb Phillips started selling shorthand lessons in the *Boston Gazette*. In the United States, as soon as the postal service was up and running, schools such as Chautauqua College of Liberal Arts of New York and the International Correspondence School proffered correspondence lessons, the old-fashioned version of self-paced learning. Meanwhile in Europe, the University of London was the first to offer distance learning degrees in 1858. Learning anytime and any place is not new!

In a self-paced course, you work at your own pace with little or no instructor input. In an instructor-led course, you follow an established schedule and interact with the other students and the instructor.

Working when it's convenient

In our opinion, this is one of the best features of online education: You get to work when it's convenient for you. Say you're a supervisor assigned to the third shift, and you work from 11 p.m. to 7 a.m. You may be able to squeeze in a morning class, but chances are your biorhythms put you in a groggy state after work. You could sleep a little and then wake up and take a night class before your shift, but then when are you going to do your homework? And, what about tomorrow night when your son has a Little League game? Wouldn't it be great to work your course around your schedule? In many cases, online education can accommodate your personal schedule. In the following sections, we define two types of timing for online courses: asynchronous learning and real-time (synchronous) learning.

Asynchronous learning

One of the most common questions related to online education is "When do classes meet?" To answer that, you have to understand the meaning of asynchronous. When a class is *asynchronous,* it does not meet at an appointed time. There is no synchronization of schedules. You don't have to be at class at any given time, such as 9 a.m. or 6:30 p.m.

That's not to say that there isn't any schedule at all. Your asynchronous class may have a very definite schedule of when assignments and activities are due. For instance, every week an assignment may be due on Monday at midnight. When you work on that assignment, however, is entirely up to you. If working at 5 a.m. when the baby wakes for a feeding is good for you, then that's when you go to class! On the other hand, if you prefer to study after the 11 p.m. news, you can go to class then. By not having synchronized schedules, students can attend to coursework when it's convenient.

You can see that asynchronous learning represents a big difference between online education and traditional education. While you may complete homework on your own schedule, very few traditional schools allow you to show up when it's convenient! On the other hand, most online schools assume you will work when it's convenient, while submitting assignments according to the prescribed schedule.

Synchronous (real-time) learning

Some online education requires a coordinated or synchronized schedule, hence the term *synchronous* learning. In this situation, you're provided a schedule of times to be available and explicit instructions concerning the software you need to connect with others.

Real-time learning most closely approximates traditional education; the meeting time is specific. Courses use synchronous time a few different ways:

✔ Some instructors require classes to meet so that they can lecture in real time. This also allows them to interact with students and determine whether students are following along in class.

✔ Other instructors host online office hours or informal times when they're available to answer student questions. These instructors may not have a specific agenda for that time, but are open to whatever the student needs.

✔ As we discuss in Chapter 12, you may be involved in a group project. Synchronous meetings are an excellent method to get a lot of work done in short order.

Keep in mind these synchronous or scheduled meetings don't require you to be in the same *physical* place. While you may have to get online at a certain time, you can do so from the comfort of your home, office, or hotel room. And, you can wear your pajamas if you want to, and no one will be the wiser!

The business world loves synchronous meetings. Companies have been saving time and money by offering part of their employee education through synchronous Webinars and online conference meetings. Although staff may be in different cities, everyone shows up at the same time online. Common Web conferencing software includes

✔ Adobe Connect at www.adobe.com/products/acrobatconnectpro

✔ Elluminate at www.elluminate.com

✔ GoToMeeting at www.gotomeeting.com

✔ WebEx at www.webex.com

No loafing!

One surprise that online students report has to do with not being able to loaf or fade into the background in an online course. Face it, in a traditional course, you could go to class, sit in the back of the room, and never utter a word. The teacher may or may not know you are present. In an online course, that's not likely. Chances are good that an instructor is tracking your logins and the quality and quantity of your discussion postings. If you don't log in for a period of time, many instructors will come looking for you. You'll receive an e-mail or possibly a phone call asking about your inactivity.

Establish a regular schedule for logging in and working on the course. We recommend three to four times a week. That way your instructor won't have to look for you.

Who Benefits from Online Education?

Ask a few of the 3.9 million students who took online classes in 2007, and they will tell you about the substantial benefits of online education. Yes, you read that number correctly! In fact, the Sloan Consortium (Sloan-C), which published that fact and conducts other research about online education, states that more than two thirds of all institutions offer some type of online course. Business is booming, but who is enrolling? This section explains what kinds of students find online classes advantageous.

Adults beyond traditional college age

If you're working, raising a family, or trying to manage many different roles, chances are you feel a little stretched when it comes to time. Busy adults, such as the ones in the following sections, flock to online courses because they can determine when and where to study.

Professionals enhancing their careers

Want to move ahead in your career? Earning an advanced degree or picking up courses that directly relate to your job can help you do so. Not only do you acquire the knowledge and skills you need, but you also appear to be much more motivated to employers. Consider these examples:

✔ Sandra's boss wanted to move company sales online, but no one in the office understood how to manage Web pages and the Internet. Sandra enrolled in a series of online courses at the local community college and became a very valued asset in her office.

✔ Karl worked as a train engineer. His job took him all over the continent and made it difficult to enroll in a traditional class. Wanting to move into a managerial role, online classes fit his lifestyle perfectly. He was able to complete a degree and stay on track!

✔ Caryn earned a masters in nursing online while working as a surgical nurse at a local hospital. Her additional degree made it possible for her to teach nursing courses and supervise others. That meant more money!

✔ Michael was a successful mortgage seller but wanted to branch into human resources. Although he had taken college courses, he hadn't yet earned his bachelor's degree. Finishing his degree online allowed him to look for work in his field of interest as competitively as any other graduate.

If you're looking for career advancement and think that taking an online course might benefit you from a time-management perspective, look for a program that caters to working adults. Take advantage of the opportunity to talk to a live representative either via the phone or online chat and ask how many students complete the course. That will give you a good idea of how many students are satisfied as well as how attentive the school and faculty are to making sure their offerings work for students. See Chapter 5 for more information on researching different schools.

Busy parents

Raising a family isn't easy. Your children need and deserve your time and attention. They also need to be fed, bathed, have their homework checked, run to tennis class, and more! But what if you're a parent and want (or need) to return to school? What are the benefits of online education over traditional schooling for you?

- ✔ Child-care savings are possible. On the one hand, we don't recommend trying to be a serious student with small children running around; you can't concentrate adequately when your attention is divided between keeping your child safe, loved, and engaged versus completing a discussion question. However, it's reasonable to think that there will be quiet times when you can concentrate on your schoolwork and not have to pay for a babysitter. Save the babysitting money for those times when you have to take an online test and absolutely cannot be distracted.

- ✔ You don't have to spend time commuting. You can study from home or from your workplace (with permission, of course), but you don't need to add travel time to school. That means more time for the family, ultimately. Many parents study at the dining room table while school-age children work on their own homework. "School" starts right after the dinner plates are cleared.

- ✔ Speaking of school-age children, studying in their presence sends a very powerful message about lifelong education, your values, and the need to balance work, family, and school. Yes, maybe they can see that if you go to night class twice a week. However, we think it is qualitatively different when your children witness you logging in daily and really keeping abreast of what's happening in class.

So, as a busy parent, when are you supposed to fit in your schoolwork? For parents of very young children, naptime means class time. Many parents who take online classes dedicate those quiet moments to getting on the computer and completing class assignments.

What if you're not home with your child during the day, but at work from nine-to-five? You have a few options:

- ✔ Get up earlier and work for an hour each morning before you wake up the kids.

- ✔ Make arrangements with your boss to work online at your desk during your lunch hour.

✔ If you're a commuter (and not driving!), consider what coursework you can do during that time. Your "green" friends might not appreciate your printing off the whole course to read on the train, but what about your textbook? How about working through a discussion question the old-fashioned paper-and-pencil way, and then posting it online later?

✔ Pull out the laptop when your children do their homework. Not only will you stay current in class, but you will model excellent study skills for your kids!

✔ Stay up an hour past your children's bedtime to catch up on your class.

Only by setting a schedule can you manage work, family, and school. That's true for traditional education, too — to survive, you must establish a regular schedule for study and stick to it. (True story: Your humble coauthors went back to school online because we were working parents, and it was the only way we could manage.)

People with transportation issues

No travel is involved with online education, so students with transportation concerns can take classes easily. For example:

✔ If you live in a very rural area and have to drive in wintry weather, commuting even 20 minutes to the local community college can become a dangerous ordeal in February. Contrast that to staying warm and toasty at home while you complete coursework. And you pay less in fuel, parking, and maintenance on a vehicle to boot.

✔ What if you have a medical condition that makes driving impossible, and you're reliant on others for transportation? Again, if you study online, you are completely independent and not in need of travel assistance.

✔ Not everyone lives where buses and trains can easily transport them to the local college. Online education cancels the need to find and fund private transportation or to hitch a ride with strangers.

✔ If you carry this a little further, you can see that online education opens the possibility to take classes from anywhere in the world. This may seem kind of silly to consider, but you can live in Iowa and take a class from a university in California with no travel costs incurred. In one university class coauthor Susan taught recently, she had students log in from Great Britain, Korea, and Dubai as well as North America.

People with disabilities

Typically, disabilities come in two major fashions: physical challenges and difficulties processing information (learning disabilities).

If you are physically challenged, whether by mobility concerns, deafness, or blindness, you may find the online environment to be more conducive to studying. Here are a few highlights:

✔ **Mobility:** Persons who use wheelchairs or other assistive devices, such as crutches, canes, or walkers, can stay at home and study. No need to worry about whether sidewalks and building entrances are accessible.

✔ **Blindness:** If you are a person who is blind and you use a screen reader such as JAWS to complete your coursework online, you may have to ask for assistance with some areas of your coursework, but your campus should have staff who can help you work around any difficulties.

✔ **Deafness:** Unless audio is a major portion of the course, such as in a language listening course, persons who are deaf can typically read their way through a class. When audio or video is part of the content for a course, alternative text versions are typically available.

Students who have documented learning disabilities can also succeed in the online environment. Most institutions have a department that students with accommodation needs can turn to. This department not only supports students, but also trains faculty and staff on how to make the necessary accommodations needed for all students to be successful in the online environment. For example, if you need additional time for testing, that can be easily addressed online.

Flip to Chapter 18 for more details on how people with physical and learning disabilities can handle online courses.

Traditional college students

According to Sloan-C's report "Staying the Course: Online Education in the United States, 2008," more than 80 percent of the people enrolled in online courses in 2007 were undergraduate students. You can probably figure that means a sizable number are in the traditional 18- to 24-year-old age group. There are some real advantages to studying online for students of this age.

Supplementing coursework

A slight variation in online education is called blended, hybrid, or Web-enhanced coursework. That means that some of your resources and activities are shifted from the traditional classroom to the online environment. For example:

✔ You might be expected to review a PowerPoint presentation online prior to coming to the traditional class.

✔ You might take all your quizzes online rather than in the classroom.

✔ You might be asked to participate in an online discussion between class meetings.

In some cases, faculty who teach blended courses eliminate one of the class meeting times. For example, if your class meets on Mondays, Wednesdays, and Fridays, your instructor may only have you meet on Mondays and Wednesdays in the face-to-face environment and transfer the Friday materials online. For a traditional age student, that means having a few additional hours available for other activities.

Taking extra credits

How would you like to finish school early and put that shiny, new degree to work sooner? If you have time in your schedule and can accommodate a credit overload, you may find that taking an extra online course could help you speed through your academic program. Or you could use summer time to catch up online.

Consider the example of Allison. Each summer she came home to her parents' house for the summer and worked as a lifeguard at a nearby camp. However, she also enrolled in six credit hours through her university. She was not a full-time student, but the extra work did require a little discipline. After three summers, she had shaved off nearly a complete year of college!

Before you try taking summer courses from a different school, be sure to verify whether the credits transfer.

Sleeping in

If you're a classic college student (unmarried and without children), not all of your time is spent studying. You may have a job, or you may be involved in campus activities that take up a considerable amount of time. We won't address what you do with your social time, but it's a significant factor in most 18- to 24-year-olds' lives.

Not many traditional-age college students like waking up for an 8 a.m. class. If you study online, you can establish a schedule that works best for you. That means you can sleep in if you need to. As long as you manage your time effectively, it's possible to be a student online and have a social life (and maybe a job!).

Seniors and retirees

Senior citizens and retirees enjoy very active lifestyles these days. That includes using the Internet. Senior Net (www.seniornet.org/), a not-for-profit organization that provides technology training to seniors, estimates that more than 35 percent of seniors use the Internet. Some of them are taking online courses for personal enjoyment or to "retool" for careers after retirement.

Seniors benefit from online education for the same reasons everyone else does (see the previous sections for examples), but convenience and not having to deal with transportation issues rise to the top. In addition, seniors have an advantage over most others in that they seem to be better at managing their time.

For young retirees, online education could provide an avenue to retrain for a new career. In particular, military personnel who find themselves looking for work in their forties can begin to prepare for their future without having to leave base. For example, First Sergeant Earl earned a special endorsement for teaching while stationed in South Korea; the university was in the United States. Once he was discharged and returned to the states, he had the credentials he needed for a successful job search.

Teachers, especially college faculty, like to retrofit themselves for teaching through retirement, as well. By enrolling in online courses, retiring faculty can update skills and acquire new understandings of the teaching and learning processes so they're more marketable as part-timers or adjuncts. A retiree can still travel and teach (with a great Internet connection, of course).

High school and homeschooled students

Perhaps the hottest area of growth and development in online education impacts high school and homeschooled students. It's so hot that Chapter 16 is dedicated to this topic, but we review the basics here, in particular, the benefits of online education for kids.

In 75 percent of school districts in the United States, one or more students were enrolled in an online or blended online course. (These estimates come from a Sloan-C 2008 follow-up of a survey of U.S. school district administrators.) Three out of four kids are learning online? Why not? In today's digital age, learning online has distinct benefits for young students:

- ✔ **It advances kids' technology skills.** Consider that most white-collar jobs now require technology skills. With the globalization of business and industry, collaborating with colleagues around the world is common for knowledge workers. Children who acquire computer-mediated communication skills already understand how to collaborate online. Online education teaches twenty-first-century skills.

- ✔ **It helps homeschooling parents plan their curricula.** In North America, homeschooling is inconsistently regulated. Having a quality source for instruction, such as the Florida Virtual School (see Chapter 20), allows parents to select and supervise the curricula. While state-supported schools still meet state mandates, parents can determine the most appropriate courses for their children.

- ✔ **It allows kids to work at their own pace.** Virtual schools for kindergarten through 12th grade are more likely to be self-paced with parental supervision. In other words, if your child is gifted and can finish algebra in eight weeks, she can move on to her next course without waiting. If your child needs more time, that can be accommodated as well.

- ✔ **It facilitates the management of health issues.** For kids with medical needs or disabilities, online education allows the family to manage health concerns without disrupting learning. For example, a child with severe diabetes can monitor blood sugar levels by snacking while learning. In a traditional classroom, the child would probably have to go elsewhere to snack, resulting in lost instructional time.

✔ **It offers greater scheduling flexibility.** Reducing the time children spend in school increases time for other activities. In some cases, teens work significant internships, acquiring additional skills that complement their online education. For kids who excel in the arts or athletics and need additional time for practice, online education fits their lifestyles. Not only can they schedule learning before and after workouts and rehearsals, but schooling doesn't stop because of travel to performances and events.

✔ **It fills specialized needs that traditional high schools can't.** One high school can only offer so many classes, particularly in rural areas. The availability and expertise of teachers and school district financial constraints sometimes determine what courses students take. For students looking for more variety, online education can serve it up. Students aren't limited to what's available at their own school, but can tap into a wide network of available courses. They may find many of these courses at a state-supported virtual school, which directly ties into graduation requirements because those courses and programs follow the same state mandates.

Advanced Placement (AP) courses allow high school students to study more challenging subject matter at a higher level than traditional high school courses. Additionally, these courses often count for college credit. Virtual high schools put AP courses within reach of those whose schools don't offer them. Even students who don't study entirely online can have access to the kinds of classes they want and need through these online programs. Of course, buyer beware: Check with your local district to be sure they'll accept the online credits.

Want to look further at online education for K-12 students? Visit the International Association for K-12 Online Learning at www.inacol.org.

Getting a Grip on Potential Pitfalls

Working online isn't without its pitfalls. One of those pitfalls, especially for kids attending online schools, is cyberbullying; we cover how to deal with this pitfall in Chapter 16. The following sections describe a couple more realities you should consider before enrolling in an online course.

Online education isn't easier

Contrary to popular belief, online education isn't easier than traditional education. As we explain earlier in this chapter, most online education is instructor-led and follows a specific schedule. While you may have the opportunity to choose when and where you study, you don't get to choose the content. If you're taking an online history course, you're going to study the same material that you would if you sat in a traditional classroom. The subject matter isn't "watered down." However, there are significant differences in the way you get the information and what you do with it.

Because online education requires students to take more responsibility for their own learning, it can be *more* challenging! You may have to work a little harder to understand the concepts, and chances are you'll be asked to do more then read a chapter and take a test. You're required to use critical thinking, to share your ideas in writing (not just by talking), and to demonstrate that you understand the material in ways other than by taking tests. We talk more about this in Chapter 14, but you should be prepared to prove that you're learning!

Also, online education is more challenging for those who struggle with time management and study skills. Some students find it easier to attend a face-to-face class because the teacher's physical presence motivates them to complete assignments. If that describes you, you may struggle with an online course. (We show you how to assess your own discipline and determine your chances of online success later in this chapter.)

If you're considering enrolling in an online course because you think it will be an easy, independent study, think twice! Read the course materials very carefully before enrolling. Chances are good that your course will require a substantial amount of dedicated time and that you will have to adhere to definite deadlines.

You can't have spontaneous, face-to-face discussions

Earlier in this chapter, we talk about asynchronous learning — accessing course materials and completing assignments on your own time. When this term is applied to discussion, a common feature of online courses, one student may post a comment at 1 a.m. and another may not respond until 5 p.m. That means discussion takes longer and isn't spontaneous. As an online student, you have to learn to be patient in these circumstances. (We discuss the importance of patience and tolerance for online success later in this chapter.)

Given the time delay, it can be more difficult to sustain a conversation in asynchronous settings. Absent of body language and immediacy, misunderstandings can also take on a life of their own. If you read something John posts and don't get what he means, you may inadvertently take the discussion off course at 1 a.m.! By the time someone notices and you all get on the same page, valuable time is lost. The focus may be lost as well.

Determining Whether You're Ready to Join the World of Online Education

So, do you think you're a good candidate for online education? In the following sections, we review some of the characteristics and qualities that will make you successful. See how you measure up!

Assessing your own discipline

One of the first areas you need to assess is the quality of your self-discipline. Some of us have more discipline than others. Use the following questions to assess your level:

- ✔ **Are you a self-starter?** When it comes to completing a task, whether or not you think you'll enjoy it, are you one who starts without a lot of prompting? If you are, you're more likely to succeed online. When you get assignments from your instructor, you will have to establish a personal schedule for getting those assignments completed. The first step is starting! Procrastinators don't do well in online education.

- ✔ **Are you persistent?** What if your computer crashes and you can't complete an assignment as instructed? What if it's supposed to be done on a word processor and you break four fingers? How likely are you to give up when tasks are challenging or things don't go as planned? There are times when technology fails, group members disappear, and documents get lost. Persistence and addressing problems creatively and expediently can carry an online student through these challenges. Just be sure to communicate with the instructor early in the problem stage. Let her know what you're prepared to do to remedy your calamity. (By the way, in the case of broken fingers, ask if you can record assignments in an audio file.)

✔ **Do you manage your time well?** What tools and strategies do you use to manage your time? Do you utilize a personal calendar? Do you schedule times or routine activities? Managing your time online will make you a successful student. You will need to dedicate study time and follow through with regular logins. You may also be juggling work and family. Online education requires effective time-management skills.

✔ **Can you work alone?** Even though a lot of online work is done in groups or collaboratively with other students, the majority of your time online will be independent. Can you follow through with tasks by yourself? Or do you need others to be present? To succeed in an online course, you need the ability to work alone and to think independently. For example: When a problem has you stumped, it's important to try to find answers independently before asking the instructor. It shows that you have an independent spirit that solves problems without whining — no one likes a whiner! It also shows a great deal of initiative — a quality that's always valued.

Knowing your learning style

Think back to how you learned in traditional school. There are a variety of ways that individuals access and process information. In this section we talk about learning styles and how they present themselves online. Knowing how you learn best can help you select the kinds of classes and practice study skills that are most effective for you.

Learning styles can be described most simply by three preferences: visual, auditory, and tactile or kinesthetic. This means that you prefer to take in information using your eyes, ears, or through physical movement. Your brain then helps you process information using your preference.

Here are several online learning style inventories you can take to help you determine how you best learn (you can find others through a traditional Web search of learning style inventories):

✔ Abiator's Learning Styles Inventory at `www.berghuis.co.nz/abiator/lsi/lsiframe.html`

✔ Learning Style Inventory at `www.personal.psu.edu/bxb11/LSI/LSI.htm`

✔ Vark at `vark-learn.com/english/index.asp`

Visual learners

People who prefer to learn visually like to read and look at images. They like to work with words that are on a page. In the online environment, visual learners prefer to read content or articles, look at charts and images, and take in information through their eyes. The page may be either a real textbook or a computer screen. For the record, most people are visual learners.

Those of you who like to access information visually will do very well with reading requirements. If you don't find enough graphics or images to help you learn, ask your instructor whether she knows of alternatives. Sometimes textbooks come with corresponding Web sites that offer PowerPoint presentations and other supporting materials.

Auditory learners

Auditory learners prefer to hear information, and their brains process the sounds. Have you ever met someone who listens attentively to you but never takes notes and still remembers what you have told them? Chances are that person is a very auditory learner. Their ears take in the information and the brain stores and processes it. Auditory learners love to hear stories, by the way. In an online course, auditory learners immediately gravitate toward programs with sound, such as slides with narration or videos.

Those who are auditory learners may struggle a little with the text-heavy nature of many courses. However, these days more faculty are including podcasts and audio files as well as video introductions into their courses. They also may narrate PowerPoint presentations to help auditory learners better understand the material.

A *podcast* is an audio file that you can subscribe to through a service like iTunes. However, you don't have to have an iPod or MP3 player or use a subscription service. Most of the time, your instructor will give you a link from which you can download the file. Then you can listen to it right from your computer. Sure, you can make it portable and listen on the road, but it isn't required. In fact, if your instructor creates *vodcasts* (podcasts with visuals like PowerPoint slides), you'll need a fancy MP3 player to view them away from the computer, in which case watching them on the computer is cheaper.

Need a couple strategies for working with an auditory preference? Read out loud to yourself. When you read your classmates' posts, give them each a separate "voice."

Don't be afraid to look for additional materials on your own. Can't quite understand Newton's Third Law? You'd be surprised what you can find on sites like TeacherTube (www.teachertube.com), such as materials that are prepared for middle school kids but still make sense and entertain at the same time.

Tactile or kinesthetic learners

Perhaps you are best described as someone who likes to take action before reading the instructions or listening to directions. If so, you may be a tactile or kinesthetic learner! People who are kinesthetic like to put their bodies into motion in order to learn. It's too simplistic to say that this means the individual has to move in order to take in or process information, but when opportunities allow the individual to put new ideas into practice, learning becomes easier. For example, say you want to learn a concept related to chemistry. You may read about it or listen to a lecture, but once you begin to experiment, it makes more sense. It's the action of *doing* that helps embed that new information.

Clicking a computer mouse doesn't count as movement. However, regardless of when or where you're working, you can get up and walk around, eat while you work, take frequent breaks, and otherwise keep your fidgeting and movement going while you work.

Being patient and tolerant

Seldom are we told that patience and tolerance are necessary qualities for academic survival. However, the classroom has gone global, and technology is now a factor. In the following sections, we describe the facets of online education that require your patience and tolerance.

Online education differs from traditional schooling in many ways. It's the twenty-first-century method of acquiring information, putting it into practice, and interacting with other learners. Having some doubts is natural, but only if you enter into the virtual classroom with a sense of wonder and possibility will you really learn.

Trying new learning methods and technologies

Online education stretches most learners. Many of the procedures and processes feel awkward, and the instructor may throw in new technology tools. How well you adapt to these additional challenges can make a difference in your overall survival online. Following is a short list of some of the tools or methods you may face online (see Chapter 3 for more details on technology and the technological skills you need):

- ✔ **Group work:** Very common online. Instructors pair up students or assign them to small discussion groups to work out a problem.

- ✔ **Wiki:** A Web page that different people can edit. It's a simple tool that is used in group work. If you can edit a Word document, you can handle a wiki.

- ✔ **Blog:** A Web page that you may use two ways. You may just be asked to go to a blog and read the entries. Or, you may be asked to keep a blog — kind of like a public journal — of what you experience in the class.

- ✔ **Webinar:** A live session where you can hear a presenter and see images. Instructors who have live office hours often use similar software.

- ✔ **Chat or IM:** Instant communication when you need to ask a question or work out a group decision.
- ✔ **Podcasts:** Audio files that you can download and play on your computer or on your portable MP3 device.

Recognizing different kinds of people in the classroom

Think back to your traditional education. Chances are there was someone in the class who was a know-it-all. There may have been a teacher's pet. And how about a class clown? Guess what? They've moved online.

If you were particularly annoyed with a certain personality type when in a traditional class, you should prepare to meet the same person online. This time, however, you'll recognize their characteristics through writing behaviors. The know-it-all will answer everyone else's posts with an American Psychological Association (APA)-formatted reference. The teacher's pet will suck up with glowing acknowledgments of the teacher's presence. The class clown will always have a pun.

There are probably many more ways to describe people. Suffice it to say, this is where tolerance comes back into play. It's important to get along when online, refrain from engaging in hurtful communication, and focus on your own work, not everyone else's. Check out Chapters 9, 10, and 12 for plenty of pointers on working well with others online.

Counting to ten when you're upset

When something doesn't go your way in the online classroom, count to ten before reacting. If you read a comment that seems unkind or downright mean, don't blast off a nasty response. We say much more about netiquette in Chapter 13, but the bottom line is that you need to write civilly in the online world. Emotions are often incorrectly "read" into written communication, and this causes definite problems.

This is where the asynchronous nature of online education is a real advantage, too. If John writes something that is borderline offensive on Thursday evening, Kelly can wait until Friday to see whether others have noticed and diplomatically said something. If not, she can then respond with a cooler head.

Chapter 3

The Technology and Technological Skills You Need to Succeed

* *

In This Chapter

▶ Making sure you have the right technological equipment

▶ Confirming your technological abilities

▶ Communicating safely online

* *

*W*hen it comes to technology and taking online courses, there are two essential components to being successful: technological inventory and technological competencies.

✔ Your technological inventory includes things like your actual computer and the programs that you use to surf the Internet, write documents, and perform other daily tasks.

✔ Technological competencies refer to the basic skills you need when taking an online course.

Don't let these words scare you. Knowing what is expected up front will help you be more successful later. We explain what you need for online education success in this chapter.

Checking Your Technological Readiness

The first thing you need to take an online course is a reliable computer that meets your course's or program's minimum standards. Most new computers meet many institutions' minimum standards for hardware and software out of the box. More technical courses, such as those focusing on media development, may require you to purchase more specific hardware and software. And, of course, you need a dependable connection to the Internet.

In the following sections, we explain what you need to meet minimum hardware and software requirements for most online classes, and we describe the importance of a fast, reliable Internet connection.

Meeting minimum hardware requirements

Each online course has minimum hardware requirements. These standards are determined by the technology used within the course. Courses using a lot of audio and video materials require better hardware than those relying solely on text-based materials.

Most institutions have a Web page where they display the minimum and recommended hardware requirements. If, after a few minutes of searching, you're unable to find the computer requirements page on an institution's Web site, don't hesitate to pick up the phone and call your advisor. Once you start classes, your instructor will provide you with a list of any additional requirements that go above and beyond the institution's advertised list.

Table 3-1 is an example of what you might see on an institution's computer requirements page. The columns note different types of hardware and what's required for both PCs and Macs.

Table 3-1	An Example of Hardware Requirements	
Hardware	*PCs — Windows*	*Macs*
Processor	1–2 GHz	G3 800–G4 125 GHz
RAM (random access memory)	1–2GB	1–2GB
Hard drive	20–30GB of free hard disk space	20–30GB of free hard disk space
Monitor resolution	1024 x 768 resolution	1024 x 768 resolution
Speakers	Sound card with external speakers or headphones	Sound card with external speakers or headphones
Microphone	Required in order to attend instructors' virtual office hours; a headset with microphone is highly recommended.	Required in order to attend instructors' virtual office hours; a headset with microphone is highly recommended.
Webcam (optional)	640 x 480 video pixel resolution	640 x 480 video pixel resolution

As we introduce different hardware components in the following sections, keep in mind that this information is simply an overview. Each operating system uses its own navigation to find information, so as we talk about whether your computer meets certain requirements, you may need to reference your computer's manual or an additional resource to help you determine how to locate needed information. We suggest looking into other *For Dummies* books specific to your computer — you can peruse available titles at www.dummies.com/store.html.

If you plan to purchase a new computer to take an online class, check with the institution to see whether you can purchase the computer at a discounted price. Many institutions have deals with computer manufacturers to provide their students with discounted hardware and software. If the institution doesn't offer discounts, you should still find out what its minimum requirements are before making a purchase. It's a good idea to print the minimum requirements and take the printout with you to the retail store of your choice. Doing so can help the salesperson guarantee that you purchase a computer to meet your educational needs.

Processor speed

The processor speed refers to how fast your computer is able to process information and provide you, the user, with the output result; it's measured in gigahertz (GHz). The more complicated the task, the longer it takes the computer to provide you with an output. Online courses that use more complicated materials, such as audio and video files, require a faster processor speed — in other words, more GHz.

Computers purchased within the last two years should have no problem meeting the processor speed requirements. If your computer is an older model, you should double-check to be sure its processor is fast enough.

Most computers have a screen that summarizes its physical makeup.

- ✔ If you're using a computer with Windows Vista, you can click on the Start button at the bottom left of your screen and then right-click on Computer. If you have the Computer Icon on your desktop, you can also right-click directly on it (see the sidebar "A quickie on right-clicking," later in this chapter) and choose Properties. This will take you to a screen that summarizes the computer's operating system version, processor speed, and the amount of memory it has (see Figure 3-1). It should be noted that other versions of the Windows operating system may require different steps to find the same information.

- ✔ Mac users can click on the Apple (top left of the menu bar) and then click on the About This Mac option to see a similar summary (see Figure 3-2).

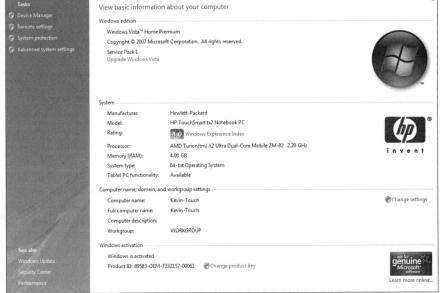

Figure 3-1:
A summary
of the
physical
makeup of
a computer
with
Windows
Vista.

Figure 3-2:
A summary
of the physi-
cal makeup
of a com-
puter with
Mac OS X.

Memory

The role of computer memory is to assist the processor by temporarily storing instructions and other information for faster processing. Computer programs, also known as applications — Microsoft Word, for example — require computers to have a specific amount of memory available for their use. Memory is measured in gigabytes (GB).

Your computer's current memory capacity can be found on the same page as the processor speed (see the preceding section and Figures 3-1 and 3-2). Most newer computers come with plenty of memory right off the shelf. However, if your computer is a few years older, it may not meet the minimum requirements for taking an online course. If this is the case, talk to either the institution's technical support team or a computer retailer about increasing your computer's memory. Depending on how old your computer is, increasing its memory may be all you need.

Hard drive

Your computer's hard drive is where all your files are stored. This includes the files required to run the computer's operating system and your installed applications. Think of the hard drive as a digital filing cabinet. How much information can be stored on your computer's hard drive depends on its size. Newer hard drives are measured in GB or terabytes (TB). Older hard drives were measured using megabytes (MB).

Institutions may require that you have a hard drive with enough space to install additional programs and store your documents such as homework assignments.

Monitor

The monitor is what displays your computer's output. A monitor's display is based on two components: size and resolution. Monitors come in a variety of sizes based on their diagonal measurements in inches. For example, a 20-inch monitor measures 20 inches from the top left corner to the bottom right corner. However, a 20-inch monitor has only an 18.8-inch viewable display. This matters because the picture is developed using pixels, and the number of pixels that can fit in a given space is measured in terms of width by height. For example, a monitor with a 640 x 480 resolution means that there are 640 pixels across the screen and 480 pixels from top to bottom. The larger the monitor size, the bigger the pixels need to be to fill the space. Most institutions require you to have a monitor with a minimum resolution of 1024 x 768. A 17-inch monitor is best; however, monitors between 15 and 21 inches should also be suitable. Even the 13.3-inch monitors on our laptops display 1024 x 768 pixels just fine.

Speakers and microphones

Many online courses use audio and video files to support the curriculum. In order to hear the speech portion of each of these files, you need a good pair of speakers or a headset. Most computers come with speakers upon purchase. These should work fine. However, your family and other housemates may prefer that you use a headset to reduce distractions. Don't rush out and buy anything expensive. The headset you use to listen to your music player will work just fine. Your computer should have a built-in sound card and a round headphone jack for plugging into. The headphone jack may be located on the front or the back of your computer. Or, if you use a laptop, the jack may be on one of the sides. Most headphone jacks have a small icon of a headset either above the jack or directly next to it.

Some instructors also may ask you to participate in a Web-based conference using Internet applications. These applications allow instructors and students to communicate in a variety of ways, including via voice over the Internet. To do this, you need to have a microphone. Many computers, especially laptops, have built-in microphones. These can work, but we recommend that you purchase an inexpensive headset that incorporates a microphone. Look to spend about $25 for the basic set.

Webcam

Some programs or courses may require you to have a Webcam, which is a camera for your computer. When you turn it on, the members of your audience see you sitting in front of the computer, as if they were looking through your screen. Webcams may be required for a couple of reasons. First, you may be required to give synchronous presentations, and you may be asked to share an image of yourself during the presentation. Usually, in this situation a Webcam is optional. However, an institution may require a Webcam if a proctoring service is used for testing. Some proctoring services have you log in to a Web site and share your Webcam so they can confirm your identity and monitor your environment during a test.

Some newer computers have Webcams built directly into the monitor. If your computer doesn't have a built-in Webcam, you can purchase one for $50, maybe less. When purchasing a Webcam, the most important thing is to make sure it's compatible with your computer's operating system. Webcams that work with Mac computers don't necessarily work with Windows Vista machines. If a Webcam is required by your institution and you're not sure which one to buy, contact the institution's technical support team. They can probably recommend one or two.

Meeting software requirements

Once you have your hardware equipment, you need to install the right software (if you don't already have it on your computer). Software applications are the programs used to complete specific tasks. The two most important applications you need to have installed on your computer to take an online course are an Internet browser and a word-processing program. However, other applications may also be required by either the institution or an individual instructor, depending on the course content.

To check software requirements for a course, check the course description. Most institutions advertise software requirements here if they go beyond the standard requirements to give you plenty of time to purchase the software before class begins. Don't forget to check the online bookstore for possible discounted purchasing.

Internet browser

The application that allows you to connect and interact via the Internet is called an Internet browser. Every computer purchased at a standard retail store these days comes with an Internet browser. Windows-based machines come with Windows Internet Explorer (IE) and Macs come with Safari pre-installed. These browsers, in most cases, work just fine. (We explain how to obtain a reliable Internet connection later in this chapter.)

For those who enjoy other browsers, such as Firefox, they should work as well. If there are browser limitations, the institution should note those in the required software section of their Web site. For example, some older programming technology only works with Internet Explorer.

Unfortunately for Mac users, many Web-based tools — including those used in online courses — require Internet Explorer in order to function appropriately. This is becoming less and less of an issue and hopefully won't affect your ability to register for an online course. However, be sure to check the institution's software requirements before registering.

E-mail access

Before you even start courses, you'll communicate with registration and advising staff via e-mail. Once your application is accepted, some institutions will provide you with an e-mail account and instructions on how to access that account. These institutions often require that this account be used for all school business. On the other hand, allowing students to use an external e-mail account of their choice is becoming increasingly popular. We recommend setting up a free account with Google (http://gmail.com) strictly for school communication. This helps separate your personal materials from your school communications. We also recommend that you choose an e-mail address that's more professional in nature than some personal addresses — for example, KevinJohnson@gmail.com rather than TheGoofster@gmail.com.

Using a free Gmail account has two advantages: Namely, it's free, and secondly, it can be accessed via the Web or other e-mail applications, such as Microsoft Outlook or Mac's iMail. Google provides step-by-step instructions on how to set up your account depending on your e-mail client of choice. The other advantage to using Gmail is that Google accounts come with a suite of complimentary resources, such as an online calendar and photo gallery.

Word processing

The assignments that you don't complete directly online will most likely be completed using a word-processing program such as Microsoft Word. For example, you may be asked to write an essay and turn it in directly to your instructor. To do this, you would use a word-processing program to write your paper, save the file, and then upload it to your instructor.

If you don't have a word-processing program installed on your machine and your institution doesn't require a specific program, you may want to consider installing the free, open-source program titled Open Office (www.open office.org). This program requires a little more work to install, but it's compatible with most commercial products on the market today.

If you would feel more comfortable with a commercial product, we recommend Microsoft Word. See whether you can get a student discount on commercial software through your institution, or try JourneyEd.com (www.journeyed.com). At JourneyEd.com, with proof of student status, you can get large discounts on software and hardware. Student status can be proven using a student I.D. or via letter from an advisor on the institution's letterhead. Other retailers may offer student discounts and just not advertise them. So never feel bad about asking whether a student discount is available.

Plug-ins

Plug-ins are applications or programs that have a very specific function. These programs are usually free but need to be downloaded from the Internet. Some plug-ins do come installed on new machines, but you'll most likely be required to download some additional plug-ins throughout your educational career. Your institution will tell you exactly what plug-ins you need or your computer will notify you when you need a specific plug-in and help you find it. Here are two popular plug-ins:

- ✓ **FlashPlayer:** Flash is a popular format for videos shared over the Web. To view these videos, you may need to download the FlashPlayer plug-in specific to your Internet browser. Even though the institution will most likely provide links directly to required plug-ins, you can get a jump on things by downloading FlashPlayer at get.adobe.com/flashplayer.

- ✓ **Java:** Even if your course doesn't require it, chances are some of the online games you want to play and other cool Internet applications require the Java plug-in. The only problem is that Java is updated frequently. To get the latest version, go to www.java.com.

Virus protection software

Whenever you're surfing the Internet, you should consider using virus protection software. Virus protection software, such as McAfee (www.mcafee.

com) or Norton Anitvirus (www.norton.com), protects your computer from malicious applications created to harm your computer hardware and files.

Once installed on your computer, antivirus software can monitor incoming communications and attachments from other computers. It can also check Web sites you're visiting to see whether they pose any danger. When viruses are found, the software alerts you to the danger.

Because computer viruses are always changing, you need to purchase an application that keeps up with those changes. Some programs have the option to update automatically, whereas others require you to manually update the software. We recommend that you update your antivirus software at least once a week.

To reduce the risk of getting viruses, follow these guidelines when surfing the Internet:

- ✔ Stay away from sites you don't know.

- ✔ Don't open e-mail attachments from people you don't know.

- ✔ Don't open e-mail attachments that seem suspicious, even if they're from people you know. For example, don't open attachments that have no name in the subject line or that seem goofy or out of context.

- ✔ Turn off your computer (or at least your Internet connection) when you're not using it.

Additional programs

Depending on what class you're taking, your instructor may require you to acquire and install additional programs. For example, if you're taking a business class, you're likely to need a spreadsheet application, such as Microsoft Excel. Or, if you're a doctorate student, you may be required to install SPSS for calculating research statistics. Courses that require additional programs often have you purchase these applications via the online bookstore. By doing this, students usually receive a discount on the software compared to typical retailers' prices.

Establishing a reliable Internet connection

When taking an online course, the Internet is your lifeline to your instructor, peers, and course materials. Therefore, reliable Internet service is essential for your success. Not only do you need a fast, reliable Internet connection at home, but you should also have alternative options just in case your connection fails.

If you're taking an online course that uses only text-based materials, dial-up connections may be okay. However, courses in which you use other materials, such as audio and video files, will take what seems like forever to download and play. Courses that use technologies such as Web-conferencing programs also will require a faster connection. We recommend a fast, broadband connection such as DSL or cable to help you connect and accomplish work in much less time.

Before signing a contract with an Internet service provider (ISP), make sure the one you choose is able to deliver the speed and service availability needed to take an online course. Some institutions will tell you the minimum upload and download speeds you need to connect to their system. Even if you don't know what this means, you can still ask prospective service providers whether they're capable of meeting those requirements.

It has been our experience that some satellite companies have a difficult time connecting to institutions where students are required to log in to systems using a more complex authentication process. The delay between earth and satellite causes the system to time out, which means that it is unable to complete a task within a specific amount of time. The result is that you can't log in.

If you live in an area that has limited options for connecting to the Internet and are concerned that the connection speed may not be adequate, you should do two things:

- ✔ Contact the institution and explain your situation. See whether their technical support staff has any ideas.

- ✔ Be sure to arrange for a 30-day, money-back trial with any prospective Internet service providers. This allows you to test the system without having to a commit to a one- or two-year contract before knowing whether it's going to meet your needs.

Trust us when we tell you that there will be times when an assignment is due and your Internet connection, even one that's typically reliable, will die. This can be frustrating and keep you from being able to turn in assignments and/or participate in synchronous meetings. Therefore, it's important to have a backup plan for accessing your course. Some ideas for backups include your public library, office, or a nearby cyber café. Of course, a laptop with wireless Internet connection capabilities is required to connect from a nearby coffeehouse, unless they also provide the computer.

Testing Your Technological Abilities

Once you have the right hardware, the right software, and a reliable Internet connection, you'll need a few technological skills to match. Understanding your technological competencies up front can help you determine whether it would be a good idea for you to take an introductory computer course or read some computer books before enrolling in an online class. The following sections describe the skills you'll need.

Reading and scrolling efficiently

Much of the information you receive when taking an online class is provided to you directly on the screen. Although printing it is always an option, you're not always provided with a word-processing file that you can save and print easily. Therefore, you need to be able to read on-screen information quickly and know how to scroll when text goes off the screen. To scroll, simply find the scrollbars on the bottom and right side of your window. The bottom scrollbar allows you to scroll left and right, whereas the scrollbar on the right provides the ability to scroll up and down.

Having your window maximized to fit the entire screen is also helpful because it reduces the need to scroll. If you're a Windows user, you can maximize the screen by clicking on the maximize icon in the top right of your active window. Mac users can click on the green plus button on the top left of the active window. Both of these buttons are located in the active window's border.

Knowing how to zoom text within your Web browser may be helpful as well. For most browsers, you can find zoom in and zoom out options under the View menu. However, your Internet browser may work differently.

Another important tip is to take breaks. This helps reduce eyestrain, which can lead to higher levels of productivity in the long run. A simple two-minute break to get a drink of water or use the restroom will do wonders for your efficiency.

Typing quickly and accurately

Because most communication in online courses occurs via text, you need to be able to type quickly and accurately. Speed and accuracy are even more important during synchronous meetings where you may be trying to answer questions in real-time. (We explain synchronous learning in detail in Chapter 2.)

Being able to type quickly reduces the time it takes to complete assignments and participate in online discussions. Though spellcheckers are a wonderful tool, accurate typing skills are always more desirable. Spellcheckers with automatic correction often "correct" misspellings erroneously, replacing the word you intended with a similarly spelled one that changes the meaning of your sentence. So, no matter how well you type or how much you use spellcheckers, always proofread your work before submitting it.

Whether you have your fingers properly placed on the keyboard or use the two-finger, hunt-and-peck method doesn't matter. No one will know how you type. However, if you need practice, you may want to consider a typing program that helps you learn how to type and provides timed tests that report your speed and accuracy. Examples include Mavis Beacon Teaches Typing at `www.broderbund.com` or Power Typing's free tutorial at `www.power typing.com`.

Dictation programs are on the market for those who may experience carpal tunnel syndrome or have arthritis. These programs allow you to use a microphone and word-processing program to translate your speech to text. These are great programs, but you should know that their accuracy rate is about 85 percent, which means you still need to use the keyboard and mouse to correct mistakes. Two common speech-recognition software programs include Dragon NaturallySpeaking (`www.nuance.com/naturallyspeaking/ products/preferred.asp`) for Windows-based machines and MacSpeech Dictate for Mac users (`www.macspeech.com/`).

Organizing folders

Have you ever gone looking for a file on your computer and not been able to find it? This tends to happen for two reasons:

✔ Students are unorganized and save their files in different places on their hard drives.

✔ Students save different files on several devices, forgetting which flash drive or folder the file was saved in.

We recommend that you have one place where you save all your course files, whether it's your computer's hard drive or a flash drive (see the nearby sidebar for more about these devices), and perform backups frequently. We also recommend that you organize your digital files the same way you would organize physical files in a filing cabinet, using folders and subfolders.

Image a three-drawer filing cabinet. In the top drawer, you want to store personal information. In the middle drawer, you want to store your work files. And in the third drawer, you want to store your school files. In the digital world, we think of these drawers as folders. Therefore, you might create three folders on your hard drive with the titles "Home," "Work," and "School," respectively.

Now imagine opening the bottom drawer where you want to store your school information. Inside the physical cabinet, you might create a hanging folder titled with the name of the institution. For example's sake, assume you're attending Smarty Pants College. Then, inside that hanging folder, you might create a file folder for each of the courses you take at that institution. Your digital file structure should follow the same concept. Therefore, inside your "School" folder, you need to create a subfolder called "Smarty Pants College" and then a sub-sub-folder inside that for each of the courses you take, for example, "ENG101."

By having a standard organizational structure on your hard drive, you can quickly and easily save and retrieve information when needed. Consistency is the key. Figure 3-3 is a screenshot of the drive structure where Kevin saves his school files. Notice for each term he creates a folder for each course. Within each of those he then creates four subfolders: "Admin" for administrative files such as the course syllabus, "Assignments" for course assignment files, "Discussions" for original discussion posts, and "Resources" for additional files provided by the instructor throughout the term of the course.

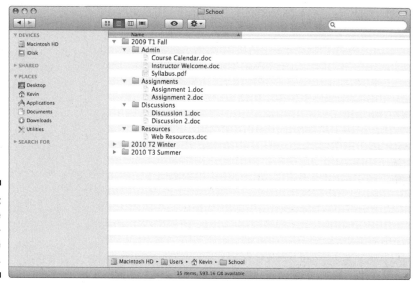

Figure 3-3:
An example of a computer's file structure.

Toting your files on a flash drive

Flash drive. Jump drive. Thumb drive. Memory stick. What are they? These are external devices that connect to your computer and allow you to store a ton of information. They are all *USB*, or universal serial bus, connections. To the average user, this just means that you can plug such a device into almost any computer and save files to it (and get them off later). These devices are inexpensive and very portable. They're so small you can stick one on a key chain. Buy one! Consider it exclusively for online courses, so that you always know your files are safe if your computer crashes.

To create a new folder in Windows, right-click inside the directory where you want to put the new folder. Choose the option New and then Folder. A new folder with the name "Untitled" will appear. Simply type over the name to rename the folder to your liking. To create a new folder on the Mac, Command-click (right-click if you have a two-button mouse) inside the director where you want to put the new folder. Choose "New Folder" and replace the default name of "Untitled" with the name of your choice. We recommend that folder names be short and without spaces or special characters.

Navigating the Web

Being able to access and navigate the Web is one of the most important skills you need to take an online course. Specific navigation skills you should have include:

- **Opening your Internet browser:** Locate and click on your browser's application icon in your Start Menu (Windows) or taskbar (Mac).

- **Navigating to a given URL:** Type the HTTP address in the address bar at the top of the browser's window — for example, `http://google.com`. In most cases, you can leave off the "http://" and simply type the address — for example, `google.com`. The browser will automatically assume you mean an HTTP address.

- **Navigating to the previous page:** Use the browser's back button at the top of the screen, which has an arrow pointing to the left.

- **Opening a hyperlink in a new tab or window:** Right-click on the link and select whether you want a new tab or window.

- **Switching between open tabs or windows:** To open a new tab or Window, click on the File menu and choose the New Window or New Tab option. To switch between tabs, either click on the desired tab with your mouse or hold down the Control (Ctrl) key and press the tab key on your keyboard. To switch between windows, click on the desired window on the task bar.

- **Refreshing the current screen:** Click the refresh button on your browser or press the F5 key on your keyboard.

- **Resizing the browser window:** Click and drag the bottom right corner to resize the window to your liking, or use the resize button in the top right (Windows) or left (Mac) of the browser window.

- **Locating and opening downloaded files:** Navigate to the Downloads folder and double-click on the downloaded file.

- **Conducting a Web search using Google or another search engine:** Navigate to `http://google.com` and enter your search criteria in the search box. Then click on any of the links provided on the search results page.

A quickie on right-clicking

Just in case you've never heard the term "right-click," a PC mouse has two sides. Most of the clicking we do when surfing the Web is left-clicking (and right-handed users do this with their index finger). But the other side works, too! You usually use the right side when you want to display a menu of options that can be executed depending on the location of the cursor. So when we say "right-click" you should hover over the words or icon, and then click on the right half of the mouse. For the "lefties"

out there, we recommend that you locate your computer's Control Panel (Windows) or System Preferences (Mac) and change the primary button to the right-side where your index finger is positioned. For you, when we say "right-click" we really mean "left-click." Confused yet?

Mac users, you can't right-click, can you? Instead, use Control + Click or place two fingers on the track pad while hitting the click bar.

If any of the preceding skills are unfamiliar to you, don't worry. None of them take long to master; it's just important that you know how to do them. If you need help, you may want to check out the latest edition of *The Internet For Dummies* by John R. Levine, Margaret Levine Young, and Carol Baroudi (Wiley).

Downloading and installing software

Earlier in this chapter we discuss the possibility of having to purchase or download and install software. It's important that you know how to do this. Most commercial software programs purchased at a retail store provide step-by-step instructions, and the process begins automatically when you insert the program disk into your computer. However, software downloaded directly from the Internet (such as plug-ins) may require a few extra steps to install. Typically, you need to download and save the software to your hard drive, browse and locate your file, run the file by double-clicking on it, and follow the step-by-step instructions displayed on the screen.

By finding out what software is going to be needed early in the process, you can better determine whether you can install it yourself or you need assistance. If you need assistance, you can try calling technical support at the institution, but depending on the program needing to be installed, they may not be able to help you. (Chapter 9 details what technical support can help you with.) However, you can always find a local retailer that has technical staff on hand who can help you for a fee.

Whenever purchasing or downloading software, it's important to know what operating system your computer uses, how much memory it has, and how much hard drive space is available. Refer to the earlier section "Meeting minimum hardware requirements" to determine your computer's profile information.

Using e-mail

One of the most common forms of communication occurs by using electronic mail, also known as e-mail. E-mail is used to communicate with peers and your instructor. Some institutions will provide you with a new e-mail account for school use. Others may require you to provide them with a personal account. In this situation, we recommend opening a free e-mail account with a service such as Google's Gmail (`http://mail.google.com`) for school use only.

Here is a list of common tasks that you should be able to complete specific to e-mail:

- **Opening your e-mail application:** Locate and click on your e-mail client/application in either the Start menu (Windows) or Taskbar (Mac) — for example, Microsoft Outlook or iMail. If you're using a Web-based e-mail account, open your Internet browser, navigate to your e-mail provider's Web site, and log in using your username and password.

- **Checking for new messages:** Click the Send and Receive or Get Messages button.

- **Checking your SPAM box for misplaced messages:** Click on the Spam folder and open for any mislabeled messages. Click the Not Spam or Send to Inbox button to reclassify the message.

- **Composing new messages and addressing them to one or more recipients:** Click the Compose New Message or New Message button. Type the recipients' e-mail addresses in the To textbox, separating each address with a space, comma, or semicolon, depending on your e-mail application. Enter an e-mail in the BCC (Blind Carbon Copy) textbox if you want to send a message to multiple people but don't want the recipients to see who the message is being sent to.

- **Attaching a document to a message:** Click the Attach Document button, browse for the desired file, and click the option to attach the file to your document.

- **Opening messages with attachments:** Click on the desired message in your Inbox. Click on the attachment and download the file to your computer. Locate the Downloads folder and double-click on the file.

- **Editing a document and resending it as an attachment:** Edit the document, click File➪Save As and save it to the desired location on your hard drive. Return to your e-mail application and click Compose New Message or Reply within an existing message. Follow the procedures for attaching a document to a message.

If you need help learning how to use your e-mail, there are a few resources you can explore. If your application is on your computer, you can use the application's built-in Help feature, found on the Menu bar at the top of the screen. If you use a Web-based mail system, you will most likely have a Help link somewhere on the screen that will transport you to a Web site with detailed descriptions and screenshots on how to use the application.

Staying Safe Online

As you start using the Internet more, it will become even more important to understand when and where to provide certain information. In the following sections, we explain how to make secure payments, remember and protect your passwords, and ensure your personal safety.

Making secure payments

You need to be sure you're truly protected when making online payments. This may be when registering for classes, purchasing books, or ordering study supplies online. Before entering your credit card or contact information into any Web page, be sure that you trust the vendor and that you're entering your information on a secure Web site. There's a quick way to assure that the Web site you're viewing is secure: Look at the Web site address. If there's an "s" after the "http" in the address, then you are visiting a secure site.

For example, if you visit Amazon.com to look at things to buy, you can see that the address, `http://www.amazon.com`, always starts with "http://." This is because you are simply looking, and you aren't being asked to share private information. However, when you're ready to check out and make your payment, you can see that `http://www.amazon.com/` changes to `https://www.amazon.com`. This means that you're now connected securely, and any information you share is private between you and Amazon.com.

The following screenshots provide examples of unsecure and secure Web sites. Figure 3-4 shows an example of a Web site that's currently on an unsecure page. Notice how the Web site address, also known as the URL, begins with "http." Figure 3-5 shows a secure page of the same Web site. Notice how its URL begins with "https." The "s" means secure. Don't forget to check for this before sharing private information, especially financial information. As this example shows, Web sites don't need to secure every page, only those where private information is being entered or displayed.

Figure 3-4:
An example
URL of an
unsecure
Web site.

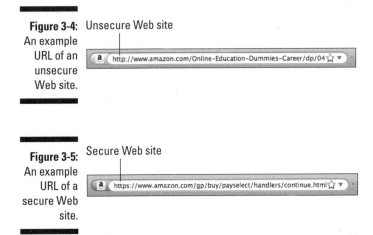

Unsecure Web site

http://www.amazon.com/Online-Education-Dummies-Career/dp/04 ☆ ▼

Figure 3-5:
An example
URL of a
secure Web
site.

Secure Web site

https://www.amazon.com/gp/buy/payselect/handlers/continue.html ☆ ▼

Remembering and protecting passwords

One thing that never fails when you become a part of the Internet community is the number of logins and passwords needed wherever you go. It's not uncommon for online students to have three or four different passwords just to access school information, depending on the technologies used.

Thinking of a password can be fun! Most institutions require 6 to 10 digits for a password, and many ask for a combination of letters, numbers, capitals, and possibly symbols. For your own security, don't choose the obvious; instead, think of something unique to you, similar to a vanity license plate. You'll have a chuckle every time you log in. For example, a ghost hunter might select "ICg0sts2!" (I see ghosts, too!). "2kds1DG*" might be perfect for someone with 2 small children and 1 big dog.

When it comes to passwords, here are a few dangerous practices to avoid:

✔ **Don't write your passwords on a sticky note that you attach to your monitor or on a piece of paper that's the first thing you see when you open the top drawer of your desk.** This is a common, but dangerous, practice. Be sure to keep your information safe from the public's view.

✔ **Don't have your computer remember your passwords for you.** This is especially true if you use a laptop that you take different places with you. If your computer is stolen, the person who stole it now has access to your secure information.

✔ **Don't use the same password for all protected sites.** Though it seems harmless and efficient, having the same password for everything makes you vulnerable if your information is ever comprised. Choose a different password for each site, and change your passwords frequently.

One way to remember all your passwords is to store them in one location. Of course, this location needs to be secure; otherwise, you're providing prying eyes with all the information needed to steal your identity. We suggest creating a single word processing or spreadsheet file in which to keep all your login information. Save that file securely with a password. Then, you only have to remember one password instead of many.

Most word-processing and spreadsheet products have a security feature. For example, Microsoft products, such as the 2003 versions of Word and Excel, have a protect document option under the Tools menu. When you choose this option, you are asked to supply a password that will be required the next time you open the document. Figures 3-6 and 3-7 provide visual examples of what protecting a word-processing document might look like:

✔ Figure 3-6 shows the first step in how to save and password-protect a document in Microsoft Office 2007 (Windows). To do this, click on File⇨Save As⇨Tools⇨General Options.

✔ Figure 3-7 shows the second step in saving and password-protecting a document in Office 2007 (Windows). Type your desired password in the "Password to open" textbox and click OK. You will be prompted to retype your password as a way to confirm that no accidental keystrokes were pressed.

Never give your password information to anyone, even technical support staff. They may have to reset your existing password in order to solve a particular problem, but they should have access to everything they need without asking you to share your password.

Figure 3-6: An example of a menu option used to protect a document.

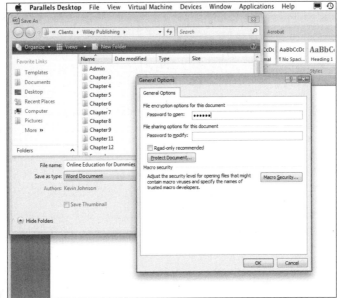

Figure 3-7:
An example
of a screen
used to
enter a
password
in order to
password-
protect a
document.

Ensuring personal security

In the previous section we discuss protecting your personal information and your passwords, and ensuring that you only provide certain information on secure Web sites. There's another type of security you should be aware of when participating in an online course: your personal security. We don't want to scare you; we simply want to remind you to stay safe when communicating online. Here are some important guidelines:

- ✔ **Don't reveal too much about yourself:** Almost every online course asks students to participate in an ice-breaker activity. Many times this includes revealing personal information about yourself, including your family, hobbies, and geographical location. Be sure to share this kind of information wisely. For example, feel free to say that you're married with two kids and live in Illinois. However, don't post your children's names or their elementary school photos. Disclosing medical conditions is also inappropriate. Your classmates really don't need to know you have irritable bowel syndrome.

- ✔ **Guard your contact information:** You may need to provide contact information to your instructor or peers when working on a group project. Again, only provide information that's necessary to complete the project. For example, you may want to give out your e-mail address and possibly even a phone number, but not your street address. If your instructor needs to mail information to your home, he should have access to that information via the academic institution. If asked to provide that information, feel free to politely question why it is needed and who it will be shared with.

✔ **Stay safe when meeting classmates in person:** Occasionally we find students who live in the same geographical location enrolled in our classes. In this situation, students often ask whether they can meet face-to-face to complete group projects. As instructors, we think this idea is fine; however, be safe when meeting classmates for the first time. We recommend always meeting in a public place, such as a restaurant or café, during common business hours. As a precaution, you may also want to notify your instructor that you're planning to meet, and provide the day and time. Afterwards, you can provide your instructor with a summary of what you accomplished.

Part II
Preparing to Be a Student

The 5th Wave   By Rich Tennant

In this part . . .

If you haven't gone to school in the past ten years, you're in for a surprise! Almost everything is online, from course catalogs to applications to live advisors. But fear not: This part takes you through the common processes involved in becoming an online student. Read this part to make sure you're making the right decisions before you invest your time and money.

We start with searching for a school or program and provide ideas for what to look for and questions to ask. Once you find a school you like, we then help you with the application process. Don't know how to pay for your online education? We have you covered there, too. Finally, we help you register for courses and get oriented to online education before you begin your first class.

Chapter 4

Discovering What's Available Online

After your appetite for learning online has been whetted, where should you go to find the right course offering? You may be surprised at the variety of institutions that offer online courses and how these courses have been packaged together for degrees. This chapter walks you through the many places you can find different kinds of online courses, and the various ways in which they are organized. Finally, we look at accelerated courses and how they work online.

Examining Different Types of Online Programs and Courses

Let's face it, most of us avoid school because it means hard work. However, there are good reasons to continue learning, including job promotions, higher earning potential, elevated status, and personal enrichment. The surprising thing is that school and learning are becoming synonymous with online education. That said, in this section we discuss aspects you should consider when looking at online programs and courses.

How important is it to you to earn college credit for your work? Do you have the time and resources to take enough courses to complete a degree? Or do you only need a few courses for professional development or skills enhancement? Would a specific certification be the professional seal of approval you need? Maybe you want to learn something to help you in your personal life, like faux painting or dog training. How you answer these questions determines the kinds of online programs that are best for you.

Earning traditional credit

If you've decided to take an online course, chances are good that you're look-ing to earn some sort of traditional credit for your work. As you should! This section describes the kinds of credit you can get for your efforts — specifi-cally, credits toward undergraduate or graduate degrees and high school credits. You can earn traditional college credits at two-year and four-year higher education institutions (which we cover later in this chapter) if you have completed your high school education. If you're still working on high school, you can earn credits through accredited online programs that serve your unique needs.

Credits toward undergraduate and graduate degrees

Yes, you can earn an entire degree online! You can find programs that award associate's (two-year), bachelor's (four-year), master's, and even doctoral degrees online. You also can use online classes to supplement in-person coursework at a traditional institution. If you follow our suggestions for searching for a course at different institutions (they appear later in this chap-ter), you'll probably see this in the marketing information you find.

Schools package courses together for an online degree just like they do for a degree you would earn in a traditional fashion. The degree consists of required courses you must take and a handful of elective courses. Only when you earn the necessary number of credit hours in the right mix of required and elective courses do you get the degree conferred. How many hours depends on the type of degree you're seeking, the state you're studying in, and the individual institution. However, in general, these are the expectations:

- An associate's degree typically requires around 60 credit hours and may represent the first two years of a bachelor's degree.
- A bachelor's degree requires 124–128 credit hours.
- A master's degree requires 32–36 hours beyond a bachelor's degree. Some programs require as many as 44 credit hours.
- A doctorate requires around 60–75 credit hours beyond a bachelor's, plus successful completion of a comprehensive examination and a writ-ten dissertation of original research.

When you enroll in a college course, the number of credit hours you'll receive upon completing it should be evident in the course schedule or the marketing information. Schools are typically very good about stating how many credit hours they attach to a particular course, because this can make a difference in the total number of hours awarded that count toward a degree. A typical semester course awards three credit hours. By looking at the course number, you can tell whether those credits are undergraduate or graduate hours:

- ✔ Anything with a 100–400 number (for example, PSY101) indicates undergraduate credit, which is what you need for an associate's or bachelor's degree.

- ✔ Courses with numbers 500 and above grant graduate level credit, suitable for master's degrees and doctorates.

You may have heard radio ads claiming you can finish your degree in as little as 18 months. These programs target adults who have previously earned some undergraduate credit and are now ready to complete a bachelor's degree. This newer twist in online education is actually a continuation of a former adult education model. These models started a couple decades ago and established a night and weekend schedule for working adults. Some programs "accelerated" their courses by compressing a 16-week course into 8 weeks, but not always. The point was that you could go to work during the day and catch up on coursework on the weekend. Today's model of online education offers even more convenience in that you don't have to push it all off to Saturday or Sunday. Because you work from the comfort of your home or office, you can engage in learning throughout the week.

One factor you may experience in online degree programs is the use of cohort groups. Simply put, this means when you begin a series of courses toward the completion of a degree, you progress with the same group or cohort of students through the entire degree. If John is in your first class, John should be in your last class — and every class in between! Many people believe that the bonds formed among a cohort group of students are more supportive and therefore more likely to influence students to positively persist through programs. If John is your friend, he might talk you out of dropping out when times get tough! Plus, from an administrative perspective, cohorts are easier to track and often allow an institution to offer more start dates so that students don't have to wait several months to begin taking classes.

High school credits

High school credit functions a little like college credit in that you need to earn the right number of course credits and the right types. This varies from state to state in the United States, however. For example, in one state you may need four years of English, whereas you may be able to get by with only three in another state. Depending on what state you live in and whether you're homeschooled or attending a traditional school, you could earn all or part of your high school credits through online schools.

Make sure that any online high school courses you investigate will count toward graduation in your state! Start by checking your local school district's policies in accordance with the state requirements. A trip or phone call to the district office should get you the information you need, but you can also search your state's department of education for policy statements concerning online education.

Obtaining certifications

Maybe you're interested in a career change or you want to branch into a new direction within your current field. A certification or endorsement may be just what you need, and you can earn many of these online.

Certificates are like miniature degrees that signify continuing education following a planned and purposeful curriculum. They offer only what you need for a specific professional field or task. For example, if you study for a certificate in Web site development, you don't have to take computer science courses in Cobol programming, but you do need graphics and multimedia instruction. If you're studying for a certificate as a dental assistant, you don't have to take an English composition course, but you need courses in radiology and diagnostics. Just the facts, ma'am.

Typically, a certificate is much shorter than a traditional degree. If you think of an associate's degree as a two-year degree (60 hours) and a bachelor's degree as a four-year degree (124–128 hours), the certification is a one-year degree. For example, you can earn a certificate in medical transcription for an average of 44 credit hours. Interested in private security? A certificate is available for as few as 50 credit hours.

Another point to keep in mind is that some certificates can lead to other degrees. For example, if you earn a certificate in elearning, some of those courses may count toward a master's degree at the same institution. Ask the school officials about this if you think the certificate may take you further!

More and more institutions offer certification online, including traditional two- and four-year institutions. Quality programs are truly beneficial in that they allow students to extend their professional development while continuing to work full-time. Every institution defines its own requirements for degrees and certificates. You need to compare carefully when looking at multiple programs. Drill down and see what courses are required and whether they hold your interest.

One of the best sources of information for a certification program is your professional association. Read professional newsletters and ask practitioners about the kinds of certificates and credentials valued in that field.

Continuing your education with a few classes for fun or profit

Online courses are not limited to degree or certificate programs. You can actually have fun online! For example, you could take a course in feng shui, an ancient Chinese practice of orienting objects to achieve desirable outcomes. You also can further your professional skills or ensure that you're meeting critical standards in your field by taking just a handful of classes. Whenever you enhance your professional skills, you stand to profit through promotions and salary boosts.

Personal interest

Ever wonder about your genealogy but don't know how to start researching and documenting your heritage? There's an online course for that. How about picking up a second language? Digital photography? These examples show the diversity of online courses.

What kinds of institutions offer such courses? To be honest, you may find a course for free or very little money by starting up your favorite search engine (such as Google or Yahoo), and typing "online course + [name of topic]". Try it; you'll be surprised! These courses may not be supported by an institution, and you won't earn credit, but you will get the information you seek. For example, coauthor Kevin recently took an online photography course where he learned the nuances of digital photography. He paid a fee to the photography school and completed the work online.

If you're looking for an institution to back you, you may find that your local college (two or four year) offers quite a few online courses geared toward personal interests. Topics may include the ones listed earlier in addition to art history, nutrition, parenting, and much more. These courses are usually part of the institutions' "community development" catalog or non-credit courses.

Professional development

In many fields, professionals are encouraged or required to complete professional development courses on an annual basis. For example, in the state of Illinois, per state funding guidelines for grant-funded adult education programs, faculty are required to complete six hours of professional development per fiscal year. So if you want to keep your job, you have to get those six hours of training somehow! If you're a practicing medical or dental professional and want to maintain your licensure, you have to earn a prescribed number of continuing education credits per year. These kinds of courses may be found at institutions that award degrees in those fields. For example, if you need credits for teaching, a college that awards degrees in education would be a logical place to look.

In addition, more and more professional associations offer professional development online. They know professionals appreciate the convenience of learning anytime, anywhere. You can find many opportunities by conducting a search for "[your field] + online courses." For example, the Young Adult Library Services Association offers its members online courses related to their professional needs. You can find these opportunities by searching for "[your association] + online courses" in your preferred search engine.

Just make sure that any professional development course credits you earn will be accepted by the professional association that requires you to earn them. To find out, visit the association's Web site and search for statements concerning acceptance of online credit. For example, if you're a dentist and you visit the American Dental Association's continuing education page, you'll see a clear statement regarding states' limits on the number of hours that can be earned through self-paced online courses.

Compliance training

In business and industry, compliance training accounts for most course offerings. What kind of compliance? It could involve ethics training, safety and material data, or emergency preparedness. Other examples include what to do with forms, processes for requisitioning funds, or must-know policies. All of these are courses you may find online. The most common provider is your company's human resource department.

Compliance training works very well as a self-paced course, so you shouldn't be surprised if you're in a course all by yourself. However, keep in mind that your participation, what pages or content you read, and how well you do in follow-up tests may be reported back to the company. We discuss self-paced courses in more detail later in this chapter.

Finding Out Which Institutions Offer Online Programs and Courses

Whether you're interested in taking one or two online courses or completing an entire degree online, the process of searching for online education offerings isn't much different from researching traditional education options. First you need to determine what kind of institution best meets your needs. Are you seeking a bachelor's degree or higher? Then you need at least a four-year school. In this section, we walk you through your choices according to the type of institution so you know what to look for.

Four-year colleges

Many four-year colleges and universities, both public and private, offer bachelor's degrees and graduate degrees online. They may also offer certificates and personal enrichment courses. Some are traditional schools with real brick-and-mortar campuses; others are completely virtual with no physical place to go. We discuss how to get course information from both of these types of schools in the following sections.

Hold on there! Before you go randomly searching, considering the following recommendations may save you time:

- ✔ **If you're completing a degree you previously started at a traditional school:** We recommend that you go back to the institution where you were a student, and talk to them about what may be available online. Jump to the section "Brick-and-mortar schools."

- ✔ **If you're starting an entire degree from scratch:** You have to decide which of the two types of institutions we talk about in the following sections you want to earn it from: brick and mortar or wholly online. Read both of the following sections to find out how to get necessary information.

- ✔ **If you simply need a course or two for personal interest or professional development:** We recommend that you look at your local state institutions. Not only do you keep your money in-state, but you're closer if you need to drive to the campus for any reason.

Brick-and-mortar schools

If you type "online courses" into a search engine (such as Google, Yahoo, or MSN), only some of the schools in the resulting list will be traditional institutions with physical campuses. For example, you might find Colorado Technical University or DeVry University. They offer their programs and classes both on a traditional campus and through online counterparts.

Traditional brick-and-mortar schools, such as your local state university, don't seem to pop to the top of the search results. They're competing against the online giants and their marketing dollars aren't going as far. However, these are still worthy of consideration — you just have to follow a different process to get the information you need:

1. **Rather than conduct an open search, we recommend you go directly to the local school's Web site.** Once there, look for links to Online Learning, Online Education, Online Courses, Distance Learning, or Distance Education on the home page. If that isn't obvious, look for a link to Academics or Future Students, and see whether online courses are mentioned there.

2. **It helps to know what kind of degree you're looking for and the school, college, or academic department it typically falls under.** For example, if you want to become a teacher, look in the College of Education or something similar. If you want a degree in business, look for the College of Business or something to that effect.

3. **Once you find your way to the correct department, you can begin sorting through the course listings.** Look for links to course schedules rather than the course catalog.

A school's catalog tells you what courses you need to put together for an entire degree, but it may not tell you whether the entire degree is available online.

4. **See whether the school gives you the opportunity to sort through the ways in which a given class is offered.** The best schools state clearly and unquestionably when a class is offered online or in a blended format. (We talk about blended learning — a combination of online and traditional teaching methods — a little later in this chapter.)

5. **Once you have an idea that the school offers online courses or a degree in which you're interested, follow up.** Send an e-mail or make a telephone call to the department you're interested in. Ask for more information.

Wholly online schools

When you look up "online courses" on your favorite search engine, other names besides those of traditional institutions pop up. Schools like University of Phoenix, Kaplan University, Capella University and other wholly online four-year schools have grown in popularity, and are now mainstream in the media and online search worlds.

Listings from the major players will come up in a general search for "online courses" plus the field you're interested in, as well as agencies that market online programs for a variety of schools. An example of an agency is EarnMyDegree.com (`www.earnmydegree.com`). This particular Web site represents universities you may recognize as well as some that may be unfamiliar.

In most cases, you're asked to complete an online form with your name, e-mail address, and some other basic information such as the type of program you are considering. You will then receive more information by e-mail.

This is a direct method of finding out what's available, but it has some drawbacks.

✔ You're put on everyone's mailing list, and your e-mail inbox grows exponentially.

✔ You begin receiving phone calls during the dinner hour.

✔ You may hear from institutions that are not accredited (Chapter 5 explains the importance of accreditation).

✔ You may have so many choices that it becomes overwhelming!

Two-year colleges

If you're looking for a two-year (associate's) degree, you'll have an easier time with your search process than you will with other types of institutions. Why is this? The short answer is that two-year brick-and-mortar colleges (also known as community colleges or junior colleges) have had the most experience with online courses. In fact, according to the researchers at the Sloan Consortium, a professional group of institutions and individuals focused on quality online education, almost half of the students enrolled in online courses in 2007 were studying at two-year colleges. They have a history, and they do it well.

The search process for online courses at a two-year college is very similar to what you would experience for a four-year school, but you're more likely to be able to go directly to course listings that specify online delivery. In short, you might see a glowing icon that says, "Online Courses Here!" on the community college's home page. That means you won't have as much difficulty finding information about what online courses are available.

If you don't see an obvious link to Online Learning, Online Education, Online Courses, Distance Education, or Distance Learning, follow the same steps that you would for a four-year brick-and-mortar school (we list these steps earlier in this chapter).

College: One word, two meanings

College of Lake County and College of Education both use the word "college," but in different contexts. Here's the lowdown:

✔ **The word *college* can be part of the name of the institution.** In North America, smaller schools, two-year schools, and schools that focus on undergraduate education are often named as colleges.

✔ **The word *college* can also describe a group of departments or programs that** **offer degrees with the same foundations but distinct expertise.** This is often the case at larger institutions where degrees are more highly differentiated. An example would be a College of Business within a university that offers degrees in entrepreneurship, administration, marketing, and accounting.

Other institutions for certificates, professional development, and training

Finding an online certification program is very similar to searching for online courses through two-year or four-year institutions. Again, you have to know what you're looking for, and you have to know what kind of institution will serve you best.

Say you want to earn a certificate in medical transcription. Using your standard search engine, you'll find that you can earn such a certificate through two- and four-year schools, some with brick-and-mortar operations, and others that are wholly online. (You'll even find programs that are sold by companies and don't offer traditional credit, but we don't recommend those.)

Here are a few pointers to help you decide:

- ✔ **Is your area of study mostly introductory and associated with a two-year degree, such as medical transcription or allied health?** If so, look to a two-year school.

- ✔ **Is your area of study more closely aligned with a field requiring a bachelor's degree?** This would include fields like computer science or education, where certificates and endorsements often mean job promotions. In this case, look to a school that can offer graduate degrees.

- ✔ **Do you need to earn Continuing Education Credits (CEUs) to maintain a license or for employment?** Maybe a professional association in your field has recommended schools. Start with the association's Web site.

- ✔ **Has your employer recommended specific skills training (for instance, database management)?** Your human resources department may already have a subscription to a provider that delivers such training online. This is big business!

When you search for any individual course, read the prerequisite information carefully so you know whether that course is available to you independently, or whether you can only take it if you're enrolled in a specific degree or certificate program.

Virtual schools for children and teens

A growing number of high school and homeschooled students are seeking online education, either to make up credits, work ahead, or study completely online as a homeschooled student. Where would you find a virtual K-12 school?

✔ **If you're a traditional high school student and need to make up lost coursework (called credit recovery), go to the school office.** Seriously, start with the local office and see whether they know of state programs that might meet your needs.

✔ **If you can't get the answer that way, we recommend you search for "your state + virtual school" in any of the major search engines.** For example, entering "Texas + virtual school" led us to the Texas Virtual School at www.texasvirtualschool.org and "Illinois + virtual school" led us to Illinois Virtual High School at www.ivhs.org.These are both state-supported virtual schools.

By the way, most state-supported virtual high schools require their faculty to have the same state credentials as any other public school teacher. Hiring state-certified instructors guarantees faculty that are familiar with state standards and helps students better prepare for successfully completing standardized tests and graduating.

✔ **If you don't find a Web site that is directly state-supported, you may see a link to a private group.** K^{12} at www.k12.com and Connections Academy at www.connectionsacademy.com are two examples. Believe it or not, a majority of the K-12 online education has been outsourced to private agencies. School districts contract with these groups to provide online courses. For the money, they get trained faculty teaching well-developed, interactive courses.

Make sure whatever K-12 program you examine will count for credit — you don't want to waste your time on courses that won't count toward your high school diploma! A good school will be able to tell you immediately what counts or doesn't count toward your state's requirements.

Imagine you're looking for specific online courses through a virtual school. Once you get to the school's Web site, you should be able to find a link to Courses or Curriculum. To be truthful, K-12 Web sites are easier to navigate than those of colleges! You can read the course description, application procedures, and more from these sites. As always, make sure you only consider an accredited program!

Flip to Chapter 16 for more about online education for children and teens.

Checking Out Different Structures of Online Courses

Once you know that you can find a class you need at your institution of choice, your next consideration should be the structure of the class. By structure, we mean whether the course is completely online or a blend of online and face-to-face time, instructor led or self-paced, and real-time or asynchronous. If you have recently searched for a college course, you may already recognize that quite a variety of structures is available. This section helps you sort through some of the differences.

Before we get to the different course structures, it's worthwhile to establish a baseline for classes in general. Every course typically has two components:

- ✔ **Content:** The guts of the course, or what you are to learn. The content of an accounting course is accounting. The content of a history course is the history of whatever you are studying, and so on.

- ✔ **Evaluation:** A nice word for figuring out what grade you earn. In many cases, testing determines your grade, but it may also be determined by a final paper or project.

Ideal courses also include a third component: Practice. In other words, some-where between content and evaluation, the student gets to practice what is being learned, either through homework assignments, short papers, or other activities.

Just you and the monitor (fully online) versus blended courses (partly online)

One big consideration for courses should be whether they're completely online or a blend of online and traditional class time.

- ✔ A completely online course means just that. You complete all the work online. You could enroll in a course at a school that's physically located across the globe because you wouldn't need to travel. (You can find other benefits of fully online classes in Chapter 2.) Because of the popu-larity of online courses, institutions readily identify which classes are online.

- ✔ Blended learning is a different form of online learning and is becoming more popular. *Blended courses* are a combination of online screen time and tradi-tional *seat time* (the amount of time a student sits in a seat in a classroom). Faculty appreciate blended formats because they can move portions of instruction online, thus freeing up class time for other activities.

For example, the instructor may ask you to read articles, complete quizzes, or watch pre-recorded lectures online. In the class time on campus, she may have groups work on projects, conduct a lab, or host a class discussion.

The major advantages of blended learning are human contact and accountability. Students aren't likely to slip through the cracks or procrastinate when a teacher has real face time with them every week. And yet, the student can work on other course materials in the asynchronous realm and may benefit from the independence and reflective thinking that often accompanies online courses.

An obvious disadvantage of the blended format is that you need to live close enough to drive to campus for the regularly scheduled meetings. If you enroll in a course at a college that is three hours from home, this could be a significant nuisance, not to mention an undue expense.

Some colleges fail to advertise the blended requirements of traditional classes appropriately. For example, you could enroll in a business management course that meets Mondays and Wednesdays, only to learn during the first week that you're also required to log in twice a week and complete activities online. For this reason, we strongly advise you to ask about the structure of a course before enrolling and putting your money down. If the academic advisor or registrar can't answer your question, go directly to the instructor.

Instructor-led courses versus self-paced courses

In Chapter 2, we briefly outline the difference between instructor-led and self-paced courses, but we look a little deeper at the differences in the following sections.

Instructor-led courses

An instructor-led course is just what you think it is; an instructor determines what happens with the content, pace of instruction, and evaluation. Here are a few distinguishing traits of this type of course, which is the most common type out there:

✔ **In an instructor-led course, there is a distinct schedule, and the whole class works through the content at the same time.** While you are reading and completing activities for "module two," so is the rest of the class. Typically, you find the schedule posted as a calendar or within the class syllabus (see Chapter 8 for more about these documents and how to locate them in your online classroom). If you're a procrastinator, an instructor-led course can keep you on task.

✔ **Not only do you interact with your peers, but you have regular communication with the instructor.** The instructor is present and virtually "visible" through regular announcements and interaction in public discussions.

Be sure to read the regular announcements posted by the instructor. Doing so not only keeps you on task and on time, but also helps you avoid looking silly by asking a question she has already addressed.

You also see the instructor through private communication. As you complete assignments and turn them in, the instructor communicates with you and provides feedback. This may come via private e-mail or by way of the electronic grade book. This communication reminds you that the virtual classroom has a live instructor, and you are not alone. (We discuss all the different methods of online communication in Chapter 10.)

✔ **You don't see the whole course at once.** This fact may be one of the most distinctive features of an instructor-led course. Many instructors prefer to "time-release" the content according to when the students need it. In other words, if you're in the fourth week of an eight-week course, you may not be able to see the content for weeks five and beyond. You only see the week you're working on. This strategy keeps all the students in the same place, and prevents discussions from becoming disjointed and confusing.

If you find yourself in a course that uses the time-release method and you know in advance that you'll be traveling, let your instructor know the dates you'll be on the road. Ask whether it's possible for you to view some of the content in advance so that you won't fall behind if you experience technological difficulties getting connected to the Internet.

Earlier in this chapter, we mention three basic components of an online course: content, evaluation, and practice. An instructor-led course is more likely to have the practice component than a self-paced course because someone is available to check your homework and smaller assignments. Your learning can be evaluated through means other than traditional testing. If you think about it, it takes the capacity of a real human to read someone's essay and determine whether it makes sense. A computer can't possibly evaluate that kind of assignment as well as an instructor. If practicing what you're learning is important to you, an instructor-led class is just for you.

Self-paced courses

In a self-paced course, you're on your own to determine your schedule, so if you're a self-starter, you may find this type of course to your liking. The content, or what you are to learn, is predetermined. When you access the course, you usually find that it has been divided up into modules or units. You click on the first unit, read the content, and move through the course at your own pace. You can spend more time in the challenging areas and breeze through those that are easier for you.

In a business setting, self-paced courses are often prepackaged with very simple software interfaces. The window loaded on your screen might look like the one in Figure 4-1.

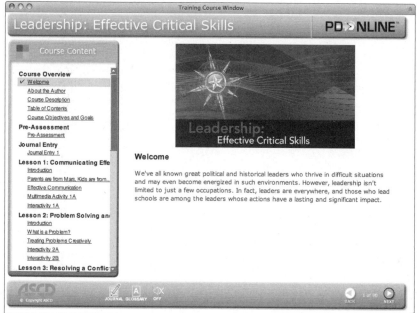

Source: "Leadership: Effective Critical Skills," PD Online course, Alexandria, VA: ASCD. ©2009 ASCD. Reproduced with permission. Learn more about ASCD at www.ascd.org. ASCD® and PD Online™ are trademarks of ASCD.

Figure 4-1: The interface of a typical self-paced course.

These courses have navigational tools to help you move through the content. You'll probably see arrows at the bottom to help you advance and a menu on the left. You use these tools to help you move through the content at your own pace.

Just because a course is self-paced doesn't mean there isn't an instructor standing by in the wings to help you with questions or concerns. Consider the case of Alex. Wanting to learn better keyboarding skills, he enrolled in an online course through his local community college. The introductory information came from an instructor who guided Alex through the process of downloading and installing special software for working through the lessons. All the lessons were made available when the course started, and they could be completed any time during the eight-week period. There were no scheduled meetings, and Alex could work at his leisure.

Even self-paced courses often have instructors assigned to monitor what's happening. What you want to know is what that person does. Will you have regular contact throughout the course or just at the beginning or end? Can you call with questions? When you identify a potential self-paced course, see whether the instructor has an e-mail address available and ask! If no instructor is assigned to the course, be wary.

What about evaluation? How does the person in charge know that you learned the content? In the business world, most often this comes through traditional testing. After you read or listen to a portion of the content, you take a short quiz that's embedded in the program. These quizzes test your ability to recall or apply what you've just heard.

Determining whether the course you want is instructor-led or self-paced

How do you know the difference between an instructor-led course and a self-paced course when you're doing the research we describe earlier in this chapter? This is where you need to drill down to course descriptions. See whether they include terms like "instructor-led." If nothing is mentioned but the name of the instructor is listed, e-mail that person and ask whether the course is self-paced. This information helps you succeed because you know what to expect. It also makes you look very savvy in the instructor's eyes!

Sometimes schools don't mention that the courses are instructor-led, and a lot of students sign up thinking they'll be taking independent-study courses. It's worth asking about before you register so you don't waste time or money.

Asynchronous courses versus synchronous (real-time) courses

As we explain in detail in Chapter 2, most online courses are asynchronous in nature. This means you do the work when it's convenient for you. As long as you meet the deadlines for assignments, all is good. However, instructors may also have synchronous components to their courses, such as weekly meetings, and some instructors require attendance or participation. For example, when coauthor Susan teaches, she hosts a weekly office hour during which she reviews assignments and introduces extra material. While her students aren't required to attend, they like the personal contact. These sessions are recorded so those who can't attend can watch a movie of the synchronous event.

This information should be available in the course description that we explain how to find earlier in this chapter. However, be sure to ask an academic advisor about this possibility if you don't see any reference to synchronous sessions. Better safe than sorry!

Finishing Your Schooling Faster with Accelerated Programs and Courses

Teachers (your humble coauthors included) would love for you to believe that learning is fun, but the truth is that it can be a major headache and very disruptive to real life! For that reason, you might really appreciate the speed at which you can finish schooling online.

Now that colleges and universities have discovered a ready market of busy students who want to learn on their own time, they want to enroll and keep those customers. A great way to achieve this is to make sure the courses hold the students' interest and move quickly. With this in mind, many institutions offer *accelerated courses,* which are traditional 16-week semester courses that have been condensed into half the time. In fact, eight weeks is a common length for an online course.

In this section, we describe the pros and cons of accelerated online education and provide a few pointers for surviving such programs and courses.

Do course catalogs and descriptions specify which courses are accelerated? Nope, not necessarily. It's up to you, smart reader, to do the math. If you see a 3 credit hour course with start/end dates indicating that it runs 8 weeks, it's accelerated. A traditional course would extend a semester, or 16 weeks.

Also, if you see marketing materials that recommend only taking one course at a time, it's probably because the courses are accelerated and very demanding. After all, you're fitting 16 weeks' worth of content into less time.

The benefits and challenges of accelerated programs

The good news is that accelerated courses generally teach you information you can apply right away. Have you ever heard the phrase "use it or lose it"? That's the mantra of instructional design for accelerated courses. Courses require students to apply the content right away through ongoing assignments. The more you use the information, the more likely you are to learn and retain it.

Obviously, if a course is accelerated, you get more information in less time. In theory, you can complete a degree in half the time. However, the reality is that how much information you take in depends on your own capacity to absorb information. In other words, if your jug (brain) is full of holes (distracted or disorganized), it won't matter how much water (knowledge) you pour in. You'll never hold it all!

So it is with accelerated courses. Yes, you receive more information in less time, but you have to be sure you have the time and the study strategies to process this information.

Tips for successfully completing accelerated classes

So how do you succeed in an accelerated course? Here are a few handy guidelines:

- ✔ **Enroll in only one course at a time until you know what you can handle.** You may even find degree programs that limit the number of courses you can take simultaneously at first for this very reason.

- ✔ **Establish a definite schedule for study.** Procrastination doesn't work well online, even for self-paced courses. We recommend daily logins. (We provide general guidelines for good study habits in Chapter 11.)

- ✔ **Set reasonable goals for participation.** You don't have to answer every post. Check your course requirements, and exceed them slightly, but not extremely!

- ✔ **If you're really crunched for time and have discussions to read, hit the first posts from the original authors.** Unless your instructor says "you must read every post," you can get by skipping a few responses here and there.

- ✔ **Develop a method for saving links and resources you want to go back to later.** For some people, this means keeping a running document where they paste links and URLs. For others, it means opening an account on a social bookmarking tool like delicious (`delicious.com`). The point is that you don't have to read everything immediately.

- ✔ **Save projects from one course to the next.** This isn't necessarily so you can repurpose them, but so you can draw on the resources, methods, and so on that you've previously utilized.

- ✔ **Work ahead if you can.** Take advantage of a slow week to get a head start on the next one.

- ✔ **Keep in mind the intensity will only last 8 weeks!** There's great comfort in knowing that it won't go on forever, even if you love the class.

- ✔ **If you're working on a degree that involves a thesis, try to connect all your assignments to your thesis.** Pick a topic early in your studies, and investigate different angles throughout the various courses.

- ✔ **Set time aside at the beginning of the course for the basics.** Read your syllabus, become familiar with the course navigation, and begin reading the text.

- ✔ **Take advantage of synchronous tools.** Using the phone, Web conferencing tools, and so forth is more productive than writing e-mails when you're conducting group work, especially during the organizing process.

Chapter 5

Doing Your Homework: Evaluating Schools

*O*ne of the hardest decisions you have to make when deciding to go back to school is which institution to attend, especially when considering online education. Unlike the early days of online education, you're no longer constrained to only the one or two colleges and universities in your surrounding area. Nowadays, you can choose one of many throughout the United States, not to mention those that are available to you internationally.

No matter what school you choose to attend, a few universal guidelines apply that can help you in the decision-making process. This chapter provides important information on what to look for and questions to ask as you evaluate various schools.

Focusing on What You Need in a School

When considering the financial investment of going to school, you should view yourself as a consumer. Approaching education in this manner helps you organize your thoughts and prioritize your wants and needs.

Consider the process of buying a car. When money is tight, what you really need is a reliable vehicle that will get you from point A to point B. Though you may want power doors and windows, keyless entry, heated seats, a navigation system, and a sunroof, you don't really need them. Therefore, you're forced to prioritize features according to what you must have, what you'd like to have, and what you can do without. You also have to decide how much you can afford to spend. By making these decisions before heading to the dealership, you ensure a smoother interaction with the salesperson and protect yourself from being swindled into buying more than you really need or can afford. You also help the salesperson better match your needs with the right car.

Preparing to go to school, especially online, is very much like purchasing a vehicle. You need to prioritize your needs and determine how much you're able to pay, whether it be now or by making loan payments later. For example, if you're a working parent with limited resources for child care, fully online courses with no face-to-face obligations may be your top priority.

In the next section, we help you develop a checklist of elements to consider when looking to participate in online programs or courses. These considerations include evaluating the program/course offerings, types and sizes of classes, how much time they take, and whether your previously earned credits will transfer.

Considering the program you're interested in

The first thing you must decide is what you want out of your education. If you want to advance professionally, check with career professionals about the kind of degree you need. For example, if you're a registered nurse (RN) who wants to teach, you may be required by your state board of health to have a Masters of Nursing. You can't get that at a two-year college. Similarly, if you want to be a paralegal, you don't need a law degree. Knowing specifically what you want can help you choose an institution with the right degree and concentration that meets your needs. The concentration is the specific area within the field you want to focus on. For example, within education, concentrations include curriculum and instruction, organization and leadership, and instructional technology and distance education, to name a few.

For those of you who aren't sure yet what you want to do professionally and want to explore multiple options, consider an institution where you can get diverse experience. One suggestion is to enroll in the general education courses that are required by almost every major and take elective courses in a variety of fields that you may be interested in.

Secondly, decide whether you want to attend any of your courses on a traditional campus. If so, research the schools in your surrounding area to see whether they offer a program that meets your academic goals. Otherwise, you need to look for programs that are offered fully online.

When researching a school (for pointers on this, see the later section "Talking to the Right People to Find the Answers You Need"), remember to find out whether the institution requires students to be on campus during any part of the program. Many institutions require a face-to-face orientation program at the student's expense. This can be a very helpful experience for the student, but attendance incurs travel and other expenses.

Determining whether or not a program is affordable

Education isn't cheap. Therefore, cost may be a big determining factor as to whether you're able to attend a specific institution. Even though different institutions offer similar degrees and courses, they may vary in cost by a large margin, especially among community colleges, public universities, and private institutions. Not only is it important to know whether you can afford to pay for tuition, but you must also find out whether the program you want to enroll in has additional fees for supplies and services. If you choose to take advantage of financial aid (see Chapter 6), you need to know the estimated cost of your program and what the monthly payments will be upon graduation. We provide some questions specific to cost later in this chapter and detail financial aid options in Chapter 6.

Checking out class size (and the student-to-instructor ratio)

Once you narrow your search to a few selective institutions that meet your academic needs, you can start focusing on other important details, including class size. You want to consider schools that offer classes that aren't too big or too small, but are just right. In the online environment, class size really matters. If the class is too big, the instructor may have a difficult time providing enough adequate feedback and managing course discussions, leaving you with little or no guidance. If the class is too small, you may struggle to keep the dialogue going and the course may seem dull and monotonous. From the instructor's perspective, we like class sizes between 18 and 25 students.

If you're looking for a more independent program with less interaction, a smaller class size may fit your learning style better. However, most research indicates that interaction, communication, and collaboration are all important pieces to successful online programs. Independent models tend to be more common in the corporate education setting, though some do exist in the academic setting. If a high level of independence is important to you, be sure to discuss this with your academic advisor up front.

When online education first hit the scene in the mid 1990s, many institutions saw it as an opportunity to make a lot of money by putting several hundred students in one class because they weren't restricted by physical space. This was disastrous. Instructors were so overwhelmed by the numbers that they were unable to provide any kind of personal attention or quality feedback in a timely manner. Courses became self-paced, and the instructor was simply used as a contact person for answering questions.

A lot has been learned since then, but some institutions still have unrealistic class sizes that prevent instructors from providing quality instruction. Therefore, find out how many students will be in your class before enrolling.

In an academic setting, we recommend classes have one instructor for every 18 to 25 students.

Knowing how much time you can commit and how it may be spent

One of the most underestimated aspects regarding online education is the amount of time needed to complete a course. The exact amount of time it takes to successfully participate in an online course is different for each person.

A common calculation for determining how much time you should expect to focus on coursework is to take the number of credits the course is worth and triple it. For example, a three-credit course should require a minimum of 9 to 12 hours of your time per week. This calculation is assuming the course runs 16 weeks. Therefore, if you're considering an accelerated program (see Chapter 4 for more information), think about how much more time this adds and determine whether your schedule allows for that level of commitment.

Several factors can affect how much time you spend on your online education. We outline those aspects in the following sections.

The technology learning curve

Most institutions have some kind of formula for determining how much time students will need to spend on assignments in order to earn the respective number of credits for a course. However, they don't consider an individual's computer proficiencies, which can have a dramatic impact on the time it takes to complete assignments. Students who take longer to navigate the Web or learn new technologies need more time to complete assignments.

When investigating programs and courses, ask about what technologies are used and how consistent those technologies are from week to week and class to class. This helps you understand what kind of learning curve you may need to account for when scheduling your time. Newer technologies take more time to become familiar with on top of your workload.

At first, learning the technology of online education takes time. However, over time and with repeated use, it gets easier and faster. Even learning newer technologies becomes easier and begins to take less time.

Real-time meetings

Even though synchronous meetings have some great advantages, they're time consuming and can frustrate students if they are unaware of them ahead of time. Therefore, it's important to know up front whether or not the program or course you're considering requires live meetings, and if so, what day and time those meetings are held. Then you can determine whether your schedule would allow you to take the class, as well as what kind of work and/or child-care arrangements you'd need to make.

Be sure to confirm the time zone as well. Most synchronous sessions are in the evening, but 7 p.m. Eastern Time is only 4 p.m. Pacific Time, and that may pose a challenge with work and commuting schedules.

Coursework requirements

Finally, and most importantly, you must be sure you have enough time in your schedule to complete the coursework. This includes reading text, reading and posting to peer discussions, and managing other important documents such as the syllabus, assignment details, and so forth. It also includes the time it takes to actually complete assignments, quizzes, and group projects.

In the face-to-face environment, the rule of thumb is for students to spend two or three hours working on schoolwork for every hour they are in class. For a class that meets for three hours a week, the total time spent in class and studying would be nine to twelve hours a week. In an online class, students should expect to spend approximately the same amount of total time. Time not spent in a physical classroom is spent participating in online discussions and completing other assignments.

The preceding calculation assumes the class is a standard 16-week course. In an accelerated program, the same amount of information is presented in half the time, dramatically increasing the amount of time required. Depending on the course, the workload could double, although that's not always the case. You might need to set aside 15 to 20 hours a week for a three-credit course in an accelerated program. Now you know why we recommend taking only one course at a time when participating in an accelerated program!

Planning ahead: Figuring out whether your credits will transfer

It pays to think about the future when deciding to enroll in a college or university. Maybe you're going to start your degree online and finish it at a traditional school, or maybe you plan to do the opposite — start at a traditional school and later transfer to an online program. Consider future possibilities and make sure the institution you choose supports those possibilities. For example, if you're a freshman and want to take your general education courses through a community college's online program, make sure your course credits will transfer to a four-year institution when the time comes.

Bringing in credits from a traditional institution

Many online programs accept credits from other accredited institutions. However, several variables are used to decide whether credits are transferrable. For example, some graduate programs simply require an undergraduate degree from an accredited school and individual course credit isn't a concern. However, other graduate programs require specific prerequisite courses that may or may not have been a part of your undergraduate curriculum.

Another variable is time. Coursework completed recently is more likely to be accepted for transfer. If several years have passed, the institution may ask that you retake certain courses.

Whether you have taken classes recently or long ago, be sure to have your transcripts audited before making your final decision about which school to enroll in. You may have to pay a nonrefundable application fee, but it's worth it to know up front whether your credits are going to transfer.

Once you are told that credit is transferrable, be sure to get an official transcript of exactly which credits will transfer. This should be a formal document on the institution's letterhead with an official seal, signed by an administrator. This provides you with protection in case you need proof of transfer due to administrative staff changes within the organization.

Switching from one online school to another

If you want to switch from one online school to another, the process should be exactly the same as that described in the preceding section. Again, the fact that your credits were earned from an accredited institution doesn't guarantee that they'll fully transfer, but accreditation will definitely be a minimum qualification.

Down the road: Will a traditional institution accept the online school's credits?

After taking courses or finishing a degree online, you may want to continue your education. Depending on what institution you decided to attend, many people reviewing your transcripts won't even know the program or course you were last enrolled in was online. This is especially the case for institutions that have both on-campus and online course offerings. Therefore, transferring courses from an online institution to a traditional, campus-based institution should be no problem. However, the same concept of preparing early applies here.

If you're transferring credits from an entirely online program and you fear your credits won't be as transferable, don't worry. As long as you do your homework when choosing an online institution, you should have no problems transferring credits — assuming the credits are aligned with the program you want to transfer into.

If you know when you enroll in an online program that you plan to transfer to another institution in a couple years, research both the online institution and the traditional school or schools you have your sights set on, and find out whether the credits you earn will transfer from one to the other. Doing a little more research and legwork up front may save you several headaches down the road.

Finding an Accredited School

Going back to school often means investing in your future. That investment isn't cheap, so you want to be sure you're getting your money's worth.

First and foremost, you should look for a school that's accredited. *Accreditation* is a process by which a school is determined to have met predetermined quality standards. These accreditation standards are determined and monitored by nongovernmental agencies that have been authorized by the U.S. Secretary of Education.

In this section, we discuss ways of determining an institution's credibility and quality.

Recognizing the two types of accreditation

Schools themselves can be accredited, and programs within schools can be accredited. (And yes, an accredited school can have accredited programs!)

The first type of accreditation is *institutional accreditation,* which means that all the parts of the institution work well together to meet its overall mission. There are both national and regional accreditation-granting organizations. Though national accreditation may sound like a higher level of accreditation, regional accreditation tends to be more credible. There are six regional accrediting agencies in the United States that serve institutions within their respective regions. (See the nearby sidebar, "Regional institutional accrediting agencies" to find out which agencies cover which states.)

The second type of accreditation is called *specialized* or *programmatic accreditation.* This means that a specific program within the school has successfully completed the accreditation process relevant to its field. For example, if you look at Eastern Illinois University's education program, you will find that it is accredited through the specialist level by the Commission on Institutions of the North Central Association of Colleges and Schools and by the National Council for Accreditation of Teacher Education for the preparation of elementary and secondary teachers and school service personnel. This means that this college meets general academic quality standards, plus standards specific to the education of future teachers. Most specialized accreditors only confer the accreditation status to programs within a regionally accredited institution. However, this isn't always the case. A few will accredit institutions that are not regionally accredited.

Regional institutional accrediting agencies

Here is a list of the six regional accreditors recognized by the U.S. Department of Education as being qualified to confer accreditation status on institutions that meet their predetermined quality standards. Different agencies provide accreditation to different types of institutions. For example, one agency may accredit vocational institutions, whereas another agency may accredit postsecondary degree-granting institutions. For a complete list of regional and national agencies, and their scope of recognition, as recognized by the U.S. Department of Education, you can visit the department's Web site at www.ed.gov/admins/finaid/accred/accreditation_pg7.html.

✔ **Middle States Association of Colleges and Schools, Middle States Commission on Higher Education (MSCHE):** Servicing Delaware, the District of Columbia, Maryland, New Jersey, New York,

Pennsylvania, Puerto Rico, and the U.S. Virgin Islands. Web site: www.msche.org.

✔ **New England Association of Schools and Colleges, Commission on Institutions of Higher Education (NEASC-CIHE):** Servicing Connecticut, Maine, Massachusetts, New Hampshire, Rhode Island, and Vermont. Web site: cihe.neasc.org.

New England Association of Schools and Colleges, Commission on Technical and Career Institutions (NEASC-CTCI): Servicing secondary institutions with vocational-technical programs at the 13th and 14th grade levels, postsecondary institutions, and institutions of higher education that provide primarily vocational/technical education at the certificate, associate, and baccalaureate degree levels in Connecticut,

Maine, Massachusetts, New Hampshire, Rhode Island, and Vermont. Web site: ctci.neasc.org.

✔ **North Central Association of Colleges and Schools, The Higher Learning Commission (NCA-HLC):** Servicing Arizona, Arkansas, Colorado, Illinois, Indiana, Iowa, Kansas, Michigan, Minnesota, Missouri, Nebraska, New Mexico, North Dakota, Ohio, Oklahoma, South Dakota, West Virginia, Wisconsin, and Wyoming, including schools of the Navajo Nation. Web site: www.nca higherlearningcommission.org.

✔ **Northwest Commission on Colleges and Universities (NWCCU):** Servicing Alaska, Idaho, Montana, Nevada, Oregon, Utah, and Washington. Web site: www.nwccu.org.

✔ **Southern Association of Colleges and Schools, Commission on Colleges (SACS):** Servicing Alabama, Florida, Georgia, Kentucky, Louisiana, Mississippi, North Carolina, South Carolina, Tennessee, Texas, and Virginia. Web site: www. sacscoc.org.

✔ **Western Association of Schools and Colleges, Accrediting Commission for Community and Junior Colleges (WASC-ACCJC):** Servicing community and junior colleges located in California, Hawaii, the United States territories of Guam and American Samoa, the Republic of Palau, the Federated States of Micronesia, the Commonwealth of the Northern Marianna Islands, and the Republic of the Marshall Islands. Web site: www.accjc.org.

✔ **Western Association of Schools and Colleges, Accrediting Commission for Senior Colleges and Universities (WASC-ACSCU):** Servicing senior colleges and universities in California, Hawaii, the United States territories of Guam and American Samoa, the Republic of Palau, the Federated States of Micronesia, the Commonwealth of the Northern Mariana Islands and the Republic of the Marshall Islands. Web site: www.wascsenior.org.

When looking at colleges and universities, investigate whether the institution is accredited and, if so, at what level. Don't be surprised if you find that community colleges are accredited at the institution level but not at the program level. It simply depends on the programs the institution offers and the level of program completion they provide. For example, most community colleges provide enough math courses to fulfill general studies prerequisites, but do not offer a degree in mathematics. Therefore, they're not likely to have an accredited math program.

In order to earn and maintain accreditation status, an institution must participate in an ongoing process that reviews its resources, programs, assessments, and self-evaluation. The bottom line is that an accredited school has to document how it is meeting quality standards. The initial accreditation process can take upwards of two years to complete. After that, the cycle repeats approximately every ten years, depending on the guidelines set forth by the accrediting agency.

Seeing the benefits of accreditation

Accreditation status is important for both you and the institution. From the institution's perspective, it provides credibility and status within the academic community, and becomes an important marketing tool. Accredited schools also have the ability to attract more higher-qualified students, like you.

The benefits from your perspective as a student include the following:

- ✔ You know that quality standards have been reviewed and met.

- ✔ You can market yourself to prospective employers who look for applicants from accredited schools and programs.

- ✔ You enhance your chances for graduate school. Having an existing undergraduate degree from an accredited institution is often a minimum requirement when applying for graduate school. Although it doesn't guarantee that your credits will transfer, it definitely helps.

- ✔ You have an increased likelihood of receiving financial aid. Students attending nonaccredited institutions may be ineligible for student assistance such as federal/state aid and tuition reimbursement programs.

Determining whether an online program is accredited

Most institutions are proud of their accreditation status and want to show it off. Therefore, determining whether an institution is accredited usually isn't difficult. In most cases, you can find out by visiting the institution's Web site and clicking on the About Us or Academics link. If you can't find it on the Web site, your academic advisor will definitely be able to share this information with you.

The demand for alternative education delivery methods to meet the needs of busy adults has increased dramatically over the last decade. Unfortunately, as a result, several institutions have tried to quickly capitalize on this by creating *diploma mills,* which are nonaccredited institutions offering quick, online degrees without quality standards or properly trained faculty. Here are few things to look for that may identify an organization as a diploma mill:

- ✔ The institution has a name very similar to a more well-known university.

- ✔ The institution is not accredited by an agency approved by the U.S. Department of Education.

- ✔ Students can earn degrees in very little time compared to other institutions. No one can get a degree in 30 days. Trust us!

> ✔ There are no admissions criteria. For example, if you're researching a Bachelor of Nursing program that doesn't require a RN degree or any clinical experience, be careful.
>
> ✔ The cost to attend the institution is much less than any other college or university offering the same program.

In response, an equally aggressive movement has arisen to establish quality standards for online courses. Organizations such as Quality Matters (www. qualitymatters.org) provide schools with benchmarks and a process they can use to assure quality in the way they offer online courses. Schools may conduct other internal reviews. Because accreditation by one of the six regional agencies is institutional and includes traditional classroom education as well as online classes, be sure to ask every school you're interested in about how they monitor the quality of their online programs.

Other factors that contribute to an institution's credibility

As you conduct your research regarding an institution's accreditation status, you should also look for other signs that the institution is a credible one. In this section, we provide you with some additional criteria for evaluating online programs and courses. These include the awards and recognition they've received, as well as the research conducted at the school. In most cases, institutions highlight this information on their Web sites as a way of enhancing their marketing efforts.

National awards and recognition

One of the best indicators of quality is recognition from nationally recognized professional organizations. Two types of awards are bestowed specifically to online academic programs or individual courses. The first type of award focuses on academic integrity and a program's overall curriculum, graduation rate, and/or contributions to the field. These awards are sponsored by leading professional organizations within the field of the program's subject matter.

Several awards may also be earned specific to the development and implementation of individual online courses. For example, Capella University's SPC1000–Public Speaking course received the 2007 Blackboard Greenhouse Exemplary Course Award, an award that's well-recognized in the field of online education. To earn this award, an organization must demonstrate that their online course has met specific quality standards based on research and best practices within the field of online education.

Other awards that you may keep an eye out for are those bestowed on faculty. Faculty awards for work within the field or excellence in teaching are both indicators of quality.

Leading research efforts in the field of distance education

Another indicator of quality is whether the faculty study the impact of online education. For example, The University of Wisconsin in Madison, Nova Southeastern University in Ft. Lauderdale, and Indiana University in Bloomington are all well-known for their research in online education. Although this research is usually conducted locally and within the College of Education, the results can be used to train faculty from other departments and institutions around the world! It can tell you a great deal about the school's attitude towards distance education: Those who research online education tend to support online education!

Consortium membership

One final consideration is membership in a *consortium,* or group of like-minded institutions. Membership doesn't guarantee quality or accreditation, but those who join are more likely to offer legitimate programs and services. By joining a consortium, schools have access to training, research in the field, and cutting edge practices that help ensure quality.

Nationally, the best-known consortium is the Sloan Consortium (`www.sloan-c.org`), a group of institutions committed to enhancing their own understanding and practices related to quality online education.

Several institutions have pooled resources regionally, as well. For example, Connecticut and Florida both have statewide consortia.

Talking to the Right People to Get the Answers You Need

Now that we've given you some things to think about in choosing an academic institution, it's time to introduce you to some important people to talk to: your academic advisor, the faculty, and other students. In this section, we provide you with a list questions you can pose to each of these people.

Communicating with a variety of people who have both an internal connection (faculty and staff paid by the institution) and an external connection (students) can help you get multiple perspectives regarding the prospective program or course. These discussions may happen over the phone or via e-mail. Either way, it always helps to be prepared and have your questions written ahead of time.

When discussing topics that impact your academic standing or financial status, request that any decisions made be documented in writing or document the conversation yourself. For example, after an advisor tells you that previous coursework will transfer, send an e-mail summarizing your discussion and request a confirmation reply. This covers you in case your advisor changes and you need to justify your actions to someone else.

Talking to an academic advisor about the school

The first contact person you will have with any institution is an academic advisor. This person's role is twofold. His first task is to serve as a liaison between the public and the institution. Recruitment of new students is usually a primary task of this person, although some institutions separate this role and have dedicated recruiters who point you to an academic advisor when you express further interest in attending the institution.

The second and more important task an academic advisor undertakes is helping you plan your academic adventures. The academic advisor will answer questions, collect your application, and step you through the enrollment process. The academic advisor should be available to help you not only during your initial application and enrollment process, but throughout your academic career when needed. Take advantage of this person and try to get as much information out of him as possible before deciding to enroll. Again, the more prepared you are before meeting your advisor, the better. So, here are some questions you should be ready to ask:

- ✔ **What courses are available?** This may seem like a simple question, but it's an important one. Knowing what courses are available and when helps you determine when you can start taking classes and in what order. For example, if you are required to take an introductory course as a prerequisite to all the other courses in a program, you must know when that course is offered next.

- ✔ **What prerequisites do I need?** Here comes that planning ahead theme again. Determining each course's prerequisites tells you the order in which you need to take courses. Paying attention to these details helps you avoid missing a term because you have to wait for one of the prerequisite courses to be offered.

  If you need additional prerequisites because some of your previous credits didn't transfer, you'll need to know whether they provide those courses. If not, you may have to take the courses somewhere else first.

✔ **What is your student retention rate?** This question is very telling. Having a small number of students drop out for one reason or another is fairly common for all academic programs. However, programs that have a retention rate of less than 85 percent should raise a red flag.

A good follow-up question to ask is whether the program documents why students drop out. If so, ask about the most common reasons for dropping out. This can tell you whether students are dropping out due to personal reasons or the program itself. If a large number of students drop out because the program is too difficult, it requires more time than expected, or the technology used is too difficult for students to learn on top of coursework, be cautious about enrolling in the program.

✔ **What kinds of student services are available?** This question is extremely important for students taking online courses. You want to be sure the institution can provide you with a variety of resources at a distance. For example, you should ask whether the institution provides access to services such as the library, academic tutoring, and career development upon graduation.

Be sure to ask *how* these services are provided. Some institutions provide online students with the same services as their on-campus students only if they come to campus. Find out whether the institution is prepared to provide these services from a distance using a variety of technologies.

✔ **What kind of placement rate do graduates report?** Asking this question is a great way to find out how reputable the program is. It can also help you evaluate the job market in the field you're considering studying.

✔ **What are the faculty's qualifications?** Whether the courses are taught by full-time, tenured faculty or by adjunct is less important than the minimum qualifications for teaching in the program. (See Chapter 2 for an explanation of the differences in faculty personnel.) Getting a feel for the faculty's qualifications helps you understand the skills and knowledge of those who will be providing instruction.

✔ **When do I have to decide and register?** When asking this question, be sure to get an idea of multiple deadlines so that you don't feel pressured into making a decision immediately. Note that some institutions may offer a discount for starting earlier if their current enrollment is not as high as they would like it to be. Even so, be sure to take as much time as you need to make the right decision for you.

✔ **How long is each term?** Students commonly ask this question because they want to know whether school will interfere with an already-scheduled vacation, family wedding, and so forth. The nice thing about online education is that as long as you have a computer with Internet access, you can still go to school. However, if you're planning a vacation where you won't have access to the Internet (or you really don't want to interrupt your honeymoon to study), don't be surprised if the institution or individual instructor asks you to take the class another time. Participation is such a large part of online education that if you're unable to participate, taking the class may not be worth it.

✔ **When do classes begin?** Some institutions provide only three start-dates per year: one each for the fall, spring, and summer semesters. Other institutions, especially those offering accelerated programs, allow students to start classes more frequently. If you need to take advantage of financial aid, make sure the aid is available when you want to start. Timing can affect whether or not you can receive aid. (Flip to Chapter 6 for more about the financial facts of online education.)

✔ **Are there any additional fees?** It's important to know whether you'll be expected to pay additional fees beyond the application and tuition fees. These additional charges may include fees for hardware, software, or campus services. Campus services may include items such as a campus e-mail address, server space for storing files, an ePortfolio subscription, or other similar services. They should not include standard fees for services only provided to campus students, such as health care or gym access — things you obviously won't be able to participate in.

✔ **What is the cost for books or other required materials?** Books are not cheap, and some people are surprised at how much a single textbook can cost. You'll be better able to budget if you know what the average cost of books and supplies will be per term. Textbooks and supplies are updated often, so you may not get an exact number, but you should be able to get a good estimate.

✔ **How many students can be admitted per course?** Remember our earlier discussion about the benefits and challenges of courses that are too small or too large? This question can help you determine whether your instructor may be inhibited from providing quality feedback due to the sheer number of students in the class.

✔ **How long does it take to graduate?** The answer to this question will depend on how many classes you take at a time and whether the institution requires you to follow a prescribed sequence of courses. You may also want to find out whether there's a maximum time frame for getting your degree. Some programs require students to complete their degree within six years.

✔ **What if I need to take a break?** Life happens, and sometimes students need to temporarily drop out of school due to other commitments. You should know what the institution's policy about this is and how it will affect your graduation date, financial aid disbursement, and so on. You'll also want to know how long you can stop taking classes and when you can reenter. Understand that stopping and restarting your education may delay your graduation for several months, depending on how frequently the classes you need are offered.

Asking a faculty member about the program

When you talk to your academic advisor, ask to speak to a faculty member about the program you want to enroll in. Someone teaching within the program can give you a different perspective specific to the curriculum, assignment types, and time commitment necessary to successfully participate in the program.

If the institution doesn't want to let you talk to an instructor, consider researching other institutions. The availability of the instructional staff before you register can be indicative of their availability once you're enrolled. However, on the other hand, be patient and give your advisor enough time to locate an instructor who is available to speak to you.

✔ **What kind of training is required of faculty members who teach for this school?** This is a great question because it allows you to find out whether instructors are required to take classes specific to online education.

Most programs require instructors to have subject matter expertise. However, not all of them require instructors to have any experience with teaching online. Institutions that require or provide additional training specific to this topic tend to have more well-rounded instructors that are better prepared to teach online.

✔ **What can I expect in terms of workload?** This question may seem repetitive, but asking a faculty member within the program gives you an idea of the instructors' expectations regarding how much time you should plan to spend on classwork.

✔ **What are the standards for faculty response time?** By asking a faculty member this question, you're kind of putting them on the spot to see how committed they are to responding quickly to questions via e-mail or phone. You should get an answer something like this: "The faculty at this institution are required to respond to student inquiries within 48 hours. However, many faculty, including myself, are committed to student success and check our e-mails and log in to the course a couple times a day. This ensures a speedy response so that students can move forward with their studies." You may not get quite that level of commitment, but you definitely don't want to hear that the faculty only check their e-mails a couple times a week, either.

✔ **How do I get help when I need it?** This question is a great follow-up to the preceding question. It lets you see whether the program you want to enroll in has an established process for getting help. When asking this question, you want to hear something like this: "Within every course, students will find the necessary contact information for the instructor, technical support, and academic advising, including e-mail addresses, phone numbers, and other important information needed to contact us for help. There's also a public discussion forum in the course where you can ask your peers questions, as well as your instructor. This way students can participate in answering each other's questions, and they may be able to respond faster than the instructor simply because there are more of them."

Chatting with other students about their experiences

To get a true understanding of what you may experience in the program, ask your advisor whether you can have the contact information of an existing student or a recent graduate of the program. This person will be able to answer your questions in a manner that no one else will, and the information you get will most likely be the most valuable to you in your search. However, don't be surprised if some institutions are hesitant to do this. It's not necessarily because they don't want to share the information; they simply want to protect the privacy of their students. You'll want them to do the same for you if you enroll.

You'll notice that the following questions are more open-ended than those we've had you ask previously. This is so that you can have a more informal conversation.

- ✔ **What has your experience been like?** Asking this question provides the student you are interviewing a wide range of options and allows him to think about what his most important experiences have been. By asking this question, you may find out about academics, time commitment, or even about the overall support network provided by the institution.

- ✔ **What has been the best part?** You really want to listen to the answer to this question and how enthusiastic the interviewee is about answering it. Someone who's excited to tell you all about the wonderful things the program has to offer can be very encouraging.

- ✔ **What has frustrated you?** In order to get a holistic picture of the program, you must ask what an individual sees as both the positive and negative aspects of the program. However, be careful with this question. Even though it's an important one, you don't want the interview to focus too much on the negative. You want open, honest answers that are direct and to the point. As human beings, we all have the capacity to find the negative in anything. Try to stay focused on the big picture and not the micro details, because every student's experiences are different.

✔ **How would you rate the quality?** Getting a student's perspective on the quality of a program is priceless. It lets you know whether that person would recommend the program to others, and why. Asking this question to a graduate who has recently entered the work field can also help you determine whether the information and skills learned in the program were transferrable to the workplace.

✔ **What is the faculty like?** By asking this question, you get one person's perception of the qualifications and teaching abilities of the faculty. Again, remember to stay focused on the big picture. Try to steer clear of finding out every negative or positive aspect of every instructor (though it doesn't hurt to find out which instructor you should look forward to having).

Narrowing Your Options

Okay, so you've been introduced to a variety of people, asked your questions, and documented your answers. Now what? It's time to decide which institution you're going to attend. Following is a list of items to consider when making your final decision. Consider making a chart that helps you evaluate the pros and cons of each institution based on these items:

✔ **Academics:** Does the program meet my academic goals?

✔ **Cost:** Can I afford to attend the institution or is financial aid available? If financial aid is required, what will my payments be when I have to start paying my loans back? Will I be able to afford them?

✔ **Workload:** Is the workload feasible based on my current work/life situation, or can my schedule be rearranged to accommodate the program's anticipated workload?

✔ **Time:** Is the length of the course or program something I'm able to sustain based on the anticipated workload? Can I graduate in a reasonable amount of time?

✔ **Resources available:** What kind of resources are available if I need help (library, technical support, academic help, advising, and so on)? Are these resources adequate based on my anticipated needs?

✔ **Independence:** How independent will I be within the program? Will there be group work? How involved are the instructors? Will I be able to work at my own pace?

✔ **Overall match:** Overall, does this program match my personality and learning preferences?

Chapter 6

Applying to School and Securing the Cash

*O*nce you've decided what you want to study and where, the next step is to apply to a school. (Of course, some people apply to more than one school at a time, but Chapter 5 helps narrow the selection.) The first part of this chapter guides you through the application process. We introduce you to the forms you'll use as well as some strategies to make your application land on the top of the applicant pool!

The rest of the chapter addresses the million-dollar question: How much is your education going to cost and how are you going to pay for it? (Okay, the tuition and other expenses may not actually cost you a million bucks, but when you're adding everything up, it may feel like it.) We give you an overview of tuition costs, as well as details about the federal financial aid program.

Applying to an Online Program

By the time you've decided which college or university to apply to, you've likely filled out a Web-based information form in order to receive more details about the school's offerings (see Chapter 4 for more details on this). After you jump through those preliminary hoops and give schools your e-mail address, they share the application process. You receive an e-mail with links to forms and instructions, including fees that may be involved. Often, you have the opportunity to receive paper versions of the same, too.

This process is very similar to that of brick-and-mortar colleges: It includes filling out application forms, writing an essay or two, and submitting documents that show your achievements and education to date. In the following sections, we describe a typical application process, one that isn't specific to any individual institution. This way you can see the kinds of information most colleges ask for and prepare accordingly.

In the following sections, we're talking about applying to online schools only. If you want to enroll in an online program through your local two-year college, they will probably ask you to complete the traditional application process, which may include testing for math or English placement.

If you apply to more than one school at a time, you have to fill out specific forms for each institution. However, you may be able to send the same resume or essay to more than one school.

The basic application forms

Your journey begins with paperwork! Forms come in a couple of types: digital and paper. Instead of working with paper-and-pencil versions, you may be completing Web-based forms. The institutions that rely on paper applications may direct you to a site where you can download and print your own forms.

Preliminary demographic information

Every college needs basic information about you. This includes

- ✓ **Your contact information:** Your home address and e-mail addresses (since now you live online as well as on-ground) and telephone numbers

- ✓ **Personal information:** Your ethnicity, and citizenship, military, and marital status

- ✓ **Your academic plans:** The type of degree you plan to pursue

- ✓ **Your previous education:** High school data and any college credits you may have earned

If you apply to a traditional school that happens to offer online degrees, this information is identical to what you would provide if you wanted to attend traditional classes. Therefore, you may also be asked about extracurricular activities, honors, family background, and work experience. If you apply to an institution that specializes in online degrees, you're less likely to be asked about these extras.

Transcripts of your previous education

You need to provide transcripts of your educational experience. Typically these need to be sent directly from the institution to the college to which you're applying. In other words, self-made copies on your home inkjet won't suffice. The good news is that, in many cases, the college to which you're applying will accept an unofficial copy temporarily as a way of keeping the ball rolling. This is called a *conditional enrollment*, which means that assuming everything else is in order, you are accepted to start the program without delay. However, you're given a deadline for supplying the institution with an original copy of your transcript. To do this, contact the high school or other colleges directly and ask them to send these credentials electronically. Follow up to be sure they were sent. If the credentials are not received in a timely fashion, you may be prohibited from enrolling for the next term. Also, during this waiting period, you won't receive financial aid.

A resume

For many graduate programs, schools request a resume to accompany your application. They want to see the connection between your work experience and your academic plans. Don't worry if these don't exactly match up, especially if you're transitioning to a new career. If you're stuck on what to write or how to organize the resume, we recommend checking out *Resumes For Dummies,* 5th Edition, by Joyce Lain Kennedy (Wiley).

Financial aid paperwork

We include this here in the list of documents that you may need, but we say much more about this in the section, "Figuring Out How You're Going to Pay for Online Classes," later in this chapter.

Application fees

You didn't think you could apply without an application fee, did you? Yes, there are applications fees even though it seems you're doing all the work. Fees vary from school to school. Most range from $50 to $100.

Your personal essay

Some institutions require a personal essay as part of the application process. Not only does this allow them to find out more about each applicant, but it gives the institution an opportunity to see your writing skills and creativity. This is especially true for applicants to graduate programs. You can't earn a master's degree without writing, and by the time you get that far in school, the school expects you to know what you're doing!

Other institutions no longer require a personal essay. For instance, schools that offer bachelor's completion programs assume that students who apply learned to write in their first two years of college, which they would have completed prior to enrolling in the online program. Likewise, private schools that don't offer remedial courses expect students to already know how to write.

If you're required to put your thoughts to paper, take a look at the next sections for a glimpse of topics you may be asked to write about, some hints about what a good essay includes, and a couple of essay excerpts.

What you may be asked to write

If you're applying for an associate's or bachelor's program or anything at the undergraduate level, chances are good that you'll be asked to give a written statement describing your past work experience or extracurricular activities. This gives the school an opportunity to get to know you a little better.

Beyond that introductory information, you may be asked to develop a longer essay. These essays are typically a page or two in length. Here are several common undergraduate essay questions:

- ✔ Evaluate a significant experience in your life and how it affected you.
- ✔ Discuss some issue of personal significance and why it is important.
- ✔ Identify and describe a person who has had a significant influence on you, and explain the influence.
- ✔ Choose your own topic.

Choosing your own topic may allow for creativity, but it does not excuse bad writing. You still have to follow standard conventions and show good grammar and organization. Be careful not to get too abstract if you choose your own topic.

Graduate essays are completely different. In a graduate essay, the schools probe your motivation to continue your education as well as your professional experience. They want candidates with prior professional exposure because this enriches the classroom experience. Working gives you stories to share and insights to offer. For example, if you seek an advanced degree in education, you may be asked to provide a philosophy statement that weaves together your personal beliefs about education with your work experience.

If you're going straight from college with an undergraduate degree into graduate school, write about volunteer or internship experience you can relate to your studies. After all, there must be *some* compelling reason you want to stay in school! Tell the reader what it is that has led you to love that field and how your experiences fit.

What the readers are looking for

Schools can tell a lot about your academic preparation and personal motivation from your written work. If your work is filled with grammatical errors or lacks basic organization, they're going to know that you need remedial help. On the other hand, if your writing mechanics (grammar, punctuation, and spelling) are fine, readers can move on to how creatively you address the topic, your ability to analyze and think critically, and your overall written communication skills. That's good!

What other pointers should you remember? Check these out:

- ✔ **Readers are not looking for formulaic essays.** Following the five-paragraph rule with an introduction plus thesis statement, three supporting paragraphs, and a conclusion is easy. Try to work a little beyond that. The people who read these essays read *a lot* of essays, so yours needs to be unique.

- ✔ **Make sure your introduction and conclusion are strong.** Readers like pieces that start with a punch and end with a bang.

- ✔ **Details count!** Be sure to support any opinions or assertions with details. Avoid vague, unsubstantiated comments. For example, if you say a lot of people take online courses, back it up with information from a trusted source (for example, "Sloan-C says 3.9 million students were enrolled in online courses in the fall of 2007").

- ✔ **Reference research methodology and theory when possible.** Impress readers by sharing your knowledge of research in the field you are studying and how you apply it currently in your work.

- ✔ **Tell the truth.** Academic honesty starts with the application process. If you trust this school to give you a decent education and a degree, they should be able to trust you to do your own work and tell the truth. For example, don't write about how facing a catastrophic illness defined your personal views if you've enjoyed excellent health your whole life. It's these kinds of lies that snowball.

For much more detailed information about writing a college application essay, read *College Admission Essays For Dummies* by Geraldine Woods (Wiley).

Samples of writing

Here is an excerpt of a writing sample for a graduate essay. The writer was asked to explain how obtaining a master's degree from that school would benefit a wide audience.

"For the past seven years, I have supported faculty and subject matter experts in both academic and corporate settings. Currently, as a Dean of

Instruction, I develop schedules for both students and faculty, provide faculty training, and supervise our institution's faculty peer-coaching program. My highest priority is to assist faculty in meeting quality standards in the areas of instructional design and instruction. To accomplish this goal, our organization emphasizes a systems approach to design and a variety of teaching methodologies to meet the needs of multiple learning styles. By accepting my application, you not only affect the lives of a single learner, but a community of educators."

An excerpt of an essay for an undergraduate program in which the author explains her goals might look like this:

"In North America, there is an unwritten rule that the senior year of high school is sacred. It is a time of morphing between childhood and young adulthood, of academic accomplishment and recognition, and of social development. So when my parents announced two months before my senior year that we were moving halfway across the world to serve in a relief agency, imagine my reaction! And yet, having to pull up stakes and establish a new identity in South Africa left an indelible impression on me. Not only did I find a new voice in myself, stronger than I had believed possible, but I learned that listening teaches more than talking. All these experiences and lessons have led me to want to earn degrees in cross-cultural communication and social justice."

Letters of recommendation

The application process includes letters of recommendation. These should come from people who know your work academically or professionally. If you're a high school graduate, you can easily ask a teacher, school counselor, or coach to write a letter for you. If you're a working professional and have a good relationship with your boss, ask her! Not only does it alert her to the fact that you're returning to school, but she'll probably be flattered to think you value her opinion. You may also want to ask a trusted colleague. It's good to get a variety of views. Be prepared to supply up to three different letters.

Be sure your references understand your academic and professional abilities and accomplishments. Friends and relatives may not be the best choice for this task, unless they've had direct experiences working with you.

Even though they adore you, the people who write your recommendation letters may not follow through promptly. Be sure to check with them to make sure their letters are sent in a timely fashion. To help speed up the process, provide each person with a self-addressed envelope and a description of the program you are applying to.

If someone asks what you want them to say, tell them typically a letter includes:

- ✔ **Information about your relationship:** For how long have they known you and in what capacity?

- ✔ **An overview of your professional abilities and accomplishments:** Here's where you could say you want them to mention certain skills or abilities. You may want to give them a resume to work from.

- ✔ **Your previous academic experience, if any:** Again, if your reference doesn't know this, give it to her in a resume.

- ✔ **A general statement of why the program would benefit by accepting your application:** This is a nice way to close the letter.

Test scores

ACT, SAT, GRE, MCAT, PDQ, ASAP . . . acronyms like these invoke fear in most college applicants. Excluding the last two, these are the monikers of standardized academic tests sometimes used to predict a student's success. Some programs require these test scores as part of the application process. However, many online institutions have dropped the test requirement because they know that your high school GPA or the number of credit hours you're transferring into their program are better indicators of future success.

If you need to take and submit the scores from one of these tests, make arrangements well in advance of when you want to start your academic program. It typically takes six to eight weeks to receive test results. When you take the test, you can indicate which schools you want to receive your scores, and the testing company will send your scores directly to those schools.

If English is not your first language, you may be asked to submit English proficiency scores from either the TOEFL (Test of English as a Foreign Language) or TOEIC (Test of English for International Communication). We address this further in Chapter 17.

When it's all due

When all this is due depends on the school. If you apply to a traditional school offering online courses that run on a typical semester schedule, there may be a deadline for admission. However, if you apply to a school that starts programs every few weeks, the deadline (and your start date) are whenever you get your paperwork sent it, and are subsequently accepted and enrolled. There are some conditions related to financial aid, so be sure to ask the academic advisor or admissions personnel about this when you first contact the school if it isn't obvious.

Lending a helping hand: The recruiter, advisor, or counselor

To gather information about online schools, you sometimes have to complete online forms (we cover this in Chapter 4). After you submit your contact information, you may receive a phone call. The people who call you are recruiters, and their job is to hook you into the process by answering your questions, providing information, and then referring you to other helpful personnel. If you're applying to one of the well-known private online schools, you should know that these people are highly trained in sales and marketing. Don't be put off by that, but ask questions. We make suggestions regarding what questions to ask in Chapter 5.

Sometimes a recruiter works with you all the way through the application process, but more often she refers you to an academic advisor or counselor. An academic advisor first helps you get together the necessary paperwork. She gives you a list of documents that you need, such as the application, transcripts, resume, and so on.

When it comes to transcripts, you tell the institution where they should come from. As we discuss in the earlier section "Transcripts of your previous education," temporary copies can help keep the ball rolling. Your responsibility is to follow through to make sure transcripts are sent and received.

Though academic advisors have a lot of answers, some decisions have to be made by others. For example, whether or not previous credits will transfer is a decision that will most likely be made by a dean or other administrator within the program you're applying to. However, the academic advisor serves as the facilitator by providing the dean with your transcripts and reporting any decisions to you. The academic advisor also helps facilitate introductions between you and other staff, such as the Financial Aid Officer.

Calculating the Costs of Online Classes

There's no easy way to break the news: School isn't cheap! According to a *New York Times* article from 2008, "college tuition and fees increased 439 percent from 1982 to 2007, while median family income rose 147 percent" (not adjusted for inflation). The reasons behind these increases are beyond the scope of this book, so we focus here only on what it's going to cost.

It's impossible for us to tell you that a two-year degree, for example, will cost you $15,000 because we don't know whether you want to go to school at a private institution, a four-year institution that awards associate's degrees, or a two-year school. In addition, as soon as we give you a price tag, tuition is going to rise (it never falls), making the number obsolete! Therefore, we look at the cost of one course in 2009.

For this baseline, consider the following costs for an undergraduate, three-credit-hour accounting course:

- **At a well-known, private online institution:** $460 per credit hour ($1,380 total)

- **At a public university that offers this course online:** $282.50 per credit hour in-state or $847.50 out-of-state

- **At a two-year community college in the Midwest that offers this course online:** $85 per credit hour in-district and in-state, $262.56 out-of-district but in-state, or $289.59 out-of-district and out-of-state ($255 to $868.77 total, depending on where you live)

In the foregoing example, you save money by taking the course through the local community college, but not everyone has that kind of option.

Now consider a three-credit-hour, graduate-level course in education:

- **At a well-known, private online institution:** $535 per credit hour ($1,605 total)

- **At a public university that offers this course online:** $294.75 per credit hour for in-state residents; $884.25 for out-of-state residents and international students

Of course, remember that the more classes you take at once, the more you'll owe at once. And, the tuition costs can vary based on the institution and program of study. For example, we've seen nursing programs exceed $600 per credit hour.

Next we break down the costs. We can't give exact numbers, but Table 6-1 shows some typical costs and where you may see differences.

Table 6-1	Traditional versus Online Costs	
Cost	*Traditional*	*Online*
Tuition	Costs vary depending on type of institution (public or private, four-year or two-year).	Expect to pay the same amount as traditional education. Typically schools charge by credit hour.
Fees	Fees can include technology fees, student activity fees, a fee for the health service, and so on. These vary greatly depending on the type of institution.	You're less likely to have the same fees online. Some schools charge for the services you use (for example, technology) while others charge no fees.
Books	Textbooks are very expensive. Spending $100 or more on one textbook is not uncommon.	Costs for online textbooks are the same. You may be able to buy discounted or used books, but you might incur an additional cost of shipping and handling. Some sellers offer free shipping above a certain dollar amount.
Room and Board	You could live at home and incur no additional room and board charges. However, if you're a traditional student enrolling in a residential college, they may require you to live on campus for at least the first year. In that case, you can add $6,000 or more to the price tag.	You can definitely live at home and incur no additional room and board charges.
Travel	If you're commuting to school, consider the cost of fuel and wear and tear on your vehicle or public transportation costs.	No additional cost! Work from the convenience of your home. However, some programs may require an annual trip to their main campus (some doctoral programs and other graduate degrees) so this would be a cost.

The end result is that you won't save money in tuition and fees if you go to school online, but you may save money in room and board and travel costs, depending on how you run your own comparison. What you save on books depends on the seller and whether they offer free shipping.

Figuring Out How You're Going to Pay for Online Classes

Cash, check, or charge? Paying for school is never that easy. It's an expensive proposition and one that no one can afford to take lightly. Once you determine what you want to study and where you want to go, you have to come up with the cash. This section introduces you to the idea of finding financial aid.

What financial aid can pay for depends on the type of aid received. For the most part, aid can pay for tuition and fees, and possibly textbooks. If you're an online student, it can't be used to pay for your housing.

Every school has a financial aid officer who can help you throughout the financial aid process. The financial aid representative may even approach you when you first inquire about the program! That person walks you through the various types of aid available at that specific institution, and what you need to do to possibly receive aid.

We should say from the beginning that every school has its own process. Therefore, we keep this discussion on a level that may be applicable to the majority of schools.

Do you need financial aid?

While earning a degree or a certificate at a two-year college is very affordable, graduate degrees and bachelor's completion programs at larger institutions carry a heftier price tag. If you're a working adult, imagine adding an additional $20,000 in debt! Few people have that kind of cash readily available, nor can they absorb those kinds of payments into their budget over the short term (the years you're studying online).

For that reason, you have to pursue the options! Further, many institutions ask you to complete financial aid paperwork when you apply regardless of your expressed need. Why is this? The institution wants you to finish the degree. It tries to remove any barriers it can, including problems paying for school.

In all fairness, you may be able to afford the education without outside assistance. Good for you! In that case, just complete the required forms and relax.

And what if you're not sure whether you need assistance? The federal paperwork helps determine this need. The government has a snazzy formula that takes all your expenses into account balanced against what you have saved, including money from a 529 savings account (the special one for education). Also, you can find an abundance of financial aid calculators and tools through a simple Web search, including resources on the Free Application for

Federal Student Aid (FAFSA) site. And, that friendly financial aid counselor the school assigns will have additional resources.

You only need to fill the financial aid paperwork out once, regardless of how many schools you're considering. However, if you receive aid, don't forget to reapply each year.

What types of financial aid are available?

Financial aid comes in a few varieties. In most cases you use this aid for tuition and fees for online courses, assuming you're attending an accredited institution. The financial aid counselor can tell you whether there are any restrictions. Here, we look at some possibilities and see how they differ.

- ✔ **Scholarships:** Gifts of a prescribed amount based on merit or circumstance. Scholarships are available for graduate and undergraduate study. You don't have to pay back scholarships. If the scholarship comes from the school or an outside agency, such as the Future Farmers of America club, it may be restricted to a certain field of study or for use only at the school giving the scholarship. Federal aid may restrict whether the scholarship is available for graduate study.

- ✔ **Grants:** Awards of a prescribed amount based on financial need. Some of these come from the federal government whereas others may come from the state. The two most common grants are federal programs: Pell and supplemental educational opportunity grants. Federal grants typically aren't available for graduate study. You don't have to pay back a grant.

- ✔ **Loans:** Money you borrow. Loans can be secured privately through your local bank or federally through Subsidized Federal Stafford and/or Direct Loans. These federal student loans do not accrue interest while you're in school. Obviously, these loans must be paid back. Any unsubsidized loans you secure accrue interest from the time they're disbursed. Therefore, if you're able to pay your tuition solely from the subsidized loans, consider declining unsubsidized loans.

Applying for Federal Financial Aid

Applying for financial aid requires diligence and an attention to detail. You fill out the form, and the government tells you how much aid you're eligible for, based on financial need. While the process requires attention to detail and searching documents (like old tax returns) for the numbers you need, it's not that awful. And the bright spot is that you only need to apply once through the government, and that information is then forwarded to the institutions you specify.

Knowing whether you're eligible for funds from Uncle Sam

In order to receive financial assistance from the federal government, you must meet certain criteria. The amount of assistance is based on a complicated formula based on anticipated need and expenses such as tuition, housing, books, and so forth.

Criteria for eligibility include U.S. citizenship, a high school diploma or GED, and satisfactory grade performance. There are other legal requirements as well, such as having a social security number (SSN), which should also be reviewed before completing the application.

Financial aid recipients are required to adhere to certain academic standards. Depending on the type of aid, students must attend at least half time and be enrolled in a certificate or degree-seeking program. Performance standards set by the academic institution must also be met. Students failing to meet these standards can be denied federal assistance.

Filling out and submitting the FAFSA

Every financial aid application begins with the Free Application for Federal Student Aid (FAFSA). Not only is the FAFSA required for federal financial aid, but it's also the benchmark for any other kind of aid consideration. Aside from basic demographic information, this form collects the details about your income or your parents' income and assets. How long it takes you to get the information together depends on how organized you are in general. Some people can find their tax returns in the snap of a finger while others have to rummage through the entire basement! Leave yourself enough time to complete the task. The form is available online at www.fafsa.ed.gov, along with more information. Figure 6-1 familiarizes you with the look of the site.

Take caution if someone is trying to charge an application or service fee. Applying for financial aid should be free. Also, answers to questions you may have about the process and help filling out the application should be available free of charge from the institution or Federal Student Aid.

The FAFSA is available online, and you can complete the application process digitally. It takes approximately four weeks for the government to process written applications. This does not count the time your institution may need to process payments and so forth based on your application results. Completing the application digitally speeds up the process. Therefore, if you're applying shortly before classes begin, apply digitally!

Figure 6-1:
The FAFSA
portal.

Once your FAFSA has been received and processed, you'll receive an e-mail from the government indicating your student aid report has been sent on to the school(s) you specified. The school takes over and administers the aid.

Starting the process of looking for financial aid early is very important. January 1 is a crucial deadline, because this is when students for the next academic year can submit FAFSAs for consideration. Each institution has additional deadlines. Be sure to meet every deadline. If you don't, you may have to wait a full year before you can apply again.

Traditional institutions and online institutions follow the same processes, so it may be worth your while to pick up a few resources, such as the book "Getting Financial Aid 2009 (College Board Guide to Getting Financial Aid)" by The College Board (available through major booksellers). You may also want to look at the Student Aid Web site at studentaid.ed.gov. Another student-friendly resource is students.gov, the student gateway to the government portal.

Chapter 7

Getting Accepted and Prepping for Class

*Y*ou've done your research, applied to an institution (or two, or more), and now you're waiting to hear back. What happens next? In this chapter, we discuss what to do once you are accepted. This process includes registering for classes, becoming familiar with the online environment, and purchasing your textbooks. Time to get started.

Finding Out Whether You've Been Accepted or Rejected

Many online institutions take less time to respond than a traditional academic institution does. When you apply to traditional institutions, sometimes you're required to wait at least two months to find out whether you've been accepted. Depending on whether the online institution accepts unofficial transcripts to conditionally admit you (admit you based on copies of your transcripts with the condition that you request original copies be sent by a predetermined deadline), you may know within just a few days whether you've been accepted.

Institutions notify students of their acceptance in different ways. Some schools choose to notify their students via a phone call from the academic advisor. Others notify students via e-mail. This not only speeds up the process, but reduces the need for paper, as well. Very few institutions choose to notify students via standard U.S. mail. If the institution's Web site or application documentation did not provide you with a timeline for notifying students of acceptance, contact your academic advisor. You can also contact your advisor once you've submitted your application to get a progress update.

One advantage to online programs is that the institutions offering them aren't restricted by physical space, so they can enroll more students. This doesn't mean the standards are lower for accepting students; it simply means that the institution doesn't need to limit the number of seats available within the program to the number of seats in a physical classroom.

You're such a smartie that we know you were accepted by multiple institutions. So, now what? How do you choose the program that is right for you? Refer to Chapter 5, where we talk about narrowing your options when searching for institutions. You should use the same checklist now for deciding which school is best for you!

Unfortunately, on the flip side of acceptance to a school is rejection. An application can be rejected for several reasons. Talking to your academic advisor will help you narrow down the reason why your application was rejected. Some of the reasons applications are rejected include the following:

- A data entry error may simply have been made.

- Previous academic history did not meet the prerequisites for the course or program being applied for.

- Previous academic grade point average did not meet the minimum standard for the course or program being applied for.

- Required deadlines were not met within the application process.

- Official transcripts were not received by previously attended academic institutions.

- Program enrollment has reached its maximum for the current term.

If your application is rejected, don't assume this status is permanent. As you can see from the preceding list, many of the reasons applications are rejected are easy to resolve quickly. Yes, you may have to delay your enrollment by one term, but don't let that deter you from accomplishing your academic goals. Here are a couple of steps you can take:

- **Sharpen your academic prowess:** If your application has been rejected because of your past academic performance, you may be asked to take remedial courses or student success classes as a way of proving your commitment and establishing your academic abilities. These courses may be available at the institution for which you are applying or you may be required to take these courses somewhere else. Also, in this situation, some institutions will place you on academic probation and conditionally accept your application. You are then required to maintain a specific GPA in order to enroll in future terms.

✔ **Meet the necessary prerequisites:** If your application is rejected because you didn't take the prerequisite courses, you'll have to postpone your application until you have successfully met those requirements. Contact your academic advisor to find out who offers these courses and when classes begin. In this situation, be sure to ask your advisor whether your application will remain on file or whether you'll have to resubmit it once you have successfully met the prerequisite requirements.

Registering for Classes

Even if the physical task of registering for classes is an easy one, you want to be sure you're enrolling in the correct courses and taking them in the right order. This section helps you determine your academic path and provides strategies for staying on course during the registration process.

Creating a plan with your academic advisor

Your academic advisor's role is to guide you through the registration process, get you started, and keep you on track throughout your academic career. The first task your academic advisor should help you do is create a roadmap of your academic career. This is a checklist of all the classes you must take within your program and the order in which you must take them. This list should also include other program requirements needed for graduation. Though each program is different, some example items include the following:

✔ All courses in program listed sequentially in the order they should be taken by term

✔ Recommended electives listed in sequential order by term

✔ Thesis, final project, and/or portfolio deadline listed, if applicable

Who cares what order you take courses in as long as you take them all, right? Well, not always. Some courses may not be offered every term. If you take courses out of order, you may find yourself in a position where the course you need as a prerequisite to the remaining courses in your program isn't available. This can force you to have to stop out for a term and delay your graduation date. It can also impact financial aid matters, because you may be required to take a minimum number of credits per term in order to receive financial aid. If you're forced to reduce your classload due to poor planning, you may not be able to receive your financial aid reimbursement for that term.

Even if communication with your advisor isn't required, and you have a very detailed roadmap, touch base with him after each term and before enrolling in the new term. This is especially important if you have failed a course or had to stop out for any reason and are ready to begin again. It ensures you're still on the right track and program requirements haven't changed since your initial enrollment. A quick e-mail exchange with your advisor should suffice.

For students who simply want to take a few classes for personal interest or professional development, the academic advisor still plays an important role. The academic advisor can serve as the first point of contact for administrative help such as registering for courses, paying for courses, or recommending other courses that meet your interests.

Picking your first classes

Most academic programs require students to take an introductory course before getting into more detailed topics. Online programs are no different. If you're enrolled in a degree program, you'll most likely have to take an introductory course as your first course. Students often complain that this is a waste of time and money if they're simply going to focus on each topic discussed in the course in more detail in future classes. However, the introductory course serves several purposes, including helping students get familiar with the field, institution, and studying (in case it has been awhile since you last had homework, or you need to develop college-level study habits). In the online environment, the introductory course also helps you become familiar with the technology used.

If you're not enrolled in a degree program or have a choice regarding the order in which you take classes, think about possible learning curves and how much you can take on. For example, if you haven't been in school for awhile, this is your first college course, or technology makes you a little nervous, you may want to take an introductory course or one with fewer credits that requires less time dedicated to coursework.

Choosing between traditional model and cohort model classes

Whether you'll be enrolling in courses that follow a traditional model or a cohort model is something to consider when looking at degree or certification program structures during the interviewing process that we describe in Chapter 5. The structure-model decision is determined by the institution and/or department sponsoring the program, and in most cases you won't have a choice of models. Here are the differences between the two:

 ✔ **Traditional model:** In a traditional model, you may be required to take an introductory class as your first course, but then you break off from the pack and choose your own path. This is where paying attention to prerequisite requirements and details such as how often a course is offered throughout a year is important. Freedom is nice, but with it comes responsibility.

The traditional model is great for students who want more control over their own destination. They can choose what classes to take and in what order. However, this model does require more planning. If you choose this model, it's important to communicate with your academic advisor often so that he can insure you're on the right track.

✔ **Cohort model:** A cohort model (which we introduce in Chapter 4) is one where you start and stop with the same people in every class. The only time students mix in this model is if the program allows students to choose elective courses throughout the program.

For example, say you want to get a Master of Education degree. Jane Smith is in your first course with you — EDD101: Introduction to Education. Jane is in the next three courses with you as well. However, after taking the four core courses, it's time for you to take specialty courses. You may choose to focus on elementary education, while Jane decides to take courses in special education. At this point, you part ways and see each other at graduation. In a cohort model, everyone who starts at the same time should finish at the same time, whether they take the same classes or not.

For many students, the cohort model is best because they like the fact that their entire academic career is already planned out. Plus, it's not uncommon for students to become lifelong friends after "surviving" an entire degree program together. However, some students prefer diversity and would rather have different classmates from one course to the next.

Whether to participate in a traditional model or a cohort model is really only a concern for those participating in a degree program. If you're taking classes for professional development or out of interest, you'll participate in a more traditional model where you choose what classes you take and when. However, you may still need to meet prerequisite requirements. If a course you want to take has a prerequisite you'd rather forgo, talk to your advisor, who may forward your request to the instructor. If the instructor is willing to consider your petition, he may ask you to provide proof that you understand the concepts presented in the prerequisite course. For example, you may have to submit your resume or take a proficiency exam. But don't be surprised if the instructor requires you to take the prerequisite course.

Deciding on other types of class structures

In Chapter 4 we introduce you to a variety of other course formats that you may want to consider when registering for courses. For example, if you're enrolled in a program that's geographically close, you may want to consider a blended program where you're provided some face-to-face opportunities with the instructor and your classmates. If distance is an issue, but you like having voice interaction with others, a predominantly synchronous class may suit your learning style better. But, if your work/life schedule provides limited study time, you may be better off taking a self-paced course.

As nice as it is to have choices, remember that course formats can be different from class to class within the same program depending on the program, course content, and instructor preference. Therefore, it's important to get a sense of the entire program's expectations when conducting your research.

Gathering the information you need to register

Whether you register online, via mail, or over the phone with your academic advisor, you need to have the following information at your disposal for each class you want to take:

- ✔ **Course Term:** The term name and year including start and stop dates, for example, Fall 2010, Aug. 10–Dec. 13, 2010.

- ✔ **Course Title:** The name of the course provided in the course catalog. This is often an abbreviated title due to the character restrictions of most catalog applications. An example of a full course title is English 101: Composition 1; a catalog may abbreviate it as ENG101 Comp1.

- ✔ **Course ID/Course Reference Number (CRN):** The Course ID is usually a letter representing the department followed by a course number. For example, E101 is the course ID for English 101: An Introduction to Writing. The CRN is an extension of the Course ID that usually includes a cohort identification and section number. For example, E100 OL1 002 could be the online version for English 101 and the second section offered to cohort 1. (We discuss cohorts in the earlier section, "Choosing between traditional model and cohort model classes.")

- ✔ **Instructor:** The name of the instructor teaching the section of the course you're enrolling in.

Most of this information can be found in your course catalog or the checklist/roadmap document you create with your academic advisor. However, you won't be able to find the CRN or specific instructor for the courses without going to the institution's course schedule page. This page is usually connected with the registration Web site so that you can determine your desired course section and register right there. Contact your advisor and ask him to show you where to find this information.

Understanding registration processes

Though your advisor helps you determine your academic path and is available for questions when needed, actually registering for classes will most likely be your responsibility. Academic institutions use a variety of Web-based applications and interfaces for registration; some institutions give you the option to register via the phone or good old-fashioned snail mail.

The two biggest differences between registering online and mailing in your paperwork are time and technology. It can take two weeks or more to mail in your registration, receive confirmation, and process the financial paperwork. Because of the added time it takes to process information, and the fact that institution staff simply enter the information into the same system that you would if you were registering online, some institutions don't allow you to register via mail.

Some institutions use the phone as a way for you to dial-in to an automated registration system. You dial a number, enter a Student ID and numeric password provided by your academic advisor, and register for courses using the same course information as previously listed.

But hey, you're signing up for an online class! The technology route is for you. It's also a great exercise for practicing Web navigation. What better time to start sharpening those skills? Figure 7-1 illustrates an example of what an online registration system might look like. In this example, you can see that all education (EDD) courses are about to be listed because all other fields are blank or have "all" chosen. If you know the course number or title, you may be able to search for those specific fields directly. Upon clicking Class Search, you would get a list of all the courses that match your search criteria, including each course's title, ID/CRN, instructor, start date, end date, and possibly more. Registering for a course is as simple as clicking on it.

Remember that each institution uses different registration technology and it make look different than what you see in Figure 7-1. However, the general information about each course will be the same.

Taking action if a course you want is full

One advantage of a cohort model (which we describe earlier in this chapter) is that you're almost always guaranteed a seat in every course you need. When a cohort fills up, either a new cohort is started or students are asked to wait one term and start during the next rotation of courses.

If you're in a traditional program and the course you want fills up, contact your academic advisor. Sometimes, he can tell you whether enough other students need the course to justify opening another section. Also contact the instructor of the course. Instructors are often given the ability to admit additional students beyond the standard enrollment. If all else fails, work with your advisor to find another course in your program and update your academic roadmap accordingly.

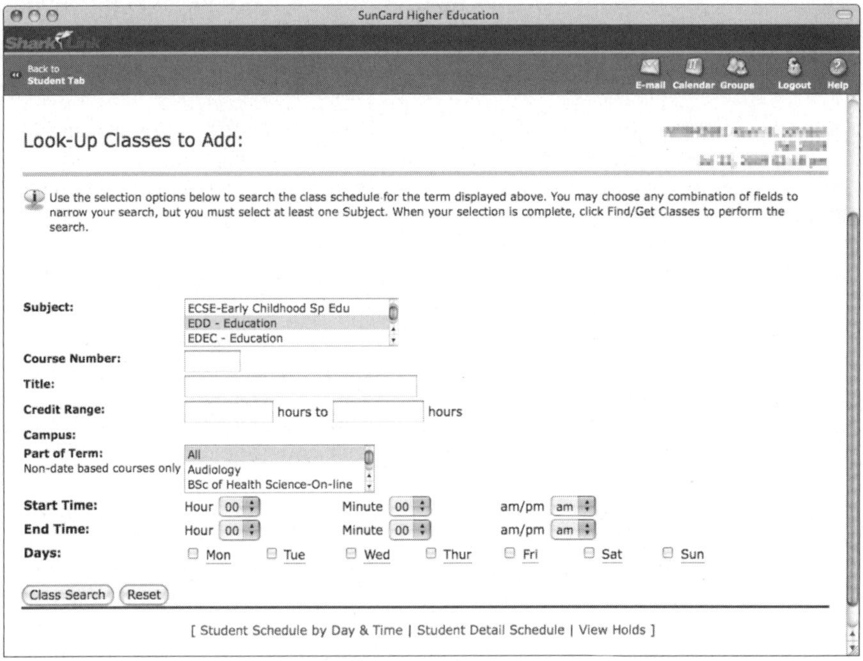

Figure 7-1:
An example
of an online
course
registration
system.

Courtesy of Nova Southeastern University

When in doubt: Talking to your academic advisor

How many times can we tell you to contact your advisor when you need something? Three, four, six, ten? We do so because this relationship is truly critical! Your advisor's job is to help you succeed. Take advantage of this and ask for help when you need it.

The assistance your advisor provides is priceless. However, never rely on one person blindly. All humans make mistakes. Be sure you understand what's going on at all times and ask questions when they arise. One of the best ways to do this is to prepare everything yourself, such as your registration schedule, and ask your advisor simply to review it and provide feedback.

Getting Oriented

Institutions typically offer orientation sessions for new students enrolling in their first online course — whether enrolled in a degree program or single course. These sessions are usually a one-time event with resources that you can access throughout your academic experience as needed. Research shows that students who participate in an orientation program are more likely to succeed academically. Therefore, many online institutions provide orientation programs, even to those who are only taking one online course. Some institutions require students to participate, whereas at other institutions participation is voluntary.

Trust us when we tell you that participating in an orientation program is worth your time and effort. It has been our experience that students who don't participate in an orientation program often are more confused and frustrated because they have to learn how to navigate within the environment while also focusing on academic deadlines.

To help you avoid becoming one of those frustrated and lost students, in the following sections we discuss how to determine what kind of orientation is available and how to participate in the process.

Determining whether an orientation is available and/or required

Hopefully, you asked about orientation during your initial interview when researching online programs (see Chapter 5 for more about this process). However, you may not have discussed the details needed to register for and participate in the orientation. This information should be provided with your acceptance information. If not, you should contact your academic advisor immediately. The sooner you know, the sooner you can start planning.

If you didn't discuss this during the interview process, again, contact your academic advisor immediately. Knowing whether you're expected to participate in an orientation program and whether it's offered online is important. It's also important for you to know the timing of the orientation and whether missing it would delay you from starting your program.

Some institutions require you to participate in an orientation program as a degree requirement. It would be a shame to skip orientation and not find out until you're ready to graduate that you're ineligible because you never took the orientation.

Distinguishing types of orientation programs

Orientation programs for online courses are provided via two delivery methods. Some institutions require students to attend an orientation at the campus, whereas others offer an online equivalent.

Face-to-face orientation

An institution may ask for you to attend an orientation on campus for a number of reasons. Being on-site provides a secure way of confirming your identity and gives you the opportunity to meet some of your faculty and support staff face-to-face. You can confirm that your paperwork is in order (financial aid, registration, and other important documents) and get to know some of your peers. This experience also helps you feel more connected to the institution itself.

Other benefits of face-to-face orientation include the following:

- **Live computer demonstrations:** Most likely, you get to learn about the online environment in a computer lab where someone actually demonstrates how to log in, navigate within the system, and perform other tasks needed to successfully participate in the institution's online classes. You may even get to log in yourself to ensure that you feel comfortable doing this on your own before returning home. This experience is priceless! It's a good thing, too, because in this situation, you're responsible for travel, lodging, and food expenses; you may as well make the most of your orientation experience.

- **Q&A opportunities:** You're introduced to policies and procedures in an environment where you can ask questions and receive immediate answers. You also get to hear the questions asked by your peers and the answers to those questions as well.

Online orientation

In contrast to a face-to-face orientation, you may be offered an orientation that is completely online. Online orientation programs are usually created one of four ways:

- **Web pages on the institution's Web site:** Institutions that don't require students to participate in an orientation program may simply develop Web pages and provide students links to those pages in their acceptance documentation. These pages may be compiled on one site (usually the technology support department's Web site) with a navigation system, or they may be randomly scattered and referenced as needed within your course. For example, separate links to technical information may lead you to a different site than links to library resources, which may lead you to a separate set of resources maintained by library staff. In this form of orientation, no one knows your progress.

- **Self-paced orientation inside the course management system:** This method is very similar to the preceding one in that the materials are available immediately and 24/7, but it's a little more authentic in that you get to work within the course management system you'll use for coursework. The institution can track student completion through the course management system.

✔ **Instructor-led orientation inside the course management system:** Some institutions require a more formal orientation program. These institutions hire an instructor to facilitate an online orientation very similar to the other online sessions of the academic courses you enroll in. The orientation lasts a couple weeks, at most. The advantage to this structure is having an instructor available to answer questions when needed. The disadvantage to this structure is that you may not have access to the materials once the course is complete. Another disadvantage is that these orientations have specific start and stop dates. If your acceptance to the institution came after the orientation class began, you may have to wait until the course is offered again before enrolling in courses required by your degree program, unless the institution allows you to concurrently enroll in both the orientation and program courses.

✔ **Synchronous Web conference facilitated by an instructor:** Synchronous Web conferencing tools may be used by some institutions to hold live sessions where the facilitator can take participants on a virtual tour of a course management system, a virtual library, and other utilized instructional tools. The advantage of this method is that you have a live person you can ask questions of, and orientation is accomplished quickly and expediently. The obvious disadvantage is working with scheduling challenges.

Figure 7-2 provides an illustration of what an online orientation program may look like. In this example, nursing students are provided with a virtual guide (talking avatar) that welcomes them to the program and provides resources to important program information, including policies/procedures, technical support, academic services, and other important information. In this specific orientation, students also get to watch a welcome video from the program's dean and the university's president. Students have access to these materials at any time by going to a Web site that is linked to the student's login portal.

Participating in orientation

No matter what type of orientation program your institution offers, be sure to play an active role. We can't stress enough how beneficial participating in an orientation program can be. This is a great time to learn how to navigate and use your institution's technology in a safe environment without the pressures of homework and assignment deadlines. In the following sections, we explain how to register for orientation (if needed) and provide pointers on how to make the most of your session.

Registering for the orientation (if necessary)

To track which students have participated in the orientation, you may be asked to register for it as if you were registering for a class; your school will provide instructions on how to do so. As a matter of fact, institutions that require this component track it on your transcript as a way of easily determining whether you've successfully met graduation requirements. Other institutions, especially those where the orientation program is not required, may not have a registration system.

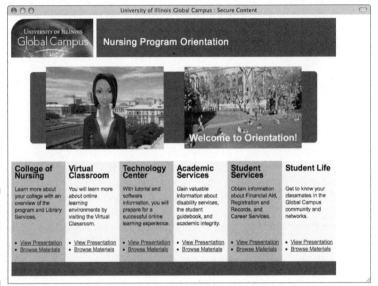

Figure 7-2:
An example of an online orientation program.

Don't get too excited about the thought of the orientation program being listed on your transcript. It's not going to boost your Grade Point Average (GPA). Most orientation programs, even those that are required, are zero-credit requirements. This means they can keep you from graduating, but they don't affect your academic standing.

Taking a virtual tour and noting important information

Most orientations, whether they're face-to-face or online, provide students with some kind of virtual tour of the learning environment. These tours can be developed using still screenshots of an example course, video, or application sharing in a live environment.

During a virtual tour, students are provided with a visual demonstration of how to log in, navigate within the course management system, and perform common, daily tasks. These may include reading new announcements from the instructor, checking for new posts within the discussion forum, replying to a peer's post, checking internal e-mail, submitting assignments, and using other software required by your academic program.

As you participate in the orientation program, be sure to note important information for future reference. Keep this information close to you when studying. Here are a few vital pieces of information to write down:

✔ Contact information for technical support, including e-mail and phone number (see Chapter 9 for more about technical support)

✔ The URL to the institution's course management system where your classes will be housed

✔ Steps for logging in and navigating to your virtual classroom (see Chapter 8 for general tips)

✔ How to navigate and log in to the library (see Chapter 11 for basic guidelines)

✔ How to start a new discussion post inside your course's discussion forum (see Chapter 10 for an introduction)

✔ Any additional tips provided for student success

This tour is one of the most valuable assets of the orientation program. If this resource is something you can get to anytime, be sure to note its location for future reference. You should also bookmark important external resources linked to from within the orientation. Finally, don't forget to bookmark other important sites, such as your institution's home page, the course management system login page, the library, and the technical support home page.

Browsers allow you to determine whether you want a bookmarked page to be displayed on the toolbar, where you see it every time you open the browser, or in the regular list of bookmarks. Put the login page on your toolbar so you can find it easily!

Buying Books

After registering for your courses, you need to find out what textbooks and other supplies are required for your courses. This section helps you determine how to find out what supplies you need and how to purchase those supplies.

Knowing which textbooks you need

Most brick-and-mortar schools have switched to an electronic registration system. As a result, institutions have also connected their registration systems to electronic bookstores. Therefore, after completing your course registration process, you see a button labeled "Buy Your Books Now" that links to the institution's online bookstore. Clicking on this link not only takes you to the virtual bookstore, it also creates a list of textbooks and supplies you need based on the courses you're enrolled in. Clicking this button doesn't obligate you to purchase your books from this site. It's just the best way to find out what books and supplies are required for your courses. Some institutions may provide a syllabus link in their course listings, which often includes required materials.

However, it's important to check the date that the syllabus was updated before using it as a reference for purchasing books and supplies.

Deciding where to buy your textbooks

Just because your institution's registration system is connected to an online bookstore doesn't mean that's where you have to purchase your gear. You have choices! Granted, purchasing your textbooks and supplies from your institution's online bookstore can be quick and convenient for many reasons:

✔ You know you're getting the right books and supplies.

✔ The process for purchasing the books and supplies is integrated with or linked to the registration system, making the purchase a quick one.

✔ The books and supplies are delivered right to your door (with a shipping fee of course).

But, are you getting the best deal, especially when it comes to textbooks? Sometimes purchasing textbooks via the institution's bookstore is more expensive. Determining where you can purchase your textbooks at the best price takes some legwork. First, you need an accurate list of all your required textbooks. You can find this information through the institution's registration system or the online bookstore. Be sure to write down the following information before searching elsewhere:

✔ Title of the textbook

✔ Edition of the textbook (some newer editions are really different from their older editions)

✔ Year of publication

✔ Author(s) of the textbook

✔ ISBN of the textbook

Local bookstores are a great place to start your hunt for a bargain. By providing bookstore staff with the preceding information, especially the ISBN number, they should be able to quickly look up prices for you. They should even be able to do this over the phone, saving you the time and gas it would take to drive all over town.

Another gas-saving technique is to check out other online bookstores, such as Amazon.com. Because online bookstores have a larger market to cater to, they often purchase items in high quantities, allowing them to discount the price to consumers. Another advantage to online bookstores is that they deliver the books right to your door. Depending on the amount of your purchase, you may qualify to have the books shipped for free.

We recommend that you shop around and look for the best deal before automatically purchasing a textbook from the institution. You may even want to purchase your textbooks for the same term from multiple vendors. When doing this, though, be sure to pay attention to taxes and shipping costs to make sure you're really getting the best deal.

Whenever you're looking for textbooks outside the institution, mention that you're a student. Some bookstores provide educational discounts to students. If your institution doesn't provide you with an ID (some online institutions don't), see whether the vendor will accept a copy of your registration as proof, or contact your advisor.

Buying new or used — that is the question

Most academic and online bookstores give you the option to purchase either new or used textbooks. Whether a textbook is available as a used book is based on whether the same book has been used in the past and whether students sold the book back to the bookstore at the end of the term.

So, should you purchase new or used books? New books are for you if:

- ✔ You like to be the first to highlight and write comments in the margins.
- ✔ You don't want to read what others thought was important (old highlighting and notes).
- ✔ You have lots of money. New books are more expensive!
- ✔ New books smell good to you (like new cars).

Of course, every issue has two sides. Used books are good for you if:

- ✔ You want to save money. You can save upwards of 40 percent of your total costs by purchasing used textbooks.
- ✔ You see value in reading what others have written in the margins.
- ✔ You don't care about reselling. It's hard to resell a used book. Buyers are more reluctant to purchase a book with more than one previous owner.

Buying used books offers some obvious benefits. But, do you know what you're getting when you buy them online?

Sites like Amazon.com or Half.com provide a venue for people to sell books they no longer need. To sell on these sites, a seller must first create a profile. Each of a seller's items is described by providing the book's overall condition and any special conditions or damages endured by the book. For example, you may read an ad that says something like this: "Book in great condition with highlighted text in 3 of the 13 chapters. No writings in the margin and no bent pages. This book is a steal." Some ads even have pictures of the book, which allow you to see proof of its condition. This feature is great for ensuring you're buying from the right person.

Another way you can determine whether you're purchasing from an honest person is to check the seller's ratings. Attached to each seller's profile is a rating system that allows buyers to rate their purchasing experiences with that seller. These ratings are public for other prospective buyers to see. They allow you to see whether the seller has provided honest information about his products, shipped them in a timely manner, and provided quality customer service. A positive rating may look something like this: "Overall rating 99%," and one of the buyer's comments to go along with this seller's rating might look like this: "Great customer service and product was in excellent shape. Fast shipping too. A+ seller."

Before purchasing a used book online, be sure to look at the seller's overall rating and the comments left by other buyers. This saves you a lot of future headaches and helps guarantee a positive purchasing experience.

Believe it or not, there is yet another method for getting physical textbooks: renting. Yes, renting. There are a few companies out there that have a system for renting textbooks and then returning them at the end of the term for less money than purchasing the book. For example, one of Kevin's textbooks cost over $90; however, at CollegeBookRenter.com (`www.collegebookrenter.com`), he can rent the book for 130 days for $47.52.

The wave of the future: Digital textbooks

Digital textbooks are available for permanent download to your computer or temporary use by logging in to a Web site. For example, the same book Kevin can rent for $47.52 in the preceding section, he can also get electronically from CourseSmart.com (`www.coursesmart.com`) for $64.82. This price includes digital access to the book for 180 days and the ability to highlight and take notes using the site's proprietary tools. Even though this is cheaper than buying the book, it requires an Internet connection and has an expiration date.

Other sites such as Amazon (`www.amazon.com`) and ebooks (`www.ebook.com`) sell electronic books that you can download and access from your computer, cellphone, or personal digital assistant (PDA). These are usually permanent downloads and often a few dollars cheaper than the print version.

Some institutions are switching to digital textbooks. You purchase the book as a computer file and read it on your computer or a digital reader such as the Amazon Kindle or Sony Reader. These devices store hundreds of books in digital format and are the size of a standard notepad. Not all titles are available via digital readers, but they're starting to gain momentum. Programs and individual courses that use digitally formatted textbooks will give you additional information during the application or enrollment process on how to purchase the books and the required reader when registering.

Part III
The Virtual Classroom: Being an A+ Student

The 5th Wave   By Rich Tennant

"I know it works on infomercials, but I still wouldn't separate paragraphs in your introduction to your online classmates with 'But wait, that's not all!' and 'Act now, and I'll include this impressive list of hobbies.'"

In this part . . .

Just as you expect a certain amount of culture shock when moving to a new country, becoming an online student can feel very foreign. In this part, we drill down to the nitty-gritty of how online courses work. We begin with the process of navigating your classroom and an explanation of who you might interact with online, such as your instructor and the other students. We cover the various means of communication and give ideas for how to write and submit A+ assignments.

Within this part, we help you understand your role as an online student. This may be a little different from what you experience with traditional courses; however, there are common themes, such as academic integrity, working in groups, study skills, and more. Finally, we leave you with ideas for creating an ePortfolio to document your academic accomplishments, and we help you with ideas for transitioning beyond your online courses.

Chapter 8

Navigating the Classroom

On the first day of a traditional class, the instructor usually passes out papers, explains the class, reviews grading, and talks a little about what the class entails. In online education, the same kinds of resources are available, but you get them in a different fashion. After you register for one or more online classes (see Chapter 7), you're ready to log in and find your way around the virtual classroom, which is where students and faculty gather together to learn. The beauty of this virtual classroom is that you don't have to dress up, you don't have to fight for parking, and you can come to school whenever it's convenient!

This chapter walks you through a typical login experience and helps you become familiar with some of the materials and activities your instructor may have for you.

Reaching Your Virtual Classroom

Your calendar tells you that class starts today. What does that mean? Do you need to log in at 8 a.m. to complete a task? We assume you're excited to begin with online education but a little anxious as to what to do first. It's not as easy as showing up to the right classroom, and all of this is new! In the following sections, we explain how to use the right Web address, set some Internet options, log in to the school's home page, and find the link for each course you're taking.

Some institutions let you log in a day or two early just to start looking around. If you're given this opportunity, take advantage of it. If you don't have time to log in early, at least log in on the first day so your instructor knows you're present.

Using the right address and setting some Internet options

Sometime prior to the start of a course, the school sends information about how to log in to your virtual classroom. In some cases, you may receive this a week in advance; in other cases, it may arrive hours prior to the start of the course. It all depends on the school. This communication includes a specific URL (Web address), a username, and a password. You type that URL (for example, `www.myschool.edu`) in the address bar of the browser, in place of whatever URL shows when you open your browser. Hit enter and the Web page should change to your school page.

Hopefully, the correspondence from your school also includes instructions explaining how to set your browser for optimal performance (see Chapter 3 for the basics on browsers). In most cases, you want your Temporary Internet Files (found within Internet Options in the Tools menu) set so that the browser checks for newer versions of stored pages every time you visit those pages (see Figure 8-1).

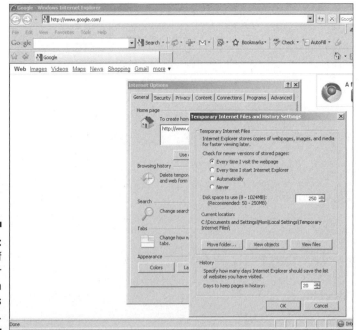

Figure 8-1:
A view of browser settings in Windows XP.

Every browser and operating system has a different method and look to it. In Figure 8-1, we show you how Windows XP looks when you're trying to set the Temporary Internet Files. Follow these steps:

1. **Notice there are seven tabs at the top. Click on the first tab: General.**

2. **That mini-page is broken into three categories: Look to the middle for the area labeled Temporary Internet Files.**

3. **Look within that area and you'll see three rectangular buttons. The one on the far right is labeled Settings.**

4. **Click on Settings and make sure the first option, "Every visit to the page," is selected.**

Logging in and checking out the portal

After you find your virtual classroom, log in for the first time by using the username and password provided by the school. These words or codes are case sensitive, meaning you cannot capitalize at will. Type the information exactly as it is on the paper (or on the screen if it was e-mailed to you).

Generally, your login doesn't take you directly to your course; rather, it takes you to a home page that includes additional information and a link to your course. (If you're taking more than one course, you'll see a link for each one.) This first home page, called the *portal,* may include information like announcements to all students, links to the library, or tutorials on common processes. It may even be the same page you used to register for classes. Figure 8-2 shows a sample of a portal from which a student would access her course(s).

If your portal looks nothing like the one in Figure 8-2, don't worry: What you see when you log in depends on the course management system software your school uses. There are several major vendors in North America and worldwide: Blackboard, WebCT, Desire2Learn®, and Moodle, for example. Whether you know which course management system your school uses may make for interesting cocktail party conversation with other online students, but it doesn't really matter in terms of getting your work done. If your school doesn't blatantly tell you in their correspondence, you will see the logo when you log into the course. Vendors love to let you know who they are!

Figure 8-2:
Desire2
Learn Home
Page: A
portal you
might see
when first
logging in.

Many institutions ask students to change their passwords as soon as they log in, and this is typically done from the portal. This is for your own security. We recommend changing your password, but not immediately. First, take some time to look around your new environment, specifically finding and printing your technical support and instructor contact information before changing your password. That way, if for some reason you get locked out of the system, you'll know who and where to call! (Flip to Chapter 3 for the basics on passwords.)

Finding your course's home page

As we note in the preceding section, your course management system software (for example, Blackboard, WebCT, Desire2Learn, or Moodle) determines exactly what you see on the application's home page when you log in. But in all cases, you see a link to your course, most often identified by the course name and catalog number (refer to Figure 8-2). Once you find the link to your course, click on it to be taken to the main page, also sometimes called the home page, of your course.

You may not be able to see the entire course at once. Some instructors like to show only what is needed in the beginning so students don't become overwhelmed. This is new, after all! However, your interface probably has links to some standard materials, such as a welcome message from your instructor, the syllabus, the calendar, and other information we look at more specifically later in this chapter. So that you know you're in the right place, Figures 8-3 and 8-4 show what you might see when logging into two different systems for the first time:

✔ Figure 8-3 shows a home page of a course taught on Angel. Notice that you see courses you have access to along with groups and announcements. Announcements might be reminders of deadlines, notes about additional resources, or basic processes that relate to everyone. This kind of opening page lets you choose to go where you need with the information that will help you succeed.

✔ Figure 8-4 shows a home page of a course taught on Moodle. In this case, you see links to content right away. You can jump directly to the lessons of the course and information about assignments. Announcements may be off to the side or contained within a special forum.

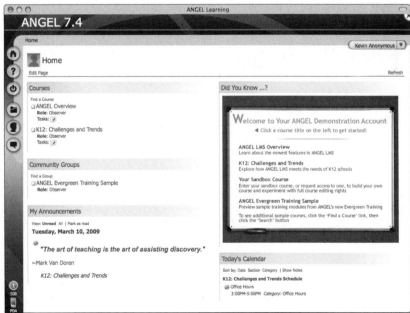

Figure 8-3:
A home
page of
a course
taught on
Angel.

Figure 8-4:
A home
page of
a course
taught on
Moodle.

Locating and Understanding Critical Documents

After you know how to get to the right home page for each course you're taking, you want to collect a few major documents you need. Think of this as a treasure hunt. Hopefully your instructor has been kind enough to put an "X Marks the Spot" on the course's home page, but just in case it's not that easy, this section walks you through what to look for — including the syllabus, calendar, and details on grading — and where to find it.

Start a notebook for each online course you take. Find the documents in the following sections and keep copies in both printed form and in a folder on your computer's hard drive. The printed copy is more portable, and if your computer crashes (it happens), you'll have the instructor's name and contact information and can continue working on the course at a different computer. You can also keep printed articles and resources as they become available in your course. It's not very "green," but many people still prefer to have a paper copy for easier reading and note taking. Most of us still like to scribble in the margins!

The syllabus

In order to teach this particular course, your instructor has to determine its goals, objectives, assignments, and much more. By putting these in writing, she creates a *syllabus*. Every course needs a plan. The syllabus communicates that plan and is therefore one of the most important documents in your course. You can think of this document as a general map of where you're headed in a course.

A link to the syllabus is often front and center on the home page. It may be a button to the left or an icon in the middle of the page, but it's generally very visible. A typical syllabus includes information on:

- ✔ **Course basics:** The name of the course, credit hours, goals and objectives, and required textbooks

- ✔ **Instructor contact information:** Name, possibly biography, address, phone, e-mail, and other contact information, such as time zone and availability

- ✔ **Course content:** Topics to be covered and possibly a schedule or calendar (see the next section for more information)

- ✔ **Grading:** How you'll be evaluated, the kinds of assignments you'll do, the rationale for those assignments, and the distribution of points (we cover details on grading later in this chapter)

- ✔ **Policies:** Academic honesty, the general expectations of logging in and participating, whether late work is acceptable, netiquette expectations, and other policies that help you understand how the instructor runs the class

- ✔ **Resources:** Links to technical support, the library, the bookstore, academic advising or tutoring, disability services, and other resources students may need

Think of the syllabus as an informal contract between you and the instructor. She has the responsibility to teach you as she planned, and you have the responsibility to follow through with what is expected. To use the syllabus to your advantage, read it and become familiar with what is expected of you. Pay special attention to how you'll be graded and the general expectations of logging in and participating.

The calendar

Even though a course might be advertised as "anywhere and anytime," you still have to complete assignments according to a calendar. Even self-paced courses have deadlines!

You can typically find calendars on the home page. On all calendars, you see the dates on which assignments are due. You may also find important deadlines and dates listed on the syllabus. Specific calendar forms depend on the course management software, but they typically fall into two camps:

- ✓ **Those that give you a graphic view (see Figure 8-5):** This calendar is found on the home page and is in a traditional chart format almost anyone can recognize.

- ✓ **Those that list assignments (see Figure 8-6):** This form lists the assignments in a linear fashion. It may be found on the home page, or as a link elsewhere.

Figure 8-5:
A graphic
calendar
view.

Figure 8-6:
A calendar view that lists assignments.

Most of us keep multiple calendars and rarely synchronize them. The calendar in the kitchen doesn't include the business trip you have planned, and your office calendar doesn't say anything about needing cookies for the PTA. Coordinate all your calendars so you know when major assignments are due and how these intersect with business and family. For example, look ahead to see whether a group project is coming up in your class and make sure you don't plan a family weekend getaway in the middle of it. Consider transferring all calendar items into your favorite calendaring program, such as Microsoft Outlook. When you do this, you can set up reminders to alert you when assignments are due or synchronous sessions are scheduled.

When coordinating your calendars and figuring out deadlines, pay attention to what time something is due and what time zone the course calendar refers to. Course management systems will timestamp all your submitted assignments for the instructor's record. For example, assignments due at midnight Eastern Time are due at 9 p.m. Pacific Time. This is a big difference and can have a dramatic affect on your grade if assignments are turned in late.

As you're coordinating dates, be sure to think about whether you need a calendar in digital or paper form. While coauthor Susan keeps an electronic calendar on Google Calendar, she also has several paper versions printed and hanging in front of her monitor. There's no shame in printing!

Don't depend on your instructor to remind you of due dates. Similarly, don't assume she uses the calendar feature within the course software. Instead, take responsibility for writing down and coordinating dates.

Finding out how you're graded

If you're going to invest a major portion of your free time in studying, we assume you want to be rewarded with a good grade. In the following sections, we describe a few key documents related to grading: the grading scale, any rubric used for your course, and the late policy.

The grading scale

You want to identify how you'll be graded and what you need to do to earn the highest score. Somewhere in your course, possibly in the syllabus but also as a separate link on the home page, should be a grading scale. Figure 8-7 shows the major components that should be included: a list of general assignments, the available number of points for each assignment, and the grade distribution based on the total number of points you earn. Notice the example doesn't include grades D or F. We were thinking of a graduate level course where typically anything lower than a C is considered failing.

Discussion (8 weeks, 10 points per week)	80 points
Weekly quizzes (8 weeks, 5 points each)	40 points
Weekly articles added to wiki (8 weeks, 5 points each)	40 points
Weekly reflections (8 weeks, 5 points each)	40 points
Midterm paper	40 points
Final project	80 points
Total possible points	**320**

** More detailed rubrics provided within course

Figure 8-7:
A view of a typical grading scale.

320-297 = A
296-278 = B
277-262 = C

When you first look at a grading scale, focus on the types of assignments, what percentage of points go with each assignment, and any projects or assignments that seem to be worth a lot more than others. Also pay attention to the proportion of points assigned to ongoing or routine activities, such as weekly discussion or chapter tests.

You can learn a lot from the example in Figure 8-7. If you read this document carefully, you can conclude:

- ✔ **Discussion is very important in this course.** It's worth 25 percent of the grade! A rubric also is mentioned. Reading the rubric will tell you exactly what is expected from the discussion portion of the course. (See the next section for more on rubrics.)

- ✔ **Quizzes are as important as weekly reflections, but only half as important as discussion.** The instructor may be using quizzes as a way to make sure you keep up-to-date with the facts of the course so you don't fall behind. This way you can also test yourself so you know where to focus your energy.

- ✔ **The final project is worth a quarter of the grade, but there is no final exam.** Plus, the paper is evaluated using a rubric. That means you should start looking for the rubric! It also means you should start organizing your time to break this big project into smaller pieces.

- ✔ **A's don't come easily.** You need 93 percent to get an A.

Rubrics

A *rubric* is an evaluation plan or a scoring tool that helps the instructor determine how well your paper, project, or participation lines up with the ideal. Rubrics are typically found in the instructions for the assignment or linked to the instructions. Rubrics typically include several categories that are deemed important to the final product. For example, in written work, the quality of your ideas is assessed along with your ability to think critically and write in a grammatically acceptable form. The rubric communicates what's important by the relative weights given to the categories. Look at the example rubric in Table 8-1, which is for the discussion portion of a course.

When you look at a rubric, you want to determine what's important and where the instructor is going to turn her attention. Most rubrics have categories that organize the evaluation. Then within each category, you'll see details about what an excellent paper or project would include. This rubric tells you the following:

- ✔ The development of ideas is twice as important as mechanics (5 points versus 2 points).

- ✔ Proper citation is expected, according to the "content" description.

- ✔ You must respond to at least two peers in order to get full credit.

Reading the rubric in detail before completing the assignment can help you prepare and self-check your assignments before turning them in for grades. We guarantee you can earn higher grades by reading and following the rubric! See Chapter 14 for more information about rubrics.

Table 8-1	A Typical Discussion Rubric
Categories	**Exceptional**
Content	The content is complete and accurate and offers new ideas for application through clear evidence of critical thinking (how does this work?). The discussion is well supported with details from the readings, which are cited properly. Postings are characterized by originality and relevance to the topic and encourage further discussion on the topic. 5 points
Interaction	Routinely responds to other students (at least twice) and offers additional insights and considerations that extend collective understanding. Communication encourages further responses, raises questions, or politely offers alternative perspectives. 3 points
Mechanics	Writing is free of grammatical errors and follows acceptable standard English conventions (spelling, punctuation, and so on). Posting is submitted prior to the deadline. 2 points

The late policy

As much as you plan to be on time with all your assignments, occasionally life gets in the way. Be sure you understand what the late policy is for your online course. The late policy may be included in the syllabus or with each assignment. Some instructors accept work past the deadline, while others don't. In every case, if you know you won't meet the deadline and have a good reason, contact your instructor! Explain the circumstances and politely ask for an extension.

Notice, we said *"and have a good reason."* Good reasons would include someone becoming seriously ill, your wife having a baby earlier than expected, a death in the family, or a natural disaster such as flooding. Good reasons would not include a NASCAR race you attended, an impromptu trip to the beach, or Mother's Day. In those situations, you could have planned in advance to get your work in on time.

Modules and More: Understanding a Course's Content Organization

Take a look at any standard textbook, and you'll see that it's divided into chapters. Each chapter covers a different topic. In some cases, Chapter 4 only makes sense if you've read Chapters 1, 2, and 3. In other textbooks, you can jump around from chapter to chapter and the content still makes sense.

Online courses are organized in a similar fashion. They're also broken down into smaller pieces, or "chapters." Your instructor probably organizes what you're going to do in the class according to weeks or topics. This way, you focus on one chunk of information at a time. Some instructors, though, organize content for a class by different functions: discussions, assignments, quizzes, tests, and the like.

You can see evidence of how the course is organized by checking out the course's home page.

✔ Figure 8-8 shows the organizational pattern on the screen. The box to the left labeled "menu" tells you that the information has been chunked into smaller units called *modules*. Each module probably contains just enough data for one or two weeks. In these courses, everything you need to complete the module can be found within the week or topic heading.

✔ In other courses, materials and assignments may be provided according to function. This situation requires a little more clicking on your part. For example, if there's no obvious link to modules organized by week or topic on the course's home page, you may have to click on a link titled "Discussions" and then another link labeled "Week 2 Discussions" in order to participate in Week 2's class discussion. Next, you may need to go back to the course's home page and click an "Assignments" link to locate Week 2's assignments. In most cases, this structure is determined by the course management system, not the instructor.

The way a course is organized affects the placement of certain documents related to assignments and testing, especially rubrics, handouts, and resources. Your instructor may leave handouts and resources in a couple locations:

✔ She may put all of them within the module for which they're needed. For example, Module One's handouts would be in Module One's folder, including the instructions for an upcoming assignment and the details on grading, including the rubric.

✔ On the other hand, your instructor may put all the rubrics and related documents together in one location and call this "Grading" or "Assessment."

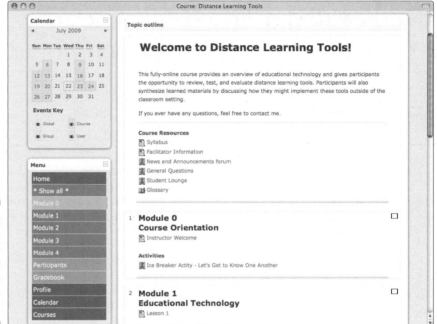

Figure 8-8:
A sample home page that shows module organization.

What can you learn from this? No two instructors are the same, and you may need to click around to find the materials you're looking for. Hopefully, your instructor will at least be consistent and you'll be able to find things more quickly after spending a little time becoming familiar with your virtual classroom. Finally, there's no harm in asking the instructor! Just say the Dummies people got you thinking there might be something you're missing.

Attending Virtual Office Hours

If you take a traditional on-ground course, your instructor will tell you about "office hours." These are established times when you can drop by the instructor's office and discuss any concerns. For example, if you really bombed the last test, you may want to go over the answers or talk about where you missed the point. Similarly, in the virtual world, instructors conduct virtual office hours as a means of staying connected to their students. In the following sections, we describe these office hours and their benefits, and we provide pointers on how to access virtual offices.

Discovering the value of virtual office hours

In the online world, the instructor may have an office in another state or country! For that reason, the office hours are *virtual,* meaning they're conducted online. Using synchronous software, the instructor makes herself available for conversation or communication at a specific time.

Instructors approach office hours a couple ways:

✔ Some make themselves available for questions and comments, and if no one shows up, they just work at their computer.

✔ Others have a specific agenda and use the time to provide additional information you may not otherwise cover in class. For example, coauthor Susan regularly previews technology tools her students may find helpful.

In many cases, these virtual office hours are recorded so if you can't attend the "live" meeting, you can watch the recording later and get the same information. The instructor posts a link after the meeting so you know where and how to access the recording. However, even if your instructor's office hours are recorded, nothing beats the live interaction — so attend if you can. You won't regret it.

You may need a few private moments with the instructor to ask a question about a grade, comment on a personal situation, or talk about anything you don't want the rest of the class to know. If that's the case, let the instructor know in advance by way of an e-mail. You can then schedule a private conversation.

Lots of students and instructors enjoy virtual office hours because they afford a kind of real-person connection that the asynchronous environment doesn't. This is your opportunity to interact with live voices! Yes, with a simple microphone/headset device (available at any office supply store; see Chapter 3 for details), participants can talk to one another! The instant gratification of communication during virtual office hours is very powerful in reinforcing a sense of belonging and presence within the class. It gives both faculty and students an opportunity to strengthen the learning community bonds.

Virtual office hours are also great for reinforcing course content. Coauthor Susan is able to demonstrate new technologies by sharing her screen with her class. Students get to see a live demonstration of how to use the technology and step-by-step instructions for doing so.

In addition to providing virtual office space for instructors, your institution may provide students with virtual office space. This space is open 24/7 for students who want to meet with other students in order to complete group projects, discuss content, and so forth. These spaces are often restricted by course enrollment and recorded for security purposes. They provide a great vehicle for collaborating on assignments in an interactive environment. We discuss this issue in more detail in Chapter 12.

Accessing the virtual office

If your college provides virtual office space to instructors and/or students, you will see a special login place within your course, typically on the home page. Often the software needed for office hours is different from your course management system, but they should be integrated. For example, you might have a course offered in Moodle with office hours occurring in Elluminate, but a link in your course should take you seamlessly to your new destination. Figure 8-9 shows a typical virtual office space. Notice there's a space for sharing slides or images in the center. To the left are a list of participants, a place for chat with text, and an audio button allowing for voice chat. These features are fairly standard with Web conferencing software.

Figure 8-9: A sample interface for an online office hour.

Courtesy of Elluminate, Inc.

No matter what technology is used for virtual office space, the institution should also provide links to tutorials on how to navigate to, and interact within, the synchronous environment. These tutorials may be a part of your institution's orientation materials, which you're hopefully able to refer to at any time. (Check out Chapter 7 for more about orientation programs.)

Chapter 9

Meeting the People in (And around) Your Classroom

In This Chapter

▶ Working well with your instructor and classmates

▶ Introducing the folks behind the scenes

*R*emember the first day of school when you couldn't wait to find out who your teacher was and who was in your class? In the online classroom, that same kind of excitement (or nervousness) exists. Unless you're enrolled in an independent study with no interaction with anyone but your professor, you want to figure out who else is in (and around) your classroom and how they relate to you.

People in the online classroom tend to fall into two camps: those who are very visible and those who work behind the scenes.

✔ **The visible people — your instructor and the other students:** You want to identify how your instructor works and the ways in which he communicates with you. You also want to get to know the other students and how you work with them as a member of the community.

✔ **The people behind the scenes:** Not everyone in the online classroom works front and center. You may encounter guest lecturers, administrative staff monitoring how the class is progressing, or technical staff. All these people help make sure the system works and that you get the best educational experience for your money. Plus, your personal support system of family and friends cannot be discounted.

This chapter helps you sort out all the people you meet in your online experience.

Getting to Know the Folks Who Are Front and Center

During your time in class, the people you interact with most frequently are your instructor and the other students. They're the folks who shape your overall online experience the most, so knowing what to expect from them and how to conduct yourself around them is important. We explain what you need to know in the following sections.

Acquainting yourself with your instructor

An instructor, simply stated, is the person who's in charge of your online classroom — he runs the show. In the following sections, we explain the credentials and training that instructors need, describe where to find your instructor in the online classroom, and provide pointers on communicating effectively with your instructor.

What you call your instructor may vary from course to course or school to school. Typically, *professor* denotes full-time, tenured faculty, whereas *instructor* or *adjunct instructor* signifies that the individual may not have full-time employment. A *facilitator* is another term some schools use to describe the instructor role, especially within the online learning environment. If the titles of instructor or facilitator have any significance (they don't always), it's to denote that the students have a lot more responsibility in making connections in the learning and the facilitator helps this happen. Throughout this book, we use the terms instructor and facilitator interchangeably to describe the role, regardless of title or rank.

Necessary credentials and training for instructors

The same requirements and qualifications for teaching in a traditional face-to-face class apply to teaching online. In the two-year or community college system, that may mean having a master's degree in the discipline; in a four-year university, institutions may require an instructor to have a doctorate degree in order to teach graduate level courses. In a virtual high school, the instructor needs to meet the state's requirements for certification or licensure, which begin with a bachelor's degree.

Online institutions also request that instructors complete some kind of online training in order to teach. The best schools go beyond showing instructors what buttons to push and include more information about how online learning is different from traditional classroom education. By exploring what makes online learning unique, your instructor can better manage the virtual classroom and teach more effectively. In fact, most higher education faculty aren't hired for their teaching skills; they're hired for their subject matter expertise (for instance, if an institution needs a geology professor, it finds someone with knowledge in geology). Therefore, if your online instructor has additional training in "how to teach," he's probably more advanced in understanding how to help students learn than he might be if he were teaching in a traditional classroom. As a student, you win!

How do you find out about your instructor's credentials? Typically, you can find a listing of faculty somewhere within the institutional Web site. This may be organized by program or discipline. Each instructor probably has a Web page that welcomes students and includes credentials. When in doubt, this is a great question to ask as you search for the right school. We talk a little more about this in Chapter 4.

Where you "see" your instructor

Rather than standing in front of a traditional class, lecturing and directing students' behavior, the person in charge of your online classroom makes information available and creatively gets students involved in thinking about and working with those concepts. He *guides* students toward understanding the material.

In the virtual world, you don't have the advantage of looking at your instructor, live and in person. Yet, a good online instructor lets his presence be "seen" in several ways:

✔ **Your instructor may communicate with the whole class by posting ongoing announcements and news.** You can typically find these postings on the main page when you log in (see Chapter 8 for details on logging in and navigating your classroom), but some instructors communicate this kind of information through e-mail. Instructors make announcements to keep students on task, remind them of deadlines, or enrich their understanding with additional resources and links.

✔ **You may see your instructor busy in the discussion area.** Many online courses require students to interact with each other by posting answers to discussion questions and extending the conversations through replies to one another. Often, instructors facilitate these discussions by raising additional considerations, asking for clarification, or extending questions that probe deeper into the material.

How much your instructor gets involved in discussions depends on the nature of the class and his own style. If you're a graduate student in an advanced seminar, chances are you and your classmates are going to need very little guidance to explore course themes. However, if you're taking an entry-level psychology course, your instructor may be much more active in guiding the discussion.

✔ **Ultimately, you see your instructor through the grades and feedback he provides.** As assignments are scored, instructors comment and leave notes in grade books. The instructor may also e-mail you this information privately. This feedback helps you close the loop so that you understand not only what you know, but what you still need to figure out.

Giving quality feedback takes a great deal of time, so be sure to read the comments your instructor leaves for you. For example, if your instructor tells you to be more careful with how you cite research (or suggests that you start citing!), check your course for tutorials and additional links to citation resources. If you really want to earn points, send a sample citation back and tell the instructor where you learned to format it. That shows you are paying attention and value the input.

Communicating effectively with your instructor

Your instructor communicates with you as a member of the class and privately, but how should you communicate with the instructor? To start, find out how he prefers to be addressed. Some instructors expect you to address all correspondence with their title, such as Professor Manning. Some prefer Dr. Manning, but check to see that you have the correct title! Others are more casual and ask you to call them by their first name.

You can usually get a sense of how the instructor prefers to be addressed based on e-mail he may have sent to you prior to the start of the class or course documents such as a welcome page or announcements he may have left in the course. Look at how he signs those pieces of correspondence. Does he refer to himself as Professor or does he sign his first name? Follow the instructor's lead.

What's in a doctorate title?

What's the difference between a PhD and an EdD when you read academic titles?

✔ **PhD** is short for Doctor of Philosophy, and is a terminal degree (meaning you can't get higher than this). It generally requires 2 to 4 years of coursework beyond a master's degree and original research in the field of specialty. People in hard sciences (sciences considered to be more scientific), such as chemistry and computer science, earn PhDs. PhDs are also conferred upon those in the social sciences such as sociology, psychology, and education. These fields are often referred to as the soft sciences.

✔ **EdD** stands for Doctor of Education. This is very similar to a PhD in that it's a terminal

degree requiring 2 to 4 years of coursework beyond a master's degree and original research in the field of specialty. Some argue that the EdD is more practice-based, whereas, the PhD is more research based. In addition, as you might expect, the EdD is specific to educators.

Other fields have their own terminal degrees. For example, the terminal law degree for professionals is the JD, which stands for Juris Doctor. Another example is the MFA, which is the terminal degree for those in applied arts. A third example is the MLS or MLIS for librarians, which stands for Master's degree in Library Science or Library and Information Sciences.

You should also figure out whether your communication should be public or private.

✔ **Public communication:** If you have a question about how the course works or where you can find some information, initiate communication in a public forum such as your discussion area. Be sure to read any FAQs or announcements before you ask, however, because many times teachers answer questions in advance.

If you choose to initiate communication publicly, be sure to *ask* and not immediately jump to the conclusion that the information isn't available. To avoid making instructors sound fickle, diplomacy goes a long way. For example, rather than say, "You haven't included instructions on . . ." an instructor would much rather read, "I can't seem to locate the instructions on . . ., although I'm sure you included these."

✔ **Private communication:** If your question deals with grades or personal issues, initiate a private e-mail. By all means, if you have a criticism or you find something in the course that isn't working, use diplomacy and communicate privately. Examples may include typographical errors or hyperlinks that don't work. For example, you could write, "I realize you have no control over Web sites that aren't part of this class, but I just wanted to let you know that one of the links appears to be broken." That's much better than, "Hey, you're sending me on a wild goose chase!"

Instructors like contact with students; otherwise, they wouldn't be in this business. You don't need to send a daily e-mail, but in some situations you should definitely communicate with your instructor:

✔ **If you'll be away:** Let your instructor know if you have an emergency that will take you away from the course for more than a couple days. Be sure to let the instructor know how you plan to make up for lost time or keep up with the course.

✔ **If you experience technical difficulties:** Tell your instructor if your computer has crashed and you're operating from a different venue, or if you've experienced some technical issue and have reported it to technical support personnel. (We discuss technical support in more detail later in this chapter.)

✔ **If you get major feedback:** When you receive individualized feedback from the instructor on a major project, consider acknowledging it and addressing any follow-up questions he may have asked. You don't have to do this for typical weekly assignments!

✔ **If you're an overachiever:** If you're one of those students who really excels and wants to work beyond course requirements, contact your instructor and ask for some additional resources and guidance. Obviously, teachers love these kinds of questions!

> ✔ **If you're having trouble:** On the other hand, if you're struggling with the course, either because the content is too difficult or life is getting in the way, let your instructor know at the first warning signs. This may be a situation in which the instructor diplomatically suggests you take the course at another time, but you save face by letting him know in advance and not failing without warning.

Interacting with fellow students

In the online education environment, you deal with your fellow classmates daily. Learning online is rarely an isolated, independent event and can be quite social! In the following sections, we explain how to get to know the other students and how to get along.

Introducing yourself and getting to know your peers

When you first register for an online course, you're given an identification name that you use to log in to your virtual classroom. This name is often a variation of your first and last names. For example, John Smith might have a login name of jsmith3. Some virtual classrooms attach this identification to all discussion posts, assignment submissions, and e-mails.

Always sign your work and begin to build your online persona under your identification name. For example, at the end of all of coauthor Kevin's posts (under the name kejohns), he writes "Have a GREAT day! Kevin Johnson, Urbana, Illinois." Without that signature, other students may never associate Kevin Johnson with the username kejohns, which makes the online environment seem sterile and unfriendly. Plus, it's kind of fun to see where others are logging in from, literally.

Once you correlate usernames to your peers' actual names, it's easy to make assumptions about cultural and academic backgrounds. It's true that your peers will come from diverse backgrounds and will be spread out around the world, but stay away from assuming stereotypical information such as gender, race, socioeconomic status, and intelligence. A lot of Pat's, Chris's, and Ryan's have had their gender identities switched mistakenly through stereotyping. These stereotypes can damage the dynamics of an online classroom. As a matter of fact, it's this diversity and the sharing of different perspectives that, when appreciated and celebrated, enrich the learning experience for everyone.

If you have a name that doesn't immediately tell your classmates that you're female or male, or if you have a name that's uncommon in American classrooms (like Uday, Kamiko, or Ping), you may choose to disclose your gender by referring to yourself as a mother, father, sister, brother, male nurse, or something along those lines. By doing this, you reduce the possibility of your instructor and classmates embarrassing themselves by using assumptive language when referencing you and your work.

Another element of identity that your peers may or may not choose to share with you is a picture of themselves. Some of your peers may choose to share a photo of them at work, with family, or even swimming with dolphins during their last vacation. Having a picture to go along with a name can provide an element of connection. You may even be amazed at how you imagine your peers' pictures in your mind when you read their posts and e-mails.

Knowing your peers can help you understand more about who they are and what amazing contributions they can add to the learning experience. If your class requires a biography-type assignment, take the time to read the introductions of your peers and get to know them better. You'll notice that some students can log in three times a day because of their lifestyles (for example, they're retired or temporarily unemployed), whereas others may barely make it to class three times a week. The biographies help explain that and allow you to be a little more compassionate toward your classmates' circumstances.

When it comes to writing your own profile, you want to make a good impression in a very small amount of space. Provide your instructor and classmates with an overview of who you are without boring them with all the micro-details. For formal profiles, it's recommended that you write in third person. However, for most classroom introductions, writing in first person is acceptable and comes across as being less formal. Consider adding some of the following information:

- ✓ **Name and geographic location:** Provide your full name and where you reside. You don't have to give your full address — your city and state are fine if you live in the states and your country/territory is sufficient if you live outside the United States.

- ✓ **Professional background:** Provide your readers with a brief understanding of what you do and your professional history if appropriate. Remember to keep it brief. Summarize your experiences into only one or two sentences, even if you've been in the field for 25 years.

- ✓ **Academic background:** Let your peers know where you are in your education and why you've chosen the program or course you're in enrolled in.

- ✓ **Personal information:** Feel free to share personal information such as whether you're married, whether you have children or pets, or what your favorite hobbies are. This reminds others that they are in class with other human beings who have outside interests and responsibilities.

Playing well with others

View your online classroom as a community of peers you don't get to see every day — like co-workers, if you will. Just like at work, sometimes you need to use a professional voice, and other times you can goof around.

Communicate formally when you submit assignments that are going to be read by the whole group. If you're required to write a summary of the main points of the unit, for example, write in a scholarly manner, with appropriate references and correct grammar, and without unsubstantiated opinion. Your classmates will figure out very quickly that you're an A student and take this seriously. If you don't, you'll quickly be read as someone who either lacks polish or just doesn't care. We say more about writing style in Chapter 14, but for now, recognize that people will judge you based on written communication.

On the other hand, there are plenty of times when you can lighten up. For example, when you respond to someone else's work, you may not need to be as formal. An example comment would be, "Hey, Molly, you're my idol. You brought up some excellent examples. I really appreciated how you. . . ."

Finally, you can just relax and shoot the breeze at times. Many online classes have a place where you can share information that isn't related to the course. It might be called the student lounge or café. Don't be afraid to help build community by sharing work examples, personal stories, and even social happenings such as a conference you attended. These experiences directly benefit learning in that they connect what you are learning to real life, and anytime you make those connections, the concepts are reinforced.

At all costs, avoid writing comments that are glib, sarcastic, or sloppy. For example, you wouldn't want to write, "You are such a princess!" if you mean to suggest that an alternative view exists and the reader just isn't seeing it. Similarly, "i no wat ur sayin" just doesn't work in a classroom context.

Students who take the time to get to know their peers, communicate often, and consistently participate go a long way toward building community. The group begins to trust one another when they realize those are real people on the other end of the computer screen. That trust comes in handy when you need to work together collaboratively. If one of your classmates needs some special consideration in a group assignment, for instance, the group is more likely to grant it to someone who has pulled his weight and contributed previously, versus someone who has only been sitting in the background and hasn't cared to interact. The same human dynamics you find in a traditional classroom play out online.

Seeing Who's Behind the Scenes

We predict you'll spend so much time interacting with your fellow students and instructor, you won't notice the following groups of people. But they're present and working behind the scenes to ensure your success. These people include guests, technical and academic support staff, and friends and family. This section helps you understand who they are and the differences they can make in your educational experience.

Noting classroom guests and observers

Much like the face-to-face classroom, you may or may not notice several outside guests visiting the virtual classroom. Outsiders can include guest speakers, support staff, and administrators. Following are some of the people you may see:

- **Teaching assistants:** Some online classes are large enough that the instructor needs help facilitating the course. In this situation, teaching assistants may be utilized to help with tasks such as facilitating discussion, answering questions, and grading assignments. Students should interact with teaching assistants in the same manner they do their instructor.

- **Librarians:** Gone are the days of thinking about librarians as the people who look over their glasses and shush you for being too loud in the library. Besides, how can you be too noisy in a virtual library? There are several instances in which you may "run into" a librarian from your institution. Your instructor may invite a librarian to guest-lecture in your classroom as a way of encouraging library use and helping you learn how to conduct research for a specific assignment. Or, you may get the chance to chat with a librarian live when you need help navigating the virtual library. No matter the situation, your institution's librarian is a great resource. Communication with librarians can be more casual, but you should still keep it professional.

- **Guest lecturers:** Hearing about different experiences from professionals within the field is important for students. After all, one of the biggest benefits of online learning is that your instructor can connect you with professionals around the world that you may not normally get to learn from. For this purpose, your instructor may ask a practitioner to join the class to share his experiences and answer student questions. This can be done using discussion boards or a live event such as a conference call or a Web conference over the Internet. In any case, do what you can to actively participate in these opportunities. Thank the guest for sharing time and talents, and then ask a question that shows a real interest in the work.

- **Administrative staff:** Have you ever taken a class where the instructor asks you to ignore the person in the back of the room taking notes, explaining that the person is there to observe the instructor's teaching abilities? The same thing happens in the online environment; you just may not know it. Because online education is rather new, institutions often set quality standards specific to an instructor's ability to teach online. The only way to know whether the instructor is meeting these standards is to log in and observe. Administrative staff may log in to your course and take note of the instructor's language use, frequency of communication, and response time to student questions. Again, you may or may not know this is going on. Either way, the process helps assure that you are getting the best education possible.

Administrative staff also interact with students when they need to resolve a conflict between the instructor and a student, when there's a question regarding a final grade that was assigned, or when they're seeking feedback regarding the quality of the overall program. It's important to know who your administrative staff are and to always interact with them in a professional manner. Administrative staff include the department chairperson of your program, the dean of the college, the institution's dean of academic affairs, and the department's administrative assistant.

All the preceding personnel are required to follow a set of federal guidelines to protect and respect your privacy. None of them are permitted to share contact information or change your grade.

Calling on technical support

The purpose of technical support is to support and complement the learning process of both instructors and students. They won't appear in your course roster like your peers, but they are there to help you succeed. In fact, technical support is so important, you'll most likely be given that contact information even before you log in to your course. In the following sections, we explain how technical support staff can help you and how to ask for that help. We also tell you when tech support can't be of service — and how to find solutions on your own.

Most institutions have information about how to contact technical support somewhere on their Web site so it's quick and easy to find. Contact information may include a phone number, an e-mail address, or even a link to chat with a live person via the Internet. Write down the technical support contact information and keep it in your wallet or purse in case you need it at work, while traveling, or when the Internet connection is down, and you can't get to your classroom's Web site.

What technical support can fix

Technical support staff focus strictly on the technology they provide for interacting with their products and services. For example, institutions provide technical support if you've lost your password for logging in to your course or if you're unable to physically access the registration Web site.

Before calling technical support, ask yourself: "Who owns the technology that I can't get to work?" For example, if you're writing a paper for your class and your word processing program keeps crashing, you have to contact the company that created the word processing application.

Here's a list of times you should definitely contact your institution's technical support staff. Call them if

- ✔ You can't log into your course.

- ✔ You can get into your course, but pages don't load.

- ✔ You can't get a synchronous tool to load (like a chat window).

- ✔ You try to post an assignment and nothing happens, or you get an error message.

- ✔ You can't access other necessary Web sites, such as the library.

- ✔ You can't remember your password, or your account has been locked after too many failed attempts.

If the technology required by a class is working but you're simply having trouble learning how to use it, contact your instructor first. Your instructor is responsible for facilitating the learning process, including the use of instructional technology. If your instructor can't help you, he will forward you to the appropriate support staff.

If, for some reason, technical support staff can't resolve a problem immediately or you've attempted to contact them several times without success, it's important that you contact your instructor. In fact, some instructors like to know *any* time you contact technical support — not because they want to get involved, but because they care about whether you're having difficulty. Letting your instructor know that you're having a problem and what you're doing about it tells the instructor you are responsible and committed. It also allows the instructor to inform your peers in the class if the problem is universal. (If the specific problem pertains to submission of homework, go ahead and submit your assignment to your instructor via e-mail when possible, to provide you and your instructor with a time-stamped submission of the completed assignment.)

Asking for help appropriately

If you need immediate help, don't use e-mail to contact technical support. You may not get a response for up to 24 hours, and it can take even longer if additional information is needed.

What is immediate? Your idea of immediate and technical support's idea may not coincide. If you find at 11:59 p.m. that you can't post an assignment that's due by midnight, that's probably not the best time to call technical support and expect an immediate response. If at all possible, call during normal working hours. You may also want to see whether live chat support is available, and what hours you can use that service.

Anytime you contact technical support, provide them with as much information as possible. The more information you can provide, the more likely your problem can be solved immediately. Here's a checklist of information you should be prepared to provide when something goes wrong:

- ✔ Your full name.
- ✔ Your student ID.
- ✔ The course ID and full course title.
- ✔ Your instructor's name.
- ✔ The Web page you were on when the problem occurred.
- ✔ A description of what you were doing immediately before the problem occurred.
- ✔ Your computer's operating system, such as Mac OS, Windows, or Linux.

Most people know the answer to this question, but they may not know what version they're using. Finding the version you're using is different on each machine, so check your manual or ask a technical support staff member to help you find it when needed. Once you know it, write it down for future reference.

- ✔ The Internet browser you were using, such as Internet Explorer, Firefox, or Safari.

Windows-based machines come with Internet Explorer preinstalled, and Mac-based machines come with Safari by default, but you can add other browsers on your computer. As with the operating system, if you need to know which version of a particular browser you're using and you don't know how to find it, ask technical support to tell you how and then document the information for later use.

- ✔ The names of other programs or applications that were running when the error occurred.

If you don't know some of the answers to these questions, that's okay. The technical support staff can help you figure it out. But, be sure to take notes and learn how to find the answers for yourself in the future. This not only helps you learn more about your computer, but also speeds up future technical support calls.

What technical support can't do (and what you can do about it)

The technical support staff are amazing people with a wealth of technical knowledge. However, it's not uncommon for institutions to hire one technical support staff to support several thousand faculty and students. Therefore, don't be surprised or disappointed if they have to send you elsewhere for help. Most likely, technical staff won't provide assistance with teaching you how to use your computer or train you on individual applications such as Microsoft Word or PowerPoint.

Your institution may offer online workshops called *Webinars* that teach you new skills. Webinars are workshops held online using synchronous technology that allows presenters to share content with participants in real time. If your institution offers such training sessions, take full advantage of them. These types of sessions can provide you with new skills, such as using advanced features of common applications like Microsoft Word or PowerPoint.

If your institution doesn't offer this type of training, you can conduct a Web search for other training sources available online. For example, if you're trying to figure out how to create a table of contents in Microsoft Word, you can go to your Internet browser and conduct a search for "Tutorial Table of Contents Microsoft Word." Often, videos and step-by-step tutorials for learning how to use a variety of applications are available, including the following:

- Check out the Training home page for Microsoft at `http://office.microsoft.com/en-us/training/default.aspx` for numerous tutorials.

- Another site that hosts a variety of tutorials is Learnthat.com at `www.learnthat.com/computers/`.

Receiving academic support

For many online students, enrolling in an online class signifies returning to school after a period of academic inactivity. In other words, as a learner, you may feel rusty. It may have been awhile since you tested your study skills. Even if you've been an active learner in some context, you're probably going to feel a little awkward in the online environment at first. After all, this is new to you! What if you get into class and find that you need some additional academic support? Academic support staff can help you through any transitional difficulties you're experiencing, including those with writing, course material, and basic student skills.

Obtaining assistance with writing

If you asked experienced online students, they would probably tell you that they were surprised at first by how much writing they had to do in an online class. But when you think about it, this is how students and faculty communicate — with their fingers. Writing skills take on increased importance in the online world. A typical course involves writing responses to discussion questions, and usually a few papers on the side. We talk more about those specifics in Chapter 14.

If you find that you're not earning the scores you want, or you receive direct feedback from the instructor about your writing skills, take action! Here are a few guidelines:

✔ **Check with your instructor or academic advisor to see whether your school offers writing services.** Some institutions are prepared to offer writing assistance to their virtual students. If this service is offered, you may be asked to submit your writing to a tutor via e-mail and receive written feedback about your work directly within your document. You may also be asked to meet with a tutor synchronously over the phone or via a Web-conference tool to review your work in more detail.

✔ **Check your student handbook and see whether your school recommends a specific writing service or program.** In some cases, schools maintain contracts with online services so they can refer students who need additional assistance. This assistance involves meeting online with a trained tutor and having that person give you specific feedback about your writing and ways in which you can make improvements. These tutors don't correct your assignments or papers, but they do make observations about the mechanics or structure of your writing.

✔ **Look for assistance online.** Run a quick Internet search on "writing assistance" to find a multitude of Web sites that provide good advice on organizing your writing. Look for a site that's specifically hosted by a college or a library. A couple excellent examples include the Guide to Grammar and Writing at `http://grammar.ccc.commnet.edu/grammar` and the Purdue Online Writing Lab at `http://owl.english.purdue.edu`.

✔ **Find assistance through in-person services.** Good writing is good writing, regardless of whether you're online. Visit an educational services provider in your area, such as Sylvan Learning (`www.sylvanlearning.com`), Kumon (`www.kumon.com`), or any similar business, and see what services they offer. They don't work only with young children.

Don't get sucked into a site that provides free research papers — this is the fastest way to end your academic career. Plagiarism is never acceptable.

Finding a tutor for your topic or basic student skills

Online courses sometimes move fast, and you're expected to keep up the pace. If you find you're falling behind because you're struggling to understand course material, you may decide you need a tutor. A tutor is a personalized teacher who helps you with specific subject matter. Finding a tutor for a specific subject is relatively easy because that person doesn't have to be online. For example, if you need help in college-level math, you can probably find someone through your local newspaper or yellow pages who provides tutoring in math. On the other hand, if you find that what you need is a refresher on time management or note-taking while reading, academic tutors can provide help with these general student skills, also. Except for dealing with the online technology, reading, note-taking, and studying for exams don't differ much between traditional and online courses.

Tutors vary in terms of their credentials, experience, and fees. How do you know what you need? Here are a couple guidelines to consider:

- ✔ **Do you need a brush-up or major instruction?** If you just need to review, a family friend with a degree in the subject area may be willing to pitch in. But if you feel you need serious instruction or more attention than a volunteer has time for, look for a tutor with teaching experience and advanced coursework in the subject matter.

- ✔ **Are you an international student who needs help with North American writing conventions?** Students who need more extensive grammar and mechanics help than subject matter knowledge may want to look for an ESL tutoring service that is familiar with strategies for teaching English as a second language.

- ✔ **How much can you afford?** A tutor associated with a corporate agency (for example, Sylvan) costs more than a former licensed schoolteacher who now works from home. In all cases, ask about credentials and experience. After all, you're paying for this service.

In some cases, online students need someone to sit beside them to help with learning the basic tasks of understanding their computers or navigation. Most likely, you can find a computer tutor in the yellow pages, but he won't be able to coach you through processes specific to your course management system. For that kind of help, you need to call your institution's technical support staff. See the earlier section "What technical support can fix" for more details.

Developing your personal support system

Going to school is a big commitment. It takes, time, energy, thought, and the attitude to succeed. Though you may feel this is your adventure to own, you must remember that every decision you make affects those around you. Therefore, involving your family and friends in your decision-making process helps them understand the role that they play in supporting your decision to go to school.

Because you won't be leaving to go to a physical classroom, your family and friends may mistakenly perceive you as being available. For example, your kids may want you to go outside with them to play, or your friends may want you to host movie night. These temptations are hard to say no to. As a matter of fact, you may feel a little guilty saying no, which can cause you to fall behind in your coursework. That's why it's important for you to set boundaries for yourself and others.

One good way of setting boundaries is to establish specific days and times for studying. During those times, go into your study space and put a note on the door that says something like "Studying in progress. Please do not interrupt." If you have young children, make time to explain your situation in terms they understand, and let them help make the "Do Not Disturb!" sign. This may give them a feeling of ownership and pride in helping you achieve your academic goals. When they feel good about helping you, you feel less guilty for soliciting their help.

The most valuable thing that family and friends can do to help you succeed is to respect your time and space when studying. Some beneficial ways they can do this include babysitting the kids, refraining from temptations that take you away from studying, and making dinner on study nights. It's also nice if your supporters can be flexible during times when your workload increases.

Supporters can also help you academically. By reading rough drafts and providing you with constructive feedback, supporters help you identify areas of your work that need polishing before you turn it in. To help them provide constructive feedback, provide the assignment's description so they know what the instructor expects. You can also ask your supporters open-ended questions after they review your assignment to see whether or not they're able to answer the questions in a manner that reflects what you are trying to convey in the assignment.

Chapter 10

Communicating Clearly Online

● ●

In This Chapter

▶ Exploring the different ways people communicate online

▶ Establishing your online identity

▶ Taking part in discussions

▶ Using social networks in learning

● ●

*I*n a traditional classroom, hashing out new concepts and debating the merits of various ideas are hallmarks of good learning. The same is true in online education. The amount of communication that occurs between students and faculty and the quality of those messages set a quality online course apart from a mediocre one.

In the world of online education, people communicate through a variety of tools, including e-mail, messaging, and discussion forums. This chapter examines how people communicate online and how important communication is to your success as a student. We consider the persona you create and present to others through your communication, and we examine the details of discussion and the influence of social networks in facilitating conversation.

Checking Out Methods of Communicating Online

In a robust online course, you can expect to see communication occurring on several different levels. Messages are directed toward the class as a whole from the instructor, individually from the instructor to single students (and from students to the instructor), and from student to student. If you were to visually plot that network of messages, a good course would look messy because there would be so many connections between learners. This section examines some of the primary ways people communicate in an online course.

Instructor-to-class communication in news and announcements

Think about the first day of school at a traditional college. Assuming security remembers to unlock the classroom door, the instructor stands at the front of the class and welcomes students. Entering the virtual classroom isn't much different. Typically a welcome message or some kind of greeting from the instructor awaits you. This communication is intended to be read by every member of the class. It may be posted on the course's home page in a "News and announcements" area, or within a specially designated discussion forum (we describe discussions later in this chapter). This kind of introductory message lets you know that you're in the right place. It may also tell you what to do next. Figure 10-1 shows "Latest News" on the course's home page, which links to a welcome. Figure 10-1 also shows the announcement itself.

Figure 10-1:
A sample announcement from an instructor on a course's home page.

After that initial announcement, your instructor may use the same public method for several different purposes. She may use announcements to

- ✔ **Keep everyone on task.** For example, if you're three days into the course and no one has been brave enough to post the first assignment, the instructor may post an announcement to reinforce the procedures and help students feel more comfortable trying the assignment. Again, this announcement may appear on the course's home page or in a discussion forum.

- ✔ **Post transitional information.** She may summarize what the class examined in the previous unit and preview what's to come in the next unit. Read these kinds of summaries with the idea of mentally testing yourself. Do you know what the instructor is talking about? If not, go back and review!

- ✔ **Reinforce news that you should know from the institution.** For example, occasionally the school needs to shut down its servers for maintenance. They may e-mail you and post a message on the portal or first page you log into, but chances are good your instructor will remind you again.

Read *all* the messages posted by your instructor, even if you're tempted to bypass lengthy messages in favor of getting to your next task. Instructors include pertinent information in their messages. Plus, you spare yourself the embarrassment of asking a question that was already addressed in an announcement.

Student-to-student communication in discussions

We hope the kind of communication you find most common within your course is student-to-student discussion about the subject matter. Why? Because a course in which students actively discuss and debate is a course where the learners are interested! It's also a course that demonstrates active, engaged learning at its best.

Many online courses follow a *social-constructivist* format of presenting information and then asking students to discuss and add to the concept. By writing about how the materials fit into the world or one's profession, everyone in the class gets a clearer picture of the subject matter. Collectively, they "construct" their understanding. For that reason, instructors ask students to engage in discussions with one another.

Discussing means having a conversation. This is a little different online than in person because your fingers do the talking. We describe online discussions in the later section "Participating in Discussions." For now, recognize that student-to-student communication should dominate your online experience!

Portal schmortal

In some cases, the page from which you log in to the school's system is called the portal. In addition to accessing your courses, you can link to the library, bookstore, and other services. Sometimes this is built into your learning management system such as Moodle, and other times it's a separate Web site created by your institution. In other cases, the first page you come to *after* you log in to your course management system may be referred to as the portal. This page usually displays links to your individual courses and summarizes announcements and calendar events in one place — particularly important if you're taking more than one course at a time. Not every school uses the term "portal" to mean the same thing. However, use of the term "home page" to represent the main page of your course is fairly consistent.

One-on-one communication via private e-mail or messaging

Private, one-on-one communication is meant for your eyes only and may come through your e-mail or an internal messaging feature if your course management system supports this.

Whenever possible, use the tools that are available within the course management system to communicate. For example, your system may have built in "messenger" type tools; these systems act like instant messaging when the other person is online. If the person isn't online when you send the message, she receives it when she next logs in. Your system may also have an internal e-mail that doesn't require you to give out your personal e-mail address. The advantage of sending and receiving messages within the system is that your academic work is all recorded in one place. You don't have to sort through your Aunt Tilda's forwarded jokes to find the instructor's note.

In this section, we describe several types of private communication: instructor-to-student, student-to-instructor, and student-to-student.

Instructor-to-student communication

Instructors communicate with students privately for several reasons.

- ✓ **They send feedback.** Many instructors like to follow longer assignments, such as papers, with comments. While these can be posted in an electronic grade book, there usually isn't sufficient space. Therefore, instructors e-mail comments and feedback.

- ✓ **They nudge.** Occasionally, you may have a really nice instructor who notices you're not making the deadlines. She may send you a little note to remind you to stay on task.

✔ **They praise and send additional resources.** Sometimes an instructor wants to acknowledge excellent work from a student and perhaps provide additional resources that the rest of the class wouldn't be interested in. This may be a case for private communication.

✔ **They communicate grades to you.** Thank goodness! Actually, your instructor must communicate grades privately by law. Your grades and feedback can't be posted publicly.

Figure 10-2 is an example of private communication your instructor may send. This was sent through an internal messaging feature. The same could be accomplished through e-mail.

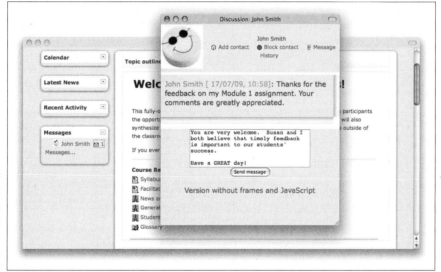

Figure 10-2:
A sample of internal private communication.

Student-to-instructor communication

Not only can instructors send students private communication, but students may also need to communicate privately with instructors. Why would you want to communicate with your instructor privately? Here are some reasons:

✔ **You're in distress.** Something is going on in your life that requires your attention and is preventing you from focusing on school or completing your assignments. The whole class doesn't need to know about this, but your instructor does. This is a case for private e-mail.

✔ **You're experiencing technological difficulties.** Whenever you have a problem with your computer, the software, or the system and need to work with technical support, it's a good idea to also inform your instructor. She may not be able to remedy the situation, but at least this alerts her to the problem.

✔ **You want to ask a question specifically about your academic work.**
Instructors cannot discuss your work publicly; it's the law! Therefore, if you ask a question in a public forum about your performance, your instructor can't answer it. On the other hand, you can discreetly e-mail the instructor to ask about your work.

When it comes to communicating with your instructor, diplomacy is the best policy. In other words, try not to push the instructor beyond reasonable expectations. Most institutions have faculty guidelines related to how quickly instructors should respond to e-mails — usually within 24 to 48 hours. If you send an SOS at midnight, don't expect a response right away!

Student-to-student communication

Students can privately communicate with one another, too. For example:

✔ E-mail is a way to continue conversations that may be of interest to only you and one other person. For example, if you read that your classmate Sarah has an interest in the culture-based health issues specific to the Polish community and you're a Polish immigrant, you may want to e-mail her privately to share some family stories. Having the opportunity to continue a conversation with one of your peers keeps you from over-posting on discussions as well (we describe the dangers of overposting later in this chapter).

✔ We talk more about group work in Chapter 12, but one way student groups work through projects is via e-mail. E-mail allows you to exchange files, send updates, and establish meetings. Plus, it's easy to copy your instructor on the e-mail so she knows your group's progress.

✔ Sometimes students exchange contact information such as instant message (IM) screen names. IMs may be another way of communicating some of the same student-to-student information, but that assumes you're lucky enough to catch each other online at the same time.

Creating and Putting Forward an Online Persona

A country song that was popular a few years ago told the story of a man who presented himself online as a suave ladies man, when in fact he was a bit of a nerd offline. Online, you can be anyone you want to be. While we don't recommend misrepresenting yourself, you may want to carefully consider the persona you put forward and cultivate lasting relationships with your peers online. We explain what you need to know in the following sections.

Depicting positive personality traits online

Written text is void of the nonverbal cues people often rely on to fill in communication gaps. Absent eye contact, facial expressions, and intonation of the voice, people only have the written word from which to judge the person on the other end of the computer connection. The persona you put forth online comes through in your writing style. How you write, the words you choose, and the frequency with which you post all say something about who you are.

Are you shy? Online, you can be as forward and confident as anyone else. Remember that the nature of asynchronous communication means nothing happens immediately, so what you say by way of posting becomes as important as what the next student says. It's not like a typical classroom where the more aggressive students get the most attention by raising their hands or talking out loud first.

Being judged by words alone may be a wonderful feature of online communication because it means you're less likely to be judged on characteristics like your physical appearance or voice. Your ideas stand on their own. We say more about writing in Chapter 14, but for now remember that the "voice" you use — casual or academic — says a lot about how you're perceived. If you write like a scholar, you'll be viewed as a scholar.

A few personality traits that come through in written communication are key to your success as an online student. The following sections explain how to depict yourself as a serious yet warm student who shows leadership skills and avoids being high maintenance.

Be sure to heed these tips as you develop your online persona:

✔ **Understand the impact of photos.** When introducing yourself to your class for the first time, you may consider attaching a casual photograph. Photos are a way of sharing who you are, but they have drawbacks, too. A photo reveals your age, weight, race, and gender; all possibilities for bias. You should never feel pressured to reveal your identity if you don't want to! If your instructor asks for a photo, e-mail it privately but request that it not be shared with the rest of the class.

✔ **Use emoticons appropriately.** We want to add a final word about emoticons — the symbolic smiley faces that pepper today's Web-based communication. As long as you use them sparingly, a wink or a frown can say a great deal. However, emoticons don't belong in the text of your academic papers. Save them for back-and-forth discussion among peers.

Finding a mix of serious and funny

The serious student posts full-bodied, articulate responses to questions. The responses are well researched and reference some of the assigned readings to demonstrate the connection between theory and practice. The serious student asks direct questions that demonstrate critical thinking as a follow-up to her peers' work. The rest of the class quickly identifies who the serious students are based on the quality of their work. (We wrote that with our serious voice.)

You may think that we're going to contrast the serious student with the class clown. Not so! In fact, it's possible to be genuinely funny, insightful, and serious all at the same time. If you see a play on words or detect a pun, go ahead and write it. This doesn't really make you a class clown.

If you think of the class clown as a "goof-off" and wonder where that person is in online education, you may not find her. Why not? Because students who goof off don't last in online education! But that doesn't necessarily mean there's no place to clown around in the online education environment. If your instructor sets up a "student lounge" for posting off-topic, you can safely post the latest hilarious viral video or clean joke of the day there.

Humor should never be insulting, sarcastic, racist, sexist, homophobic, or directed toward any one individual or group. Because it can be easily misconstrued, be careful if you have a twisted sense of humor — keep it to yourself.

Adding warmth to your words

Establishing the right amount of "presence" online can be a challenge, especially when you're balancing multiple roles and have limited time. We acknowledge this! You don't have to be a social butterfly and respond to everyone when interacting with your class. However, being a social recluse and posting only the bare minimum probably isn't the way to go, either.

What sets a recluse apart from a social butterfly isn't just the amount of posting but also a lack of warmth. Even if you can't respond to many of your peers because of time limitations, a few warm messages go a long way toward establishing you as a friendly classmate and not a recluse. To warm up your communication, you may want to try these tips:

- ✔ **Always address the person by name.** "Jane, that is an intriguing point you brought up. . . . "

- ✔ **Introduce just a touch of personal information.** "Your analysis reminds me of the time we vacationed in New Jersey. . . ."

- ✔ **Compliment freely.** "I love how you wove the reference to *MacBeth* into your description of the current conflict. . . ."

Showing off leadership qualities

Leadership is a quality you might not expect to see online, but it definitely shows! Leaders are students who:

- **Post early (or at least on time).** If you have several days to submit a public assignment, see whether you can be one of the first posters. The others will follow your lead.

- **Volunteer to be leaders when assigned to groups.** Just be sure you have the time and skills to carry through. That generally means coming up with a plan; it shouldn't mean doing all the work.

- **Present themselves as serious students.** Our earlier discussion of serious students explains that they post thoughtfully and back up their ideas with research. They set examples for the rest of the class.

Avoiding a reputation as a high-maintenance person

No one wants to be remembered as high maintenance. How can you avoid this?

- **Report problems, but save the drama for another setting.** Everyone has problems. You might be experiencing computer issues, a life event, or a broken link in the course. High-maintenance students tend to describe each of these problems as if they had equal weight. They also tend to post these problems publicly, when sometimes a private message to the instructor would be a better choice. (We explain when to properly use private messaging earlier in this chapter.)

- **Try a few things on your own before calling a full-blown SOS.** Try to find your own resolution before posting publicly that you *can't* do something. For example, if you're assigned to read an article online and the link doesn't work but you know the title, try running a quick search for it on your own. Then you can score points with the instructor by posting that the original link didn't work, but you found an alternative.

When it comes to pointing out typos or instructions that don't work, send those notes privately to the instructor. Just as you wouldn't want everyone in the class reading the feedback your instructor gives you on assignments, your instructor doesn't want the feedback you give her shared with everyone else, either.

- **Establish boundaries regarding what and how much you share.** The public forum isn't the place to explain your messy divorce. Your classmates came to learn, not counsel. The educational experience you share should be the basis for your interpersonal relationships.

- **Have a backup plan or a personal technician if you start to experience a computer issue every week.** Everyone has computer issues periodically. However, we observe that high-maintenance students tend to have them weekly. If that's you, and you tell everyone within shouting distance, your classmates will begin to question your competency. While you can't see people rolling their eyes online, we believe it happens!

Developing relationships

Think about the nature of work in the twenty-first century. Many of us routinely collaborate with colleagues in other cities, towns, and countries. We send e-mails, attach files, and make phone calls. We depend on each other to get work done. No one says these relationships aren't real!

The same is true for online education. Students interact through technology and come to depend on one another to get work done. In the process, very real and lasting relationships form.

When you present your ideas to the class, your intellect shines, not your gray hair, thick glasses, or skinny legs. Friendships develop based on the quality of your ideas, as well as some of the characteristics we describe earlier in this chapter. The serious students tend to hang together, while the ones with active senses of humor banter among themselves. Birds of a feather flock together.

This is not to say that the online classroom is polarizing! Putting aside some of the biases that may creep into a traditional classroom, students form online relationships based on what and how they think. It's not uncommon to see a young student who is technologically comfortable befriend an older learner when they have the same academic goals and share similar insights.

A special bond forms with cohort groups. *Cohorts* are groups of students who start a degree or certificate program together and stay in the same group for their entire time online. These students may be together for a year or more. Our observation is that they disclose more personal information as time passes and therefore provide more support and understanding when trouble arises. (Flip to Chapters 4 and 7 for more about cohorts.)

Some of you may question whether these online academic relationships are real and lasting. They are very real as long as both parties make an effort to maintain the relationship, and it can easily move from academic cohort to friendship. As your friend discloses information in posts or e-mails, take the time to send a private message to commemorate a birthday or a child's T-ball success. Or, send a good-luck e-card right before you all hunker down for finals. Touch base after class if you wind up in different courses, and keep up-to-date on professional accomplishments. Most people agree that it's nice to be remembered!

Participating in Discussions

Some instructors describe discussion as the heart and soul of online education. For academic courses that require participation, there's little doubt that discussion is a cornerstone. In this section, we look at why discussion is important, how discussions are organized, and how you can determine what's expected of you to succeed in online discussions.

Understanding why you're asked to discuss

No doubt, you've heard the expression "practice makes perfect." This makes perfect sense if you're studying keyboarding skills or French pronunciation, but seeing how this works is a little more difficult when you're studying something like economics or world literature. Furthermore, in an online course, it's impossible for the instructor to see students practicing, right?

Not so! Online discussion is one of the methods instructors use to witness your learning. Here's why:

- ✔ **Discussion shows you are reading.** When you answer a discussion question and refer to your assigned readings or textbook, you demonstrate to the instructor that you're actually reading the material.

- ✔ **Discussion shows your ability to think critically.** Many instructors want you to take the content and break it down, analyze it, put it back together in a way that is meaningful, and add an interpretation of how this works in the real world. This is critical thinking! When you participate in discussion, you show your ability to think critically.

- ✔ **Discussion helps you learn better.** It's not enough to read, cite, and move on. Instructors want you to personalize and internalize the information. In fact, this is one of the ways adults learn better and faster.

- ✔ **Others benefit from discussion, too.** In the constructivist classroom, everyone wins when you take a topic and develop it fully. When you add your insights and interpretations, the rest of the class is able to consider whether they agree or disagree and, most importantly, why.

Organizing discussions in different ways

Discussion is a conversation that occurs online and requires more than one person. For example, John puts forth an idea to which Chris responds with an example supporting his idea. Others join in the conversation, too. Sally suggests an alternative view to what John has written with an additional reference to the literature. Pat asks a question for clarification, forcing John to find another way to explain his original idea. All of this gets rolled together for a more complete understanding of the content. By the time the discussion runs its course, the readers and authors have looked at the subject matter more thoroughly because of the diversity of views.

Depending on the course management software, you may see your conversations displayed as small pieces connected to one another in a couple ways: chronologically or threaded. Each piece comes from an individual speaker and is a piece of written text, or post.

✔ **Chronological posts:** The posts may be connected in a linear fashion, following one another in chronological order. Figure 10-3 shows what this looks like.

✔ **Threaded posts:** A threaded discussion displays the conversation in a different graphic fashion. When you look at the display, you're better able to see how ideas connect to one another. The dates may seem out of order, but not if you follow the conversation as if it were in outline form. Text that's indented is directly related to the post above it. Figure 10-4 shows a threaded discussion.

Does it matter whether your software shows the discussion in threaded or chronological fashion? Not really. What matters is that conversations are occurring between students and that you can follow these conversations.

Many course management systems allow you to change how you view discussions. You control whether you see them in threaded or unthreaded fashion according to your settings. If you have this option, play around with the settings until you find the system that works best for you.

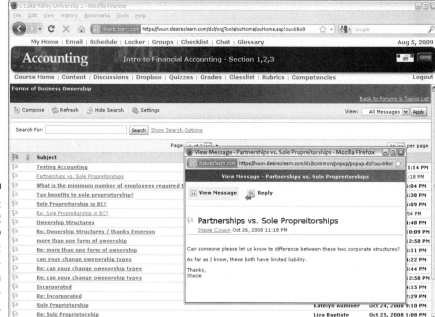

Figure 10-3: Desire2 Learn® Discussions: A discussion in chronological order.

Courtesy of Desire2Learn Incorporated

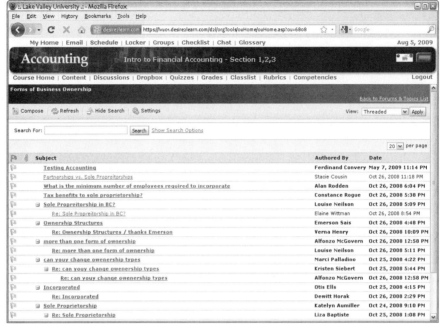

Figure 10-4:
Desire2
Learn
Discussions:
A discussion
displayed
in threaded
fashion.

Courtesy of Desire2Learn Incorporated

Figuring out discussion requirements

Each instructor has her own expectations regarding discussion and participation. You may find these expectations in several places:

✔ **The syllabus:** Chances are good the instructor lists discussion as a component of your grade in the syllabus. She may say something like "Participates in discussion by posting an initial statement and responding to two other peers each week." Read those statements carefully to determine what is expected. (Chapter 8 describes a course syllabus in detail.)

✔ **The instructions:** You most likely have a page in your course that describes what you should do in the discussion area; you should be able to find a link to this page from the course's main page. The questions you're expected to answer may be listed here. Often this is where the instructor reminds you of how much to write and how to post. For example, you may read, "Answer one of the follow questions in 300 to 500 words. Be sure to reference one of our assigned readings. Before the close of the module, respond to two of your fellow students' posts."

✔ **The grading scheme and rubric:** These may be on a separate page within your course, or they may be woven into either the syllabus or the instructions. A rubric spells out what counts. For example, a rubric may state that you need an on-time post of 300 to 500 words with proper citation, and you must respond to two peers. See Chapters 8 and 14 for full details on rubrics.

Avoiding overposting

Overposting can occur in two manners: writing too much and responding too frequently. Both have consequences.

✔ **Writing too much:** When your instructor asks for 300 to 500 words and you submit a three-page essay, you have overposted! The result is that your classmates won't read through your ideas, and no one will want to discuss them. You may be penalized for overwriting, too.

Before posting, count your words. You can do this in Word 2003 and earlier editions by going to File and then Properties. There you'll find a tab labeled Statistics or Word Count. You may need to isolate (highlight) the paragraph you want counted. In Word 2007, click on the Review tab, and then click Word Count in the lower right-hand corner of the Proofing group.

✔ **Responding too frequently:** You don't need to respond to everyone's posts. When your instructor asks for a minimum of 2 responses to others, she may be hoping for 4 or 5, but not 15 or 20!

Think of this in terms of the traditional classroom. How do you react to a student who has something to say to everyone's comments? Doesn't that person seem to be an attention-seeker? After a while, aren't the ideas a little self-serving? Do students begin to roll their eyes when the commenter opens her mouth?

The same happens when students overpost. However, in the world of online education, you can avoid reading what those who overpost have to say. This is not a good thing.

We like to encourage good discussion with quality posts. Think of contributing 10 percent of the comments. Discussions can grow exponentially, and you don't want to be the student whose posts no one reads because you're too prolific.

Tapping into Social Networks

What's popular online waxes and wanes. Remember when everyone had to have a Web page? Services popped up allowing for easy Web page creation.

The members of these services wanted more widgets and features, and they began to communicate with each other. Thus, the idea of social networking was born.

A social network starts with a Web site, like Facebook (`www.facebook.com`), MySpace (`www.myspace.com`), and LinkedIn (`www.linkedin.com`), that allows users to find other people like them, send messages to each other, and share bits and pieces of information. Say you're interested in cooking. A social network connection in Facebook could result in recipe swapping, sharing culinary do's and don'ts, discussing a few favorite kitchen tools, and even getting recommendations for good culinary schools, which could lead to a new career! This section addresses how to use social networks to your advantage academically and what to avoid.

The benefits of communicating outside the virtual classroom

Because social networks are built on the principle of connecting people, and learning is largely social in the online classroom, using a social network in connection with your online education has several advantages:

- ✔ **Supporting schoolwork:** Social networks can be very helpful in organizing study groups, sharing notes, and communicating with your classmates. Some of the sites include instant messaging features, e-mail, and shared calendars. You can also establish a group so that only class members can interact. Within that group, you can talk about what's going on in your class, such as upcoming assignments, and answer each other's questions outside of your class site. Some faculty are organizing class groups and using the tools to continue conversations about class themes. If you're already a social network user, you can easily toggle between your personal life and school. Figure 10-5 shows a social networking site used academically.

- ✔ **Help after graduation:** Several social networking sites focus on professional connections more than personal ones. For example, LinkedIn (`www.linkedin.com`) promotes itself as a network for professionals seeking to maintain job-related contacts. The site organizes information by company so you can find other people who may be helpful in job searches. Not only can you ask to add them to your network, but you can give and receive recommendations. After you complete your program or degree, you could ask classmates to become part of your network so you can exchange ideas about job seeking, new prospects, and so on.

Figure 10-5:
A social network used academically.

Avoiding distractions

Social networks can be distracting. Isn't it always more fun to talk socially than to study? If you think you would like to use a social network to embellish your online education, consider these ideas to limit distractions:

- ✓ **Keep your profile private.** Only let your immediate classmates know your username and contact information. That way strangers won't seek you out.

- ✓ **Don't add extra widgets and tools.** For example, you can add an application that allows you to save the rain forest or play trivia games, but these probably aren't related to what you're studying.

- ✓ **Create separate accounts.** If you already use a social network and your class suggests establishing a group, consider signing up with a different e-mail address and username. Keep your personal account and your school account separate so you won't be tempted to jump from school to personal issues.

  If you do comingle personal and academic accounts, be aware of how to set privacy limits within the tool. For example, in Facebook, you can control who sees your "wall," whether they can post to it, and who your other friends are. It's good to know how to set those limits.

Chapter 11

Developing Good Study Habits for Online Courses

● ●

In This Chapter

▶ Scheduling time to study

▶ Surfing the Web with ease

▶ Reading course materials efficiently

▶ Using the virtual library

▶ Studying offline

● ●

*M*any students taking an online class for the first time are not accustomed to the amount of self-discipline it takes to succeed. The most important habits you must establish when taking an online course are setting aside time to study and developing patterns of good studying behavior. In this chapter we provide strategies for organizing and using your time wisely.

Setting Aside Time to Work

When taking a traditional, face-to-face course, having class in a physical building on a specific day and time each week forces you to prioritize class time in your schedule. Friends and family understand why you are unavailable to hang out, make dinner, or go to the movies.

Other than the occasional synchronous (real-time) session, in the online environment, you are responsible for determining the days and times you will participate in class by logging in, reading and responding to discussion, and performing other academic tasks. As long as you meet deadlines, your schedule is really up to you. Therefore, you must have good time management skills to succeed.

Once your class begins, take time to review the workload and assignment deadlines; you can typically find this information in the documents we describe in Chapter 8, such as the course syllabus. Use this information to help you set a weekly schedule and make a commitment to stick to it. This section focuses on strategies to consider when determining how to plan your weekly study schedule.

Regardless of what you're working on, your study time should be scheduled (not incidental) and uninterrupted.

Working at your peak times

Knowing when you're the most productive is important when scheduling study time. Studying when you're tired can lead to frustration and poor performance. For some, peak times are mornings before the kids get up. Coauthor Susan starts many of her mornings writing and grading student papers a few hours before the family wakes up and the school-prep frenzy begins. Coauthor Kevin, on the other hand, takes time during the late morning or lunch hour to complete his academic tasks. Whether you're an early bird or a night owl, set aside time that fits your schedule and lifestyle.

Checking in every day for a short time

To help you stay on top of classroom discussions, instructor announcements, and other basic course activities, set time aside to log in several times a week — daily if possible. Sometimes you only need to set aside fifteen to thirty minutes to keep up on what's going on. During these quick check-ins, do the following:

- ✔ Check for new announcements from the instructor.
- ✔ Check the course calendar to confirm you are on track.
- ✔ Read new discussion posts from peers. Only respond to posts that you have time for. If you need to take longer to think about a response, print those posts and jot down a few bullet points as you think about what you want to write.
- ✔ Print any assignments that you plan to work on soon for reference purposes.

Calculating how much time you need to finish longer tasks

Some tasks require the allotment of a significant amount of time. For example, it may take longer to compose an original response to a discussion question (not a reply to what someone else wrote), complete assignments like projects or presentations, or take online quizzes.

When we talk about estimating study time, we're not only referring to computer time. The fact that you're taking an online class doesn't mean you'll be learning only when you're in front of a computer. You'll complete many tasks off-line as well. What you do off-line is just as important as what you do online when scheduling your study time. (We discuss off-line activities in more detail later in this chapter.)

Be sure not to make too many assumptions when estimating study time. For example, when calculating how much time it takes to complete an essay assignment, don't forget to count the time it takes to research the subject before sitting down in front of your computer to write it. Students often overlook these details and scramble to complete their assignments at the last minute.

Though no two students require the same amount of time to complete any one assignment, here's a list of things to consider when calculating the time it will take to complete an assignment:

- ✔ **Understanding the assignment:** It takes time to read the assignment description and absorb what's being asked of you. More time may be needed if you have questions that need to be answered by the instructor.

- ✔ **Prep time:** This refers to the time it takes you to lay the groundwork for the assignment. For example, some instructors require that all essays be completed using a specific document structure. Therefore, you have to set up a document with specific margin settings, a title page, page numbers, and a reference page. Those less familiar with these word processing features may take longer to do this before even focusing on the assignment details.

If your instructor requires you to use a specific document format for each assignment, create a template that you can use over and over again. For example, during his studies, coauthor Kevin was required to turn in all assignments using the institution's standard document structure. This included a title page with the assignment's title, course

ID, course title, instructor name, student name, institution name, and assignment due date. The document was also required to have one-inch margins and page numbers in the upper right-hand corner, be double-spaced, and have a references page at the end. So, Kevin created a document with all this information, leaving the assignment title, course ID, course name, instructor, and due date blank. For each new assignment, he opened the document and immediately clicked File, Save As, and saved the file in the appropriate course folder on his computer with an obvious file name. It took approximately 30 minutes to an hour to create the original template, but only one minute to customize it for every assignment.

✔ **Research time:** For most assignments, you can't just sit down and write without having some background information. This involves doing research like reading chapters within your assigned textbook, conducting interviews with professionals in the field, watching a video, or conducting database searches at your virtual library. Graduate programs, especially, require you to write about more than just your opinions and experiences. You're required to back up your thoughts with theory and research analysis conducted within the field being discussed.

✔ **Editing:** Editing refers to checking spelling, grammar, document formatting, and editorial style. Editorial style refers to the technical formatting in documents, including reference citations, punctuation, abbreviations, numbers, and more. Two common editorial styles are Modern Language Association (MLA) and American Psychological Association (APA). Becoming familiar with these styles can be time-consuming and require a true attention to detail; flip to Chapter 13 for more about these styles.

✔ **Learning new technology:** Some assignments may require you to use a technology you're unfamiliar with. Therefore, it takes additional time to learn how to use that technology. You may have to set time aside to watch tutorial videos, practice using the technology, or read instruction documentation.

Rewarding good study habits

Rewarding good study habits is a great way to encourage yourself to stick to a schedule and accomplish your goals. These don't have to be fancy, expensive rewards — just small incentives you look forward to once you meet milestones. For example, maybe you have to schedule your study time during your favorite television show. Record the show and reward yourself by watching the show commercial-free once your homework is complete. Don't forget the popcorn!

Blocking off enough study time each week

Within the first week or so of an online class, you should establish a routine for studying. At first, set aside as much time as you can to read the syllabus, review the course calendar, and complete your first set of assignments. Make a mental note of how long it takes you to log in, navigate your virtual classroom, and complete assignments.

After the first week of class, plan out your weekly schedule, taking into account both daily check-ins and the larger blocks of time you'll need for finishing longer tasks. In Chapter 8 we talk about synchronizing your course, work, and personal calendars. Here, we ask you to take it a step further by adding specific tasks to your calendar. For example, if you set aside study time on Friday night from 7 to 9 p.m. in your calendar, you can divide that time into parts. From 7 to 7:30 you can check in with your course, read new posts, and confirm assignments. From 7:30 to 8:30 you can conduct research for the essay assignment due next week. And from 8:30 to 9 you can develop an outline for the essay based on your earlier research.

One way to help you determine how long it takes to complete a task is to simply jot down the start and stop times when studying. This is especially helpful within the first few weeks of a course. By doing this, you can better estimate how much time you really need to set aside on your calendar. It's amazing how little time most people think tasks are going to take.

Navigating the Web Efficiently

As you become more familiar with your virtual learning environment, you'll begin to spend less time focusing on navigation and more time actually completing assignments. This section provides some timesaving tips on navigating the Web.

Keeping multiple browser windows open

When you're quickly checking in with new course happenings and responding to peers' posts, you may want to conduct some quick searches for resources to share. Keeping your course page open in your Internet browser while going off and searching for those resources in another browser window can help you to quickly search for and then copy and paste information from one window to another.

With most Internet browser applications, new windows can either be opened in a floating window or a tab within the existing window. Both methods are helpful:

✔ Figure 11-1 shows multiple floating windows. To open multiple windows in most Windows-based browsers, hold down the Ctrl key and press "n" for "new" (Ctrl+n). Mac users hold down the Command key and press "n" (Command+n).

Figure 11-1:
A full task bar showing multiple floating windows.

With many of today's web-savvy students preferring online courses, online-only universities and electronic offerings at traditional colleges are becoming very popular.					stout	73
EDIT | DELETE		onlinelearning	OLO	book	podcasting	54
20 JUN 09 The English Blog: Vocabulary					onlinelearning	52
Internet resources, reviews, news, tips and trivia for learners and teachers of English					OLOSummer2007	51
EDIT | DELETE				esl	OLO	49
					web2.0	49
19 JUN 09 The 10 Hardest Jobs To Fill In America - Forbes.com				14	K12	47
Manpower survey found that employers are having a very hard time filling jobs for skilled workers in specific niches.					secondlife	33
EDIT | DELETE				personal_sites	▼ All Tags	169
					accessibility	1
17 JUN 09 Wired Campus: Students Prefer Real Classroom to Virtual World - Chronicle.com				10	adjunct	7
College students were given the chance to ditch a traditional classroom for an online virtual world. Fourteen out of fifteen declined.					adult	1
					assessment	6
EDIT | DELETE				secondlife	audio	5
					Aurora	2
More and More Baby Boomers Embrace Technology					blended	1
EDIT | DELETE				generations	blogs	11
					Bloom's	6
Volunteer Power: Recruiting and Managing the Younger Volunteers				2	book	18
Done						
🏁 Start | 🗔 🌐 W » | 🌐 University Library :: ... | 🌐 :. Desire2learn .:. O... | 🌐 :. Desire2learn .:. O... | 🌐 smanning's Book... | 📷 Macromedia Firework... | « 🔲 🔊 🔵 2:43 PM						

Floating windows

✔ Figure 11-2 shows a single window open with multiple tabs. To open a new tab within a window in most Windows-based browsers, hold down the Ctrl key and press "t" for "tab" (Ctrl+t). Mac users hold down the Command key and press "t" (Command+t). We feel that the tabs are more organized and easier to keep track of.

How would you actually go about using this? Imagine reading a discussion post by one of your peers discussing a topic you recently researched for another assignment. You decide that you want to share a white paper with him that you found during your previous research. While on your course page, you would open a new browser window (either a floating window or a new tab on your existing window), locate the resource on the Web, copy the URL (Web address), return to the window with your course information, and paste the URL in your reply. This saves you from getting lost in cyberspace by having to hit the back button endlessly to find your course site.

When viewing course information, you may come across links to external resources. When you click on these links, they may open in the same window, overwriting your course information. You can force the link to open in a new window by right-clicking (Command + Click for Mac users) and choosing either the "Open in New Window" or "Open in New Tab" option.

Multiple tabs

Figure 11-2:
A single
window
with
multiple
tabs.

Permission for the use of this Screen Shot granted by the Board of Regents of the
University of Wisconsin System on behalf of University of Wisconsin-Stout

Avoiding time wasted by chasing links

Occasionally, when navigating within your virtual classroom, you'll click on
a link and it will go to a page with an error on it. This happens no matter how
hard your instructor tries to share up-to-date information or how often he
tests those links before sharing them with you. It's just one of the challenges
of utilizing Web resources. Instead of spending a lot of time searching for that
information, notify your instructor immediately (privately, please, to spare
embarrassment; see Chapter 9 for methods of private communication) and
move on to other things.

When notifying your instructor about broken links, be sure to paste a copy
of the link in your message and tell him what page the link was on inside the
course. The more information you can provide, the faster your instructor can
address the problem.

If you're able to conduct a quick Web search and find the working address, be sure to share this with the instructor via e-mail. You can also share this with your peers if your course is set up with a public forum for questions and answers. When posting the updated link, be sure to use language that doesn't make the instructor look bad or place fault on the instructor. Simply mention that the link on a given page didn't work for you and that an alternative address was found.

Using social bookmarking tools

How many times have you come across the perfect resource on the Web and then forgotten where you found it? This can be very frustrating, not to mention time-consuming when searching for it again. We have an easy fix for you: Social bookmarking tools are Web-based tools that allow you to bookmark your important Web addresses and store them in cyberspace, not on your computer (see Figure 11-3). Yes, this means another login and password, but it's well worth the effort. Trust us! Here are a few major benefits of social bookmarking tools:

- ✔ **You can categorize your bookmarks using common search phrases called tags.** Each bookmarked URL can have multiple tags assigned to it, making it easier to find in the future.

- ✔ **You can choose to make each bookmarked address public or private.** If public, other Internet users can see your bookmarked addresses; some may find you because they use the same keywords you used to tag your resources. If marked as private, only you will be able to see that bookmark associated with your account.

- ✔ **You can get to your bookmarks from anywhere with an Internet connection.** So, if you want to get some homework done while on your lunch break at work, you don't have to worry that your bookmarks are on your home computer. A quick navigation to your social bookmarking tool will bring all your tagged bookmarks to your fingertips.

Depending on your tech saviness, you can either have your social bookmarking Web site open in a separate tab or window and copy bookmarks to that site as you find them, or you can see whether a browser plug-in is available for your browser. A browser plug-in allows you to add a toolbar to your browser whereby you can click a single button on any Web page to add that page's address to your account.

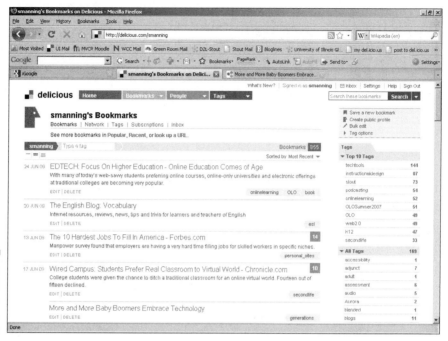

Figure 11-3:
A social
bookmark-
ing account.

Here's an example of a practical use for social bookmarking tools. Imagine researching the topic of conducting business in a foreign country. As you can imagine, tons of resources are available on the Web about this topic. Some are good and others aren't so good. As you browse the Net and find resources you want to read in more detail later, you can bookmark them and tag them with keywords (tags) such as "Business," "ForeignAffairs," and "BUS120" if the assignment is for your Business 120 course. Later, when you're ready to review the resources in more detail, they're all in one place. Carry this a step further by looking at who else saved the same URL and seeing whether they have additional resources stored in their accounts. You may find new material for your paper or project!

By the way, you may have noticed that "ForeignAffairs" doesn't have a space between the words. This is because tags often don't allow spaces. Therefore, you can either put multiple-word phrases together or separate them with a special character such as an underscore. If you choose the latter, your tag would be "Foreign_Affairs." This tends to be more pleasing to the eye.

Several social bookmarking tools are available on the Web. Most of them have similar features. Two commonly used tools include Delicious (`delicious.com`) and Diigo (`www.diigo.com`). Both of these tools provide adequate bookmarking functionality. However, Diigo offers a few additional features, including highlighting Web text. We discuss this feature in more detail later in the chapter.

Reading Wisely

Because a majority of the information you receive online is text-based, your ability to read efficiently is of the utmost importance. We're not just talking about reading comprehension here. We're also talking about your overall ability to navigate to and read important documents and posts quickly, as well as your ability to retain what you've read with note-taking and keep track of everything you've read so you don't waste precious time rereading.

Finding the stuff you need to read

You can save time by knowing what information is in an online course and where to find it. The following sections introduce you to the type of information you find online and gives ideas for managing that information more efficiently.

News and announcements

Every instructor-led course has some kind of news and announcements section. This is often a one-way communication from the instructor to the students, and it's required reading — no exceptions. Instructors use this feature to welcome students to the course, remind them of deadlines, share additional resources, and assure students of the instructor's presence. (See Chapter 10 for more information about this method of communication.)

As instructors, this is one of our most utilized features within the virtual classroom. Our students should expect to read a new post at least once every 48 hours — more during the first week or two of class. However, other instructors prefer other methods of communication like e-mail or posts within discussion forums. No matter what method your instructor uses, it's important that you read his posts and respond if necessary. You may be thinking that this could be a lot to manage, but usually these types of communication don't require response and are for your benefit. Checking in with your class on a daily basis, as we suggest earlier in this chapter, and developing good tracking techniques can really help. Tracking techniques include filing messages in folders in your e-mail and marking discussion posts as read (a feature found in most course management systems).

Discussion postings

The heart of any online course is the content discussions. For example, one activity we use to engage students is to assign each student a discussion question pertaining to the current module's content. Students are required to respond to their assigned question, read other students' posts, and respond to at least two different student posts. Students are encouraged to read all posts, but only respond to those that interest them.

Using this example, simple math tells you that if you're in a class of 20 students, there should be a minimum of 60 posts at the end of this activity. Our experience says that there will be closer to 200 posts. This is a good thing, assuming the posts are evenly distributed and don't come from 4 or 5 boisterous students. It means that students are engaged and dialoguing about the topic. However, it can be quite overwhelming if not managed correctly. Here are a few tips to consider when participating in such an activity (see Chapter 10 for additional information on discussions):

- ✔ **Focus on your assigned question as soon as possible:** As soon as you know your assigned question, begin reading, researching, and formulating your response. The sooner you do this, the more time you have to focus on reading and responding to your peers (and the more time your peers have to respond to you).

- ✔ **Set time aside to check in and read new posts:** When possible, take 15 minutes every day to check-in and read new posts, as we suggest earlier in this chapter.

- ✔ **Respond to posts:** If it's easier for you, based on your time schedule, respond to two students in one sitting.

- ✔ **Check responses:** Take time to check and see whether anyone has responded to your initial post and whether a reply is needed. Also check the threads you responded to and determine whether further discussion is appropriate.

Most discussions occur while you're working on other course assignments in the background. Be sure to schedule enough time to manage both.

At times, you and/or your peers will want to discuss things that don't relate to the course content. Most courses have a social forum for this purpose. This keeps off-topic discussion from interrupting the flow of content discussions. This can be a great resource, but don't feel bad if you're too busy to read any new posts in this forum. Feel free to ignore them. You can always go back and read them later when you have more time.

Assigned readings

Just like in the face-to-face environment, each online course uses a variety of course materials to support the curriculum. You may be asked to purchase one or more textbooks, download Internet-based resources, or link to "lectures" written by the instructor. It's not uncommon to be asked to read 60 to 100 pages per week. We estimate that our students need to dedicate approximately 2 to 4 hours to reading the assigned materials in an eight-week, three-credit course. If you want to succeed in your course, don't skip these readings! Be sure to block off plenty of time in your study schedule for them, as we suggest earlier in this chapter.

Depending on the course structure, you may find course readings in the syllabus, course calendar, or at the beginning of every module. For example, in our course, you would find the readings in two places: in the syllabus and in an introduction page at the beginning of every module. This allows our students to read ahead if they want (they have access to all the readings in the syllabus) without being able to post discussions early (content modules are opened one at a time as needed).

Deciding whether to print online reading material

Printing is not a requirement when working online. If you feel comfortable downloading everything to your computer and reading it from there, go for it. Portability is probably more important. If you're one of those students who likes to read whenever you get a free minute, printing will definitely help. Printed documents are easier to take on the bus, stash in your backpack or briefcase, and pull out during downtimes. Printed documents are also easier to highlight and jot notes on. As a mother of two very on-the-go children, coauthor Susan is well-known for reading between chauffeur duties and during athletic practices. (We have more to say about working offline later in this chapter.)

Feel "green" with guilt? For the more environmentally conscious, simply print on recycled paper and print on both sides. You can also print everything in "draft" form and save ink.

Increasing the font size in your browser to help you read more easily

In an effort to get as much information on a page as possible, some Web designers use smaller fonts. Internet browsers allow you to expand the text size so that it's more manageable to read. You may have to use the scrollbars more, but that's better than eyestrain. Figure 11-4 shows how to zoom your text inside a Web browser. In most browsers, the zoom feature is under the View menu in the application's toolbar at the top of the screen.

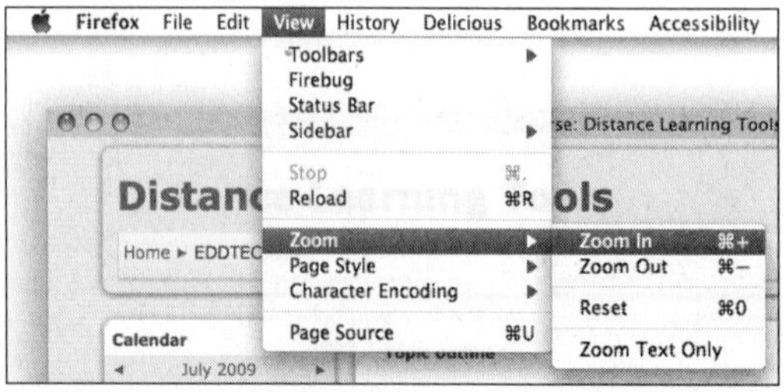

Figure 11-4:
The View and Zoom options inside a browser.

🍎 Firefox File Edit View History Delicious Bookmarks Accessibility
Toolbars ▶
Firebug
Status Bar
Sidebar ▶
Stop ⌘.
Reload ⌘R
Zoom ▶ Zoom In ⌘+
Page Style ▶ Zoom Out ⌘−
Character Encoding ▶ Reset ⌘0
Page Source ⌘U Zoom Text Only

Taking notes on what you read

Taking notes while reading helps you organize your thoughts, recall information, and reduce the amount of rereading. Here are some guidelines for this task:

- ✔ **Get the main ideas:** As you read, take note of the main ideas presented in the materials. Paraphrase this information in your own words and quote anything that you use directly from the materials.

- ✔ **Test your knowledge:** While taking notes, ask yourself why you are reading this chapter and see whether your notes are able to provide you with a correct answer. Still not sure? Read the abstract or conclusion, which summarizes the material. Then go back and reread for more details.

- ✔ **Note your opinions and experiences:** As you read, if you have an opinion about something or recall an experience that relates to the information, write it down.

- ✔ **Decide whether to write in your book:** If you plan to resell your textbook, remember that highlights and handwritten notes in the margins decrease its resale value. Consider purchasing a notebook for each course for the purpose of taking notes while reading.

- ✔ **Bookmark Internet resources:** As you search the Web, bookmark articles you may want to reference again. Bookmark Web sites even if you decide to print the information (see the next section). Nothing is more frustrating than trying to find an article you remember reading last week.

- ✔ **Save articles and citation information:** When conducting database searches within your virtual library, you won't be able to bookmark results pages. Therefore, it's important to download the actual article if possible and/or document the citation information for future reference.

- ✔ **Keep track of reference information:** Don't forget to write down the source information based on your instructor's preferred editorial style, such as APA or MLA. You'll need this information to give proper credit when referring to concepts and ideas gleaned from the source. We say more about citation tools in Chapter 13.

By this time, it should be no surprise that there's a digital answer to note-taking. For those who prefer to read everything online, you can use products that allow you to highlight and annotate documents, including PDF files and Web pages. Some of these tools even allow you to make your notes public for others to read. Figure 11-5 illustrates an example of a Web-based program, Diigo (www.diigo.com), that allows highlighting. Diigo has a browser plug-in that adds a toolbar to the top of your browser. One of the tools is a highlighter tool that allows you to highlight text on the Web page you're currently browsing.

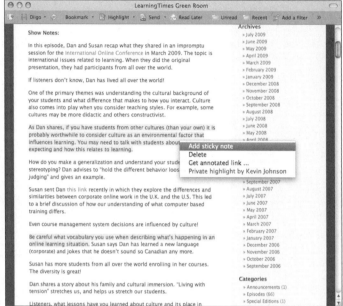

Figure 11-5:
Highlighting
a Web page
within a
browser
using a text
highlighter
tool.

Keeping track of everything you've already read

In the earlier section "Checking in every day for a short amount of time," we discuss the need to establish a pattern of logging in. Well, this is where it really pays off. To give you a little perspective, we want to share with you the number of discussion posts alone that make up our classes. After eight weeks of teaching, an average of 2,500 posts have been submitted by students and the instructor. This includes discussion posts, announcements made by the instructor, and social conversations held in the virtual student lounge. As you can imagine, it's important to know how to determine what's new and how to track what you've already read.

Most course management systems have an information section on your course's home page that alerts you to any new information posted since the last time you logged on (see Figure 11-6 for an example). This summary usually includes links directly to that information. Once you click on the link, it takes you directly to the unread information. The system automatically tracks where you have clicked and updates the new information summary accordingly.

Other course management systems provide you with more control by requiring you to manually mark information as read or unread. Either way, find out
how your institution's system identifies newly posted information and take
advantage of this feature. To find out whether your system has this feature,
review the support materials often found by clicking on a help button on
the screen, contact technical support, or ask your instructor. Because your
instructor must be able to manage a lot of information within the system
(student posts, assignment submissions, and so forth), he's probably fairly
versed in using the tool efficiently.

Another feature your system may have is the ability to have new information
e-mailed to you. Depending on your personal preference, this can help you
keep up with new information as it's posted, or it can be a distraction from
your daily activities. To find out whether your system has this feature, again,
review the support materials often found by clicking on a help button on the
screen, contact technical support, or ask your instructor.

Visiting the Library

During the course of your class, you'll be expected to complete assignments
that require you to conduct research and summarize your findings. Trust
us when we say that searching on Google is not enough. As a matter of fact,
most graduate courses are now adding a "No Google" clause in their sylla-
buses to discourage students from citing sources that are not reputable.

So, you have a choice: Jump in the car and drive to your local library, or sit comfortably in your PJs at your computer and log in to your institution's virtual library. Don't get us wrong, we love libraries and feel they're an asset to any community. However, as an online student, you may need access at times when your local library isn't open. Knowing where your local library is and its hours of operation is a great backup plan, though.

This section explains how to access your online institution's library, provides some basic pointers on using an online library for research, and clues you in on the value of library tutorials.

You should access the library whenever you need external resources to support opinions or positions and/or to provide cited materials as required by the instructor. Your experience helps you apply theory to practical situations. However, you shouldn't rely on your experience alone. Instructors want you to reference course readings and external resources so they know you understand the materials.

Accessing the library

Each institution has a different way for you to access the library. Some have a link to the library on their students' home pages, while others have links to the library in every course. If you didn't learn how to access the library in any of your orientation materials and it's not obvious within a few minutes of looking around, ask your instructor. When you find the link, it will most likely take you to the library's own home page or portal. Depending on how the institution connects to the library, you may or may not be required to log in using a different username and password than the one you use to access your class. Figure 11-7 provides an example of an online library portal. Notice there are sections with tutorials, databases, and information specific to distance education students.

The nice thing about libraries today is that most of them provide 24/7 access to their online databases and resources. Therefore, the times that you can access the library aren't controlled by strict hours of operation. However, if you think you may need help, knowing the availability of help staff is important. Libraries use a variety of telecommunication devices to provide support to students and faculty. For example, coauthor Kevin's favorite method for contacting help from his institution's library is via the text-based, instant chat messenger. If he has a question when browsing the library site, he simply clicks on the "Chat with a librarian" button, which immediately connects him to a live person.

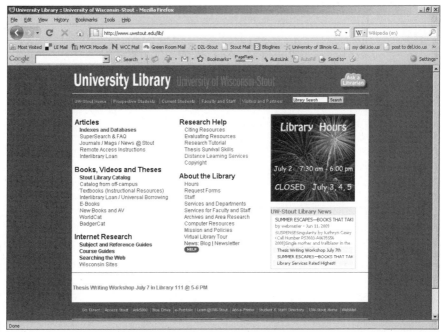

Permission for the use of this Screen Shot granted by the Board of Regents of the University of Wisconsin System on behalf of University of Wisconsin-Stout

Figure 11-7:
An online library portal.

If your library has a chat button, it's usually on the library's home page or a static section of the site that follows you from page to page, such as the header or sidebar navigation menu. Most live chat buttons use text to tell you whether a librarian is available. For example, when available, the button may read something like "Chat with a Librarian Now," but it may say something like "Chat is currently unavailable" when staff are not logged in. Sometimes the button disappears completely when librarians are unavailable. Check your library's home page for hours of operation. You can usually find staffing hours, including live chat hours, there.

Doing research online

As an online student, you're going to need the library primarily to conduct research for papers and projects. You may be surprised by the similarities between a virtual library visit and a visit to a physical library. You determine the kinds of materials you need, you search for them through databases and the card catalog, and then you determine what's worth checking out to take home. These processes require decision making and knowledge of what makes a source credible and useful.

Begin the research process as early as possible. Just because you have access to the institution's online database doesn't mean everything you want will be available in a format you can download immediately. You may be required to have materials mailed to you, get them from other sources such as your local library, or find an alternative resource. This process can take time.

Figuring out the type of material you need

Before you begin to search for resources for a course or assignment, consider the type of material best suited for your research. Scholarly literature is often most appropriate for college-level research, so you should be able to identify it.

Scholarly materials appear in journals. They're academic or scholarly in nature and may be available in print or online. Scholarly journals can be easily accessed through academic library databases and usually have at least some of the following features. They

✔ Have long articles (5 or more pages).

✔ Are written by scholars or authorities in their fields (and aren't anonymous).

✔ Have a bibliography, references, citations, or footnotes.

✔ Contain jargon (language that pertains to the field).

✔ Often (but not always) contain graphs or charts.

✔ Report original, scholarly research.

✔ Are written to relay information to other scholars in the field.

✔ Are often peer-reviewed or -refereed. This means that the article must go through a review process of scholars in that particular field to be accepted into the journal.

Accessing online library databases

Databases are electronic collections of information. Periodical databases provide citations and full-text articles for journal, magazine, or newspaper articles. Online catalogs are also databases that allow you to search for materials in a library by author, title, subject heading, keyword, or call number.

When your instructor assigns you the task of finding a journal article in your discipline, look first in a database specific to that field. In most cases, your institution's library portal will have specific links to find different types of resources, such as books, articles, reserves, and/or media, directly on the home page. These links will take you to a search form that often allows you to search by keywords and subject. You will also have an advanced search option that will allow you to search by other variables, such as author, journal title, year, and so forth.

Conducting searches by subject or keyword

When you search for materials on a specific topic, you'll most likely need to begin with a subject or keyword search.

✔ When you search by subject, you're searching for items that have been identified with a specific and standardized heading. If a subject heading is available that is closely related to your topic, this will often produce more useful and relevant results than a keyword search. Subject headings are usually generic field titles such as Business, Education, Engineering, Physical Science, Social Sciences, and so forth.

✔ Searching by keyword allows you to use a combination of keywords that may appear in any of the fields within a record. The keywords you use might appear in the titles, authors, subject headings, publishers, or abstracts, so your results will usually be broader and may be unrelated to your topic. Keyword searches are more flexible, though, and subject headings may not always exist for your topics.

When doing a keyword search, it's very important that you use only the most relevant keywords for your topic. Don't include words like "effect," "cause," "relationship," "pros and cons," or prepositions (like "of," "at," "to," "in," and so forth), because these will ineffectively limit your search. For example, imagine you need to research the current state and perceived effectiveness of the No Child Left Behind Act. It's best to focus on the act itself and leave out the extraneous details in your search. Figure 11-8 illustrates an example of a keyword database search on this topic. Notice how the words "No Child Left Behind" are in quotes. This means that the search will look for and display results that have the words in this exact order mixed with the word "Act."

Determining the quality of your sources

When conducting research, you'll find several sources of information about your topic. However, don't just accept information at face value. As you search the Web or library databases, critically evaluate each resource to ensure its quality. Here are a few questions you can ask yourself to help assess the quality of the resources you find:

✔ **Accuracy:** Are there footnotes, citations, and/or a bibliography? Is the information free from error?

✔ **Authority:** Is there an author? What are his credentials? Is the author well-known in his respective field?

✔ **Objectivity:** Is there a minimum level of bias? Is the author trying to sway the reader's opinion? Why was the document created?

✔ **Currency:** When was the document created? Is the information up-to-date for the subject?

✔ **Coverage:** Is the information in-depth? Is the information valuable for your topic?

✔ **Readership:** Who is the intended audience? Is the material appropriate for college-level research?

Watching tutorials on the library site

Most libraries have links to tutorials that provide additional tips on how to conduct database searches and check for quality. Take time to review these tutorials. The time it takes to review the search tips alone will be returned two-fold in the time they save you when conducting research. Pay attention to tips and tricks on searching using Boolean commands and truncation methods of searching. These help make searching more efficient and help you get the information you want by reducing the number of unnecessary search results.

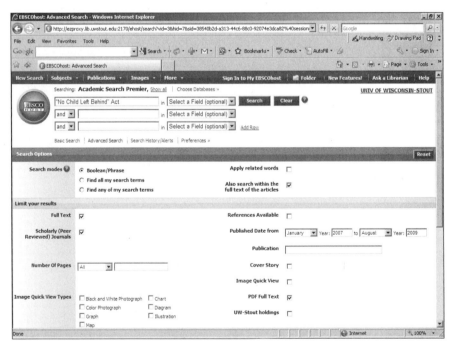

Figure 11-8:
An example of a keyword database search.

Working Offline

The fact that you're taking a course online doesn't mean that you're learning only when you're logged in to your class. As a matter of fact, you may find that you spend more time thinking about your class and working on assignments off-line than online. Working off-line has a lot of advantages:

- ✔ **Reading offline:** Printing documents or reading texts away from the computer allows you to take documents with you when you're on the go. It also saves on eyestrain from reading your computer screen. You can also take notes more easily on printed materials.

- ✔ **Writing offline:** Some course management systems time out and cause you to lose your connection if you sit on the same screen too long. This means that you may lose all your hard work if you take too long to write a discussion post before posting it. Therefore, we recommend that you first type all your assignments, including discussion posts, in a word-processing program of your choice. By doing this, you can save as you go and then paste the final product into the course management system when you're finished. This process automatically creates a backup copy of all your work. If for any reason the system fails to accept your post, you can quickly repost by opening your document and copying and pasting the information again.

Chapter 12

Getting a Handle on Group Dynamics

· ·

· ·

Do you smile or cringe when you hear the words group project? We find that students have extreme views: Either they truly appreciate group projects or they really detest them. Those who appreciate working in a group have had positive experiences and see the value multiple people can bring to a project. Others have had a bad experience working with peers who have done nothing, leaving them to pick up the slack.

One of the biggest questions we get from students and other instructors we train is "Why group work?" Besides the typical "because we said so" or the overused cliché "two heads are better than one," educational research supports the use of groups as a means of helping students construct and retain knowledge. Not to mention the opportunity it gives them to learn and practice marketable skills.

This book serves as a testament to the power of distant collaboration. Not only do we, your humble authors, live in different parts of the same state, but the editors and other technical staff live and work out-of-state. Some of us have no idea what the other contributors look like. Most communication occurs via e-mail and phone. So, when we ask our students to complete online group projects, we truly are helping them learn marketable skills that easily transfer to the workplace.

Online collaboration takes time, communication, organization, and dedication on the part of all group members. This chapter provides you with strategies for successfully participating in online groups and communicating effectively with peers, including in times of conflict.

Making Your Online Group Successful

So how do online groups work? Just like in the face-to-face classroom, an instructor may ask students to create a common document or product as a team. Students may be able to pick their group members, or groups may be assigned by the instructor. (In most cases, the instructor assigns groups to save time.) Students contribute to the final product by sharing research, writing, and editing responsibilities. The difference for online students is that they must be organized enough to do this from a distance. The following sections talk about how to make the overall collaboration process successful.

Keep in mind that you'll do some of the following steps at the same sitting. For example, you may make your introduction and initial posts about establishing roles one right after the other — before others even have time to reply. Otherwise, the time it takes to wait for replies in the asynchronous environment can delay your progress to a point of no return. Take initiative, and don't be afraid to be the first to post your thoughts regarding next steps and the process for taking those steps. In most cases, others go along with ideas presented first as a way of moving forward with the project. Be sure to post in a manner that is respectful and doesn't seem pushy. Otherwise, your plan may backfire.

Introducing yourself in a group forum

After your group has been given its assignment, it's time to introduce yourself to your fellow group members so you can begin organizing the project. Most likely your instructor will provide you with a private discussion forum to communicate with one another. From the students' perspective, these forums look and function like any other discussion forums (see Chapter 10 for an introduction to discussions). The only difference is that only you, your fellow group members, and your instructor can access it.

You can organize this forum by creating new discussion threads specific to conversation topics. For example, your first thread might be titled "Group Introductions." Figure 12-1 illustrates an online discussion forum that's organized in this manner.

Before you jump too deep into the content of your assignment, it's important to set a collaborative tone among your teammates. We recommend introducing yourself as soon as possible. Your introduction should be brief and provide essential contact information. Provide the following information in your introduction:

✔ **Name and brief introduction:** Include a brief background of any experi-ence you may have in the subject matter, your professional goals, and any skills that may help complete the assignment.

✔ **Contact information:** Include as many methods for contacting you as possible, including your school e-mail address, phone number, and instant messenger ID.

For security purposes, we don't recommend providing home addresses. If by any chance your group is able to meet face-to-face, choose a public location, such as a library or an Internet café.

✔ **Available times to meet synchronously:** Provide your peers with the days and times you're able to meet synchronously. (We discuss having real-time meetings in more detail later in this chapter.)

✔ **Your desired role:** If you have a preferred role you would like to take, this is the time to share it. Whether you want to be the group leader, editor, or take on some other role, let the group know. The sooner you do this, the more likely you are to get what you want. (See the next section for more about the roles of group members.)

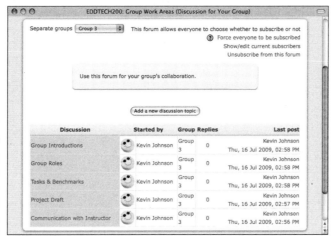

Figure 12-1:
An example
of a discus-
sion forum
for a group.

Establishing a leader and other roles

After group members' introductions, the next task you need to accomplish is to work with your group to establish roles within the group. By establish-ing roles up front, you reduce conflict later when bigger decisions need to be made.

No matter what role you assume within your group, every member is expected to contribute equally. Therefore, tasks such as research and writing are the responsibility of all members. Establishing roles helps organize the group by making different members responsible for extraneous tasks such as content structure, time management, and content review.

Here are a few roles to consider when establishing your group:

- ✔ **Leader:** The group's leader is responsible for the overall management of the project. The leader's job is to facilitate the processes for setting deadlines, delegating tasks, and staying on track.

- ✔ **Editor:** The editor's job is to critically review each group member's contribution and comment on grammar, spelling, content quality, consistency in language usage, and so on.

- ✔ **Submitter:** The submitter's role is to format and submit the final draft of the project to the instructor on behalf of the group.

If your group is communicating via the discussion forums, one member will need to initiate some kind of voting process for deciding on roles. We recommend that you take the initiative and post your preferred role as soon as possible in the appropriate discussion topic. For example, if you have leadership skills and would like to volunteer for this role, simply write something like "Hey, everyone! I'm really looking forward to working with each of you on this project. I'd be happy to take on the leader role if no one is opposed to it. I recommend that we post our preferred roles and vote on them by Wednesday so that we can move forward with the project. Let me know what you think." If there are more workers than there are roles, that's okay. What's most important is that each person's complete workload is equal to the other members of the group. So, the editor may do less research and actual writing as a way of leveling the playing field.

Setting up a group schedule

Whether your group plans to meet in real time (see the next section) or communicate solely in an asynchronous fashion (via e-mail and your private discussion forum), creating a group schedule is important. Your schedule should include task benchmarks, deadlines, and formal progress check-ins. Be sure to document the schedule and post progress information in a location where your instructor can see it (such as inside a topic titled Group Progress). One way of making sure everyone understands the schedule and their responsibilities is to post the schedule within a discussion topic and ask all members to reply to the post with a simple statement such as, "I have read and agree to meet the deadlines provided within the posted schedule." This makes everyone accountable for completing their part. Table 12-1 is an example of what a group project schedule might look like:

Table 12-1	Example Group Project Schedule
Day	**Task**
Monday, January 25	Everyone conducts initial research on topic
Wednesday, January 27	Everyone submits three ideas to include in project in private discussion forum
Thursday, January 28 Synchronous Session Scheduled for 8:00 – 9:00 p.m. (Central Time)	Leader compiles submissions to a single document and distributes the document via e-mail to all members before synchronous session

Everyone votes on top five items to include in project in Elluminate (Synchronous Session) |
Friday, January 29	Leader delegates research topics to group members in private discussion forum
Saturday, January 30	Everyone conducts research
Friday, February 5	Everyone posts draft of research in GoogleDocs
Sunday, February 7	Editor edits draft and submits for group comment in GoogleDocs
Wednesday, February 10	Everyone posts comments on draft in GoogleDocs
Friday, February 12	Editor makes final edits in GoogleDocs
Sunday, February 14	Submitter posts final project to public forum

Meeting in real time

Completing tasks in an asynchronous environment can take awhile as you wait for peers to reply to posts, answer e-mails, and so on. Therefore, we recommend you find a way to meet synchronously, or in real time, especially during the initial organizing stage. And, if you and your group have the ability to meet synchronously multiple times throughout the project, take advantage of it. (See the later section "Web conferencing" for details on methods you can use to meet synchronously.)

By scheduling a definite start and stop time for your meeting and then sticking to the schedule, you force yourselves to stay on task.

During your synchronous meetings, you should briefly introduce yourselves and then get right down to business. Your first meeting should include an overview of the project to make sure all members of the group are on the same page. You should also review your established roles and begin to break the project down into manageable tasks.

Once everyone knows what the project tasks are, the leader can delegate them to the group and set deadlines for each. Future meetings can be used to check in on each other's progress and discuss any problems or issues you may be having. These meetings are usually very short and keep everyone on track.

Want to really impress the group and make your meeting run even more smoothly? Create an agenda ahead of time that provides your interpretation of the project and your recommended tasks and deadlines. The more you bring to the table, the faster you'll be able to get through your meeting and focus on completing the project. Consider doing this even if roles have not been determined yet and no one has been elected as the group's leader. A quick message to the group via e-mail or discussion forum post to let them know you are planning to do this will help communicate your dedication to the project's success and reduce the chances of someone else duplicating work.

If your Web conferencing tool has a record option, be sure to record your meeting so that your group and your instructor can review it later if needed. If recording is not an option, a group member should be assigned the role of secretary and that person should post a brief overview of each meeting, outlining tasks and deadlines, in your group's private discussion forum. This helps your group and your instructor to stay up-to-date on your group's progress.

Speaking of your instructor, feel free to invite her to your group's synchronous meetings. She may not be able to attend, but at least you're keeping her in the loop. If she does attend, conduct your meeting as usual and allow her to lurk in the background. However, don't be afraid to take advantage of her presence by asking questions if needed.

Using collaborative tools

As you find out in the following sections, you can use quite a few Web-based tools to collaborate and communicate with your group. These tools are often external to your course management system. Many of these tools are free for public use.

The key is to either use tools that are very simple to learn or *only* use tools every member of the group is already familiar with. Trying to learn a new tool in the middle of a group project can be frustrating and distract you from completing the project on time.

Document collaboration

Suppose you and your fellow group members are asked to produce a written document, an essay. In the "old" days, one person would write something and forward the document to all other group members. Then, everyone would provide feedback and send back their comments individually. The originator would have to open several documents and do the best job possible of combining the input of the others.

No longer is this necessary, thanks to Wiki technology. A *Wiki* is a collaborative tool that is Web-based and allows multiple people to contribute to the same document. In a group-project situation, this means that you can collaborate on the same document at the same time as your fellow group members. You go to a Web site and log in (after you have created an account), and the Web page looks just like a common word-processing, spreadsheet, or presentation program. You create a page and invite group members to join. Once they join (and create their own accounts), you can all log in at the same time and view the same page simultaneously. It doesn't matter what software you have on your individual machines because everything is handled through that Web page! Each of you can edit and save the copy. Eventually, one of you can save a final copy and turn it in for your assignment or link your instructor and class to the page. Wikis can be used for group projects, company policy documents, and much more.

One of the more common Wiki applications on the Web right now is GoogleDocs (`http://docs.google.com`). With GoogleDocs, you can collaboratively create a word-processing document, spreadsheet, presentation, or Web form. This service is free and allows a document originator the ability to invite others to either view only or edit the document. Figure 12-2 illustrates a document created using GoogleDocs.

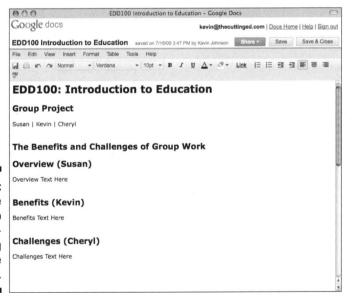

Figure 12-2:
An example of a group project document using Google Docs.

For your essay assignment, one group member or the instructor would start the document. Then, that person would invite the other group members to view the document as collaborators in order to provide them the permission needed to edit the document. Based on your group's organizational meeting, the editor might add headings to the document as a way of visually dividing it into pieces. Group members would then go in and begin filling in the blanks as they completed their research.

Web conferencing

If your group decides to meet synchronously, a few tools are available to help facilitate the process. Consider the following variables when choosing a synchronous tool:

- **Availability:** Don't spend extra time looking for tools if your course provides them for you. For example, one of the institutions we teach for provides each class with a virtual office space via Elluminate. The space is open to students 24x7 and students access it directly from inside their course.

- **Functionality:** Some tools are limited as to what features they offer. For example, the telephone provides voice communication, but you can't share documents via the phone. Skype combines voice and text-based chat only. Other tools, such as Elluminate, provide interactive features that allow users to share voice, text, whiteboards, each others' computer screens, and more. Choose your tools according to what you need, or learn to work around your chosen tool's limits.

- **Cost:** Unless your institution gives you access to some of these tools, you're not likely to be able to justify the cost of purchasing comprehensive services like Elluminate as an individual. Some of these tools can cost upwards of $400 per user per year. Other tools, like Skype, are free and can meet your needs just as easily for the project at hand.

Two available synchronous communication tools are Skype and Elluminate.

- Skype (www.skype.com) is a text and audio chat program that allows users to chat with one another either through text or voice. Currently, Skype allows you to conference up to 50 people via chat and 5 people via voice. The service is free when connecting computer-to-computer. The program also allows you to dial landline and mobile numbers from your computer for a minimal per minute fee.

  To efficiently use this tool, each group member needs to establish an account. (Yes, that means yet another login and password; see Chapter 3 for an introduction on keeping everything straight.) Once everyone has an account, they share their account names with each other just like phone numbers. At the time of the meeting, each group member logs in to the group's Wiki (see the previous section) and Skype. A designated group member initiates the Skype conference, calling the rest of the group members. Figure 12-3 illustrates a conference call using Skype.

  Once connected, the group can use the voice feature just as if they were talking on the phone, except this time it's free and doesn't cost you any minutes. Because GoogleDocs allows multiple people to edit a document at the same time, one group member can be taking notes and editing your group's document as you talk. The other group members can see the changes as they are made.

For conferencing tools such as Skype, users need a microphone and speakers. We recommend a combination headset with microphone.

Figure 12-3:
A group call with Skype.

Courtesy of Skype Limited

✔ Multi-modal tools, such as Elluminate (www.elluminate.com), are for groups wanting a little more interaction capabilities within their Web-conferencing tool. *Multi-modal* refers to the user's ability to interact using a variety of methods. For example, Elluminate allows users to interact using voice, text, video, whiteboard, application sharing, and more.

Tools such as Elluminate can be very expensive. They're often licensed by the institution for instructor and student use. However, depending on your group size, you may be able to use the tool for free even if your institution doesn't have a license. Elluminate offers a free service called Elluminate vRoom (www.elluminate.com/vroom) that allows you to sign up for a free virtual space and invite up to two other people into that space at one time.

To use such a space, each group member clicks on a link that takes them to a virtual meeting space. The meeting's organizer could prepare a few slides in PowerPoint and load them to the whiteboard where all participants could see them. The slides would have the meeting's agenda on it and possibly space between each agenda item to take notes.

Each attendee uses a speaker/microphone combination (headset recommended) to talk to and hear the other participants. During the course of the meeting, one member of the group could share their computer screen with the other attendees, projecting the shared document.

This way everyone could see and comment as one of the members edited the document. Figure 12-4 illustrates an example of a group meeting occurring in an Elluminate virtual office.

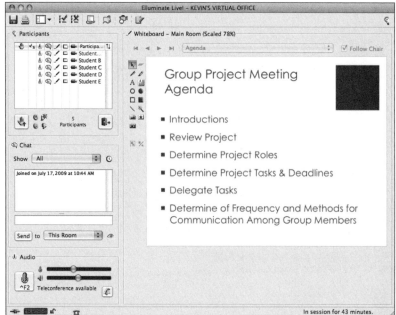

Figure 12-4:
A group meeting in Elluminate.

Courtesy of Elluminate, Inc.

Being patient

Okay, time for a reality check. Even if you do everything we tell you to do in the preceding sections, not everybody in your group will be able to dedicate the same amount of time to your project. Inevitably, life happens: Kids get sick, work is busy, and other life events distract your group members from participating at the most desirable level. Therefore, patience is a must! Even the most dedicated group members may have a different work schedule or live in a different time zone. Therefore, communication may be delayed.

The sooner you can organize your group, the sooner you will feel more relaxed. Once you are organized, you can work independently on your own time schedule — just as long as you meet established deadlines (see the example of a group schedule in Table 12-1). As you work alone, you need to trust that your fellow group members are doing the same. That's why having periodic check-ins is important. You definitely don't want to find out that a group member has done nothing the day the project is due.

Resolving Conflicts

Whenever people are asked to collaborate, the potential for conflict exists. The ability to be patient and strategically resolve conflict is an important skill when participating in an online course. The lack of participation of a group member or the misinterpretation of written text can lead to frustration and resentment — distracting you from the objectives of the course. As you read this section, don't just think about how to resolve conflict; consider how to prevent it as well.

Understanding the conflicts you may encounter (and handling them)

In our experience, conflict occurs between students in the online environment for three reasons: They disagree on the subject matter; a student says something that others find offensive; or resentment sets in when one or more students are perceived as not pulling their weight.

Disagreeing on the subject matter

Sometimes students disagree on the subject matter. In a classroom, you would think this would be the most prevalent source of conflict. However, this type of conflict rarely occurs online, and when it does (typically in a discussion forum), the instructor should step in to help facilitate a resolution.

If the conflict is initiated via text, contact your instructor and provide her with the specific forum where she can find the post. If the conflict occurred during a synchronous session, contact your instructor and provide her with as much detail as possible, even if you are merely a witness to the conflict. Use your instructor's phone number for issues that need to be resolved immediately. If you have to leave a message, follow up with an e-mail as well. Some instructors, like us, get their e-mail on their cellphones and get information faster that way than from voice mails on our office phones. Information should be presented in a factual and professional manner.

Finding a submission offensive

One student may write something that other students consider offensive. Very rarely are these incidences intentional. Students sometimes write before thinking about how others might interpret their written words.

If you encounter a post that you feel is offensive, don't assume that it was an intentional attack. Politely respond by asking for clarification, and explain why clarification may be needed without pointing fingers. For example, "Jane, thanks for your response. I'd like to ask for clarification about your point on . . . the way I read it made me think you were saying. . . ."

If a post is blatantly offensive, don't fuel the fire by responding further. Contact your instructor immediately and allow her to facilitate the resolution process (see the next section for tips on how to communicate effectively with your instructor in this situation). The instructor will most likely delete the post and deal with the situation behind the scenes.

An ounce of prevention here is worth a pound of cure. To avoid offending others, think before you write and reread your posts before submitting them. A simple slip of the comma can really change the meaning of a sentence.

Simmering over slackers

Resentment tends to build when one or more students don't pull their weight. This often occurs when organization or communication within a group is lacking. Even the most understandable situations can lead to conflict if not communicated correctly. For example, we have both witnessed a student who has had a family emergency to attend to, requiring the student to step away from class momentarily. However, because the student did not communicate this to the group, the other group members started resenting her, which began to destroy the entire group dynamics. Had the student explained the situation to the group before removing herself, most likely, the other students would have supported her lack of participation. Not only would they have provided emotional support, they would have gladly picked up her share of the work.

To avoid this situation, be sure to communicate with your group on a consistent basis, even if it's just to say "hello." Your virtual presence will reassure your group that you are on task and on time. On the other hand, if you find that a group member is not participating, try contacting that person semi-privately. We recommend that you include your instructor on all communication, especially when you're dealing with lack-of-participation issues, hence the phrase "semi-privately." If your instructor wants to be less involved in the day-to-day communication, she'll let you know. Write an e-mail to the group member who is not participating, and copy your instructor. Do not blind copy the instructor because you want the instructor's involvement to be known by your fellow group member.

If, after two attempts, you don't receive a response from your peer, let your instructor take it from there. Start making backup plans for completing that person's share of the project and move forward. Don't let one person's lack of participation hold you up from completing the project and having a positive group experience. However, continue to keep the non-participating member in the communication loop as a way of documenting that person's lack of participation.

One activity the group's secretary (or other designated group member) should consider when first delegating tasks is to create a spreadsheet of what is to be done, who is to do it, and when it's due. Then as tasks are completed, the secretary can document who actually completed the task and when.

This encourages all group members to be responsible for completing their part of the project and provides the instructor with a clear picture of each member's level of participation.

Bringing problems to your instructor's attention

A good instructor will most likely know when a problem is brewing from having observed goings-on in the background, especially if you include your instructor in your group communications as we suggest in the preceding section. However, a good instructor will also provide the group with some time to resolve conflicts on their own without stepping in at the first signs of a problem.

Whenever you need to contact the instructor about a group member not living up to expectations, you may feel like a tattletale, but it's okay. The classroom is a good training ground for people to learn responsibility and the social repercussions of not living up to that responsibility. A good instructor will be able to handle the situation professionally in a manner that doesn't reflect poorly on you or other group members. Instead, the instructor will focus on the unwanted behavior and coach the student on how to improve that behavior.

The way you approach your instructor when you're dealing with a group conflict is very important. Use the following guidelines when communicating to your instructor:

- ✔ **Communicate privately.** When you reach the point where you feel that communicating directly with your peer isn't working, communicate the situation privately to your instructor so that you can focus more on you and the next steps you should take to move forward.

- ✔ **Be direct and use facts.** Politely explain the situation, and share with the instructor any communication you have had with your group member. The more information you can provide the instructor, the better. Hopefully, the instructor already has some idea about what's going on, but it never hurts to be thorough.

- ✔ **Don't complain.** Your instructor understands the repercussions of someone not participating in a group project. Complaining about the situation only distracts you from moving forward and makes you look needy to your instructor.

- ✔ **Have a backup plan.** Ensure your instructor that you're ready to move forward with a backup plan and ask whether this plan should include the group member who is failing to participate.

- ✔ **Ask for direction.** End your communication by thanking your instructor and confirming that it's okay to move forward with your backup plan.

You may be asking yourself who should ultimately be responsible for reporting conflict to the instructor. Generally, the leader should be the person who contacts the instructor about problems within the group. However, sometimes, other group members have problems with the leader. In this situation, if the other members of the group are communicating with one another, it's best if only one person is chosen to contact the instructor. Otherwise, if you feel there is a problem that no one is addressing, you have a choice: You can either report the situation to the instructor privately, or you can politely initiate the group deciding on who should contact the instructor by posting something like "Hi, all. It seems that we may be at an impasse, which is blocking our ability to complete our tasks effectively. I'd like to propose we ask our instructor for guidance. I'd be more than happy to contact her on our behalf, unless someone else would rather do it. I'm confident with the proper guidance we can work this out and create an amazing project to turn in."

Chapter 13

Understanding Netiquette and Ethical Behavior

Remember the Robert Fulghum book *All I Really Need to Know I Learned in Kindergarten*? In it, he states some of the simple rules from childhood, including to play fair and not take things that aren't yours. In a nutshell, that's what this chapter is about! Online education should be a place where students are fair to one another and honest in their interactions. We look at how this plays out digitally and what tools you can use to help you stay true to your word.

Defining and Using Netiquette

Netiquette is computerese for a set of rules or standards people follow to keep the online environment pleasant and safe. The word combines *etiquette* with the Inter*net*, and, just like its parent definition of etiquette, netiquette is all about communicating respectfully and politely and avoiding stereotyping.

Most good instructors convey their interpretation of netiquette along with expectations for its use in the early days of the course. You may see a list of "do's and don'ts" or a policy statement, and this may be referenced in the syllabus (a document we describe in Chapter 8). Setting those ground rules early can prevent misunderstandings and hurt feelings later.

Communicating politely and respectfully

What makes discussion board postings, e-mails, and instant messages polite? A few standard conventions work on all communication fronts, no matter the audience (Chapters 10 and 14 feature additional guidelines for discussion posts):

✔ Always fill in the subject line for discussion postings and e-mails. Mystery messages make people nervous.

✔ Address the reader by name, if possible. Who doesn't love reading their name in print, and how else will others know you're talking to them?

✔ Make sure you sign your name at the end of your posting. Own up to whatever you write.

✔ Follow basic writing conventions and don't mix popular text-message lingo with your academic work. Not only is texting inappropriate for scholarly work, but many in your class will not understand the code.

✔ Don't type in all caps! It's the equivalent of shouting.

✔ Okay, if you need to add emphasis, you can do it *this* way (by adding asterisks before and after the text you want to emphasize) or use all-caps occasionally.

✔ Too much colored font or busy images can detract from your message. Keep the look of your postings, e-mails, and messages simple and clean.

✔ It goes without saying that name-calling is out. Diplomacy is in. If you disagree with something, say "I politely disagree and here is why. . . ."

✔ "Please," "thank you," and other courtesies work really well online!

✔ Those little emoticons like smiley faces and winks can be used judiciously in replies to one another. However, be sure you're not punctuating every sentence with an emoticon; a little goes a long way. For that matter, avoid overuse of !!! and ???, too.

✔ Be forgiving. Anyone can make a mistake and accidentally shout with all caps or forget to say thank you. Rather than publicly humiliate your peers by pointing out a transgression, politely disregard the occasional offense. If it gets to be a habit, you can raise the question with the offending student (privately and politely, of course!) and carbon copy the instructor. Is it possible that your instructor will be the offender? Not likely, although he may forget to address you by name in an e-mail, or a reply may seem uncharacteristically short. If that's the case, let it go. Pointing it out will make you look like a high-maintenance student.

✔ Proofread your work before hitting the send or submit button. You'll save yourself embarrassment.

All the preceding guidelines go a long way toward showing respect for others, but we make a few additional notes concerning student-to-student communication and student-to-instructor communication in the following sections.

Showing respect for other students

In the academic world, discussion should involve critical thinking, which means ideas have to be taken apart and reconstructed. In short, not everyone is going to agree! How you communicate those disagreements speaks volumes about how much you respect the other party.

Your tone shouldn't suggest shouting at or belittling the original author. You should simply offer another view and the reasoning behind it. To strengthen your point, supporting your opinions with course materials and additional research is helpful. We demonstrate with a few examples in the list that follows. These are polite ways to disagree in discussion forums as well as e-mail and instant messages.

- ✔ I hear what you're saying, but I see it another way, and here's why. . . .
- ✔ That's an interesting point you make about the causes. Have you also thought about (fill in the blank) because I think. . . .
- ✔ Respectfully, I'd like to add a few thoughts that might reshape your thinking. Here are my ideas. . . .
- ✔ I'm still thinking about what you said. One of the issues (or points) I struggle with is (fill in the blank) because. . . .

Next, we contrast the preceding tactful examples with some that could be misread. Any of the following examples can be written tongue-in-cheek and with a note of humor. However, they can also be terribly insulting. In fact, we encourage students and instructors to use humor sparingly. What you think is funny may be interrupted as offensive by others. This doesn't mean that you should leave your personality at the virtual classroom door (Chapter 10 explains how to put forward your online persona). It simply means to post carefully and respectfully. Remember, online communication is void of nonverbals and can easily be misinterpreted.

- ✔ You're so wrong and don't even know it!
- ✔ How can you miss the other side of the argument?
- ✔ What are you, goofy?

If you do feel strongly about what someone wrote, don't reply immediately. Draft a response and sleep on it. The next day, reread what you wrote and see whether you need to tone it down or whether you still feel the message needs to be sent. Swift and emotional responses almost always backfire.

One more note: Most of your communication will occur within a course management system or at least within the parameters of class. Therefore, forwarding chain-letter e-mails to your class is inappropriate. If you do make friends with one or two students and want to share something like that, ask their permission first and use discretion.

Respecting your instructor

Of course, you know your instructor is a real person and therefore subject to the same feelings as your classmates. While you're exercising diplomacy with your peers, extend the same courtesy to your instructor. Teaching is a very public activity, and it's impossible to get everything "right" when dealing with technology. You may also want to approach your instructor when you disagree with a grade. Here are a few circumstances in which you may want to respectfully approach your instructor:

✔ When you see typos or broken links, e-mail the instructor privately. Sometimes he has no control over these, and a link that works one day can be broken the next. Say something like, "I'm having trouble opening the link to X. It says 'page not available,' and I can't tell if the whole site is down forever or if I'm just hitting it at a bad time. Do you know an alternative URL?" Or, "Dr. Manning, I noticed you have the word 'resource' twice on the first line of the second paragraph on the instructions page for the assignment this week. Just thought you'd want to know."

✔ If you disagree with a grade or a score, approach the instructor calmly and with respect. After all, he has more content knowledge than you. Asking for clarification without going overboard emotionally yields far more positive results. In these cases, try something like, "Dr. Manning, I wondered if I can get a little more clarification on my grade on the last paper. I want to make sure I can incorporate the feedback into the next round. Can you please tell me more about how I can improve in the area of. . . ."

Before you ask about a score, determine the overall relevance. Is it worth haggling over 1 out of 15 points?

✔ If you need more specific feedback, ask for examples. Say something like, "I'm trying to better understand how I can improve in the future. Could I please have an example of what you consider an excellent post/paper/project?" Likewise, if your instructor gives individual feedback, take the time to read it!

Avoiding stereotyping

Many people realize that stereotyping is harmful. It may be obvious that comments of this nature do not belong in online discussions. And yet, sometimes we inadvertently carry our stereotypes into the classroom. For example, if you assume that someone with the last name of Gonzales can interpret the cultural significance of homeopathic remedies in a community nursing course, you may be surprised to find out that that person married into the family and is a member of the dominant culture, not the minority. (Furthermore, Gonzales could be a surname from either a Latin American or Asian country!)

You simply cannot stereotype. In an online course, it's important to get to know your fellow students as individuals. Take time to read any icebreakers or biographies that are posted, and, rather than assert a stereotype, ask questions.

Recognizing the Importance of Online Ethics

In the early days of online education, the primary concern for many faculty, administrators, and students was that it was too easy to cheat with technology. They feared that the value of the degree would become meaningless because you could copy papers, make up resources, and get your cousin to do your work. Of course, the same could be said of traditional education, so a renewed awareness of the importance of ethics has evolved.

Ethical behavior should govern how (and what) people communicate with one another, what work people submit with their names attached, and the extent to which they are true to their word. We examine these themes in this section.

Being honest in the written word

Because written communication is the primary way ideas are exchanged in an online class, what you say and how you say it must belong to you. Here are a couple of examples in which honesty is absolutely important:

- ✔ **Presenting ideas:** Your instructor may ask you to read an author or theorist and then give your ideas about the work. If you answer a discussion question or write a paper for this kind of assignment, you're expected to give credit to the original authors when you use their ideas. If you don't, you're not being honest about your work; you are plagiarizing. (Later in this chapter, we discuss plagiarism in much more depth.)

- ✔ **Being yourself:** Occasionally, a student misrepresents his ability or life experience. For example, suppose John writes that he is a certified public accountant. Later, the class learns that John barely finished his associate's degree and lied about his achievement. John's integrity is now shot because he wasn't honest. It's true that you can be anyone you want online, but if you're in an academic setting, we suggest that you become a serious scholar and not a dishonest participant.

Showing integrity by following through

You may be part of a study group in an online course. That means that others depend on you to do your share of the work. If you say you'll contribute, your group expects you to follow through, and rightly so. If you fail to do your part of the work and become a "social loafer," you will quickly lose trust and respect among your peers by your lack of integrity. Your grade will probably suffer as well, because most instructors give credit for group participation. (We give many more details about participating in an online study group in Chapter 12.)

At some point in time you may need to step away from the computer and focus on personal issues. In this situation, you may "contract" with your instructor to extend deadlines or receive an "Incomplete" grade until you have caught up on work by a specific date and time. You may be surprised at how many students do this and then never finish the work. Don't make it your instructor's responsibility to manage your time. Follow through with integrity by completing the work by the determined deadline, and communicate with the instructor privately regarding your status.

Respecting privacy and confidentiality

As we explain throughout this book, students develop personal relationships in online courses. They communicate outside of the parameters of the course management system through private e-mail and messages. You may receive confidential information about one of your peers, and this needs to stay between you and your friend. For example, if Jane writes about her ugly divorce, you have no right to bring that up in a discussion forum. Even if you're a law student and the topic is divorce, this is Jane's business, not yours.

The same is true for information you receive from your instructor. Your instructor will handle your progress and grades as confidential matters. Please do not post this communication publicly nor share it with your friends.

Asking before you repurpose prior work

If you're enrolled in a degree program, chances are good that assignments you complete in one course will flow nicely into another. For example, in an introductory course you may be asked to write a paper that requires research on a certain topic. That background research may be very helpful in your second class as you extend the theme. Is it wrong to take your first paper and repurpose it for your second assignment?

The answer to that depends on your instructor. While we would say that building on prior work is very efficient and shows impeccable organization, your instructor may not agree with us. Therefore, always ask before you rework an old assignment. Tell the instructor what part and how much of the old assignment you would like to repurpose, and what new information you plan to add to complete the new assignment.

If you don't ask before you repurpose prior work, you may find your instructor won't accept the work. In some programs, instructors coordinate assignments and will know if you try to pass off an assignment from another course. You don't want a failing grade!

Avoiding Plagiarism

Is plagiarism more rampant today, and has technology made it easier to borrow another person's ideas? Faculty wrestle with these questions routinely because, unfortunately, plagiarism happens all too frequently.

The only way you can completely avoid plagiarism is to write every word without ever thinking about, borrowing from, or referencing another person's work. Examples of original work may be original poetry, a musical composition, or an essay about your summer vacation that only you could have experienced. However, this isn't the case in most academic courses in which you're asked to research the topic or back up your ideas, so we need to scratch away at the topic a little further. In this section, we define plagiarism, take you through the process of writing without plagiarism, and provide tools and tips to guide you. We also explain what happens if you're caught plagiarizing.

Defining plagiarism and related concepts

Plagiarism is . . . well, without looking, coauthor Susan can tell you that plagiarism is stealing someone else's ideas and passing them off as if they were your own. Does she need to quote someone here? Is this common knowledge and therefore something that can't be attributed to a single source? A little investigating may be worthwhile.

If you research the definition of plagiarism and come to the Web site Plagiarism.org, you find a very similar definition at `www.plagiarism.org/plag_article_what_is_plagiarism.html`: "In other words, plagiarism is an act of fraud. It involves both stealing someone else's work and lying about it afterward."

If you want to quote a source, as we have here, you need to provide enough of a reference so that the reader can go back and check it. Even if you're going to summarize or use this publication as evidence to support your own ideas, tell readers where you found the information. The act of providing that reference is called citing or giving a citation. This keeps academics honest. (We describe how to cite sources properly in more detail later in this chapter.)

Two important concepts that work hand-in-hand with plagiarism are copyright and intellectual property.

- ✔ **Copyright is the legal status that says someone else owns the work.** You see it in the front of books, on the bottom of Web sites, and on the back of your CD cases. It denotes that the creator is legally protected from you or anyone else stealing his work or any portion of his work.

- ✔ **Intellectual property is creative work.** When you write a paper for Introduction to Psychology, that paper is your intellectual property. And once the work is in a fixed state, including blogs and Web sites, it is automatically under copyright protection.

Getting the facts on plagiarism

Having a thorough understanding of plagiarism makes you less likely to make a mistake. The resources noted in the following sections are places to which you can turn to further educate yourself.

Using online tutorials

Teachers really want students to succeed, and for this reason you may be surprised at the number of resources available online to help students understand and avoid plagiarism. Run "plagiarism tutorial" through your preferred search engine and see what comes up. Here are a few of our favorites:

✔ **The 21st Century Information Fluency site** through the Illinois Math and Science Academy maintains a page full of additional links, resources, and interactive self-tests to help you learn more about avoiding plagiarism at `http://21cif.com/resources/links/plagiarism_links.html`. The page was written primarily for teachers, but it can be used by students as well.

✔ **The University of Southern Mississippi's tutorial** at `www.lib.usm.edu/legacy/plag/plagiarismtutorial.php` is very straightforward. We like this tutorial because it allows you to ascertain your understanding through several self-checks. You begin by taking a quiz. Once you finish the quiz, you have to enter an e-mail address in order to access the rest of the tutorial.

✔ **Purdue University's online writing lab (OWL)** dedicates a portion of its Web site to plagiarism. At `http://owl.english.purdue.edu/owl/resource/589/01/`, you can find links and activities to help you better understand how to avoid plagiarizing as you write your assignments.

✔ **The Media Education Lab** at `http://mediaeducationlab.com/code-best-practices-fair-use-media-literacy-education` can't be beat for background information on copyright and fair use. This site provides information for teachers, but if you drill down to some of the fun videos and songs, you can find a lot that applies to student work.

Finding help from the school library

Get to know your school librarian, and when in doubt, ask this person to guide you toward understanding how to avoid plagiarism. Many school Web sites contain their own tutorials and resources. For example, the University of Wisconsin at Stout maintains a page full of resources and links at `www.uwstout.edu/lib/reference/citation.htm`.

Citing sources properly

When you give credit to an original author within the body of your writing, you are citing his work. Proper citation demonstrates that you have a respect for the author's intellectual property and understand the standard conventions of citation. In this section, we describe the information that goes into a citation, explain when to use citations, note some popular citation formats, and list some tools to help with citations.

What goes into a citation

A citation typically includes the author's name, the date of the publication, and possibly the pages from which your reference came. Most often, this information is included within parentheses after the quote or concept from the original author, but it can be referenced in an endnote or footnote, as well. The citation tells the reader that you used a source to support your work, and points the reader toward that source if he wants to follow up.

You may be curious as to why we didn't say that the citation includes the title and publisher (and possibly volume, journal number, and so forth). Those details are included in the "Works Cited," "References," or "Bibliography" page, the detailed listing of all the citations mentioned in the document. That's where the reader turns for the details needed to find the original source.

Taking good notes results in better citations. As you prepare to write any assignment, take careful notes as you read each source. Copy quotes exactly and note page numbers. Summarize ideas separately. Be sure to document all bibliographic information you need according to the style you are told to use.

When to cite

The rules for citation are pretty easy. You need to cite work when

- ✔ **You quote the work.** A quote may be a one-liner or a lengthier portion, such as a paragraph. An example: According to Manning (2009), "Just because you embrace online education, doesn't mean you like gadgets."

- ✔ **You summarize a portion of the work.** This means putting it in your own words, not just changing a phrase here or there! An example: Manning (2009) says it is possible to learn online successfully with relatively few technology gadgets.

- ✔ **You refer to the work.** You may have previously quoted or summarized the work, or this may be one work of many on the same issue. An example: One of the authors who argues against frivolous use of technology tools is Manning (2009).

If the idea was not originally yours and is not a well known fact (for example, the fact that George Washington was the first president of the United States), you need to provide a citation and a reference.

Citation formats

The style you use to cite sources depends on your instructor and your academic discipline. Your instructor should tell you which style he prefers at the beginning of class or the start of an assignment. This information is often included on the syllabus, but you may also find it within a rubric. Some of the common styles for citing work include:

- ✔ **American Psychological Association (APA):** This format is common for the social sciences, education, psychology, and sometimes nursing. You can find out more about APA style at www.apastyle.org/.

✔ **Modern Language Association (MLA):** The humanities and arts are more likely to use MLA formatting. Check out `www.mla.org/style`.

✔ **American Medical Association (AMA):** Students in medicine, biological sciences, and other health-related fields may use the AMA format. See `www.amamanualofstyle.com//oso/public/index.html` for further information.

✔ **Chicago:** This is what the real world uses. When you read an article in a weekly news magazine, its references are in Chicago style. For more details, go to `www.chicagomanualofstyle.org/home.html`.

✔ **Turabian:** This is a generic style that can be used by any of the disciplines. You can explore Turabian style at `writing2.richmond.edu/WRITING/wweb/tura.html`.

Tools for citing

You are so lucky: Internet tools can do the formatting for you when you need to write a citation! (We used to have to buy the manual and learn the system on our own.) Once you know which format your instructor prefers, visit one of the many free Web-based services that formats your citation for you. At most of these sites, you select the style (APA or MLA, for instance) and then the type of media you need to cite. Is it a book, a periodical, or a Web site, and how many authors are listed? In addition, you fill in other information like the date or page numbers and eventually you push a submit button. Voilà! The site tells you the appropriate formats for inclusion within the text and for the end of the document in a "Works Cited" or "References" page.

Here are a few of our favorite tools. You may also find your school's library has a tool built into its Web page. Whichever tool or method you use, double-check the results.

✔ Landmark's Son of Citation Machine at `http://citationmachine.net/`

✔ North Carolina State University Libraries citation tool at `www.lib.ncsu.edu/lobo2/citationbuilder/citationbuilder.php`

✔ Citation Center at `http://citationcenter.net/index.php5`

Checking your own work

If the best defense is a good offense, then the best way to avoid plagiarism is to learn how to write correctly. However, even good writers question their own work. After you finish an assignment, take the extra time to verify your sources and citations. You can do this using online tools or by having a friend check your work.

Using online tools

You may have heard about Turnitin (www.turnitin.com), a Web-based service that schools subscribe to so that faculty can check student work for possible plagiarism. Before your instructor sends your papers through the cycle, why not check your own work? Here are a couple of tools:

- At WriteCheck (http://writecheck.turnitin.com/static/home.html), you can sign up for a free account and run your papers through the same database Turnitin uses. The service tells you if there are areas of your paper that are suspicious, so you can make changes and be ethically correct about your work.

- Another free tool that is simple to use is Plagiarism Checker (www.dustball.com/cs/plagiarism.checker/). You input your writing and send it through the tool, which probably uses a common search engine to look for matches. If it finds something that appears to be plagiarized, it warns you, but it doesn't necessarily tell you how to fix the mistake.

Finding a classmate to help

If you prefer to rely on the human eye rather than a digital check, you can ask a friend or classmate to help. In fact, you and a classmate could agree to read one another's papers and ask each other questions of verification. This practice not only provides a service, but you also learn a lot about plagiarism when you have to look for it in someone else's work. In the end, you come out a better writer for having done this.

Looking at the penalties for plagiarism

Can you *accidentally* plagiarize? Is this possible? Quite a few schools say no; there are no accidents, just sloppy writers. After all, the cornerstone of academia is the idea that students create new understandings of their own, based on integrity and truth. If you plagiarize, your ideas are not your own and there is no truthfulness.

If you mistakenly fail to cite someone else's work and someone notices, you *may* be in serious trouble. Every institution has an academic integrity or academic honesty policy for students. You can find this in the student handbook and in the orientation materials. Your instructor may link you to the policy as part of the syllabus or resource materials in your course. Trust us, the policy exists, and by enrolling, you agree to abide by it!

Every institution also has a process for handling possible infractions. While the details change from one institution to another, the basic procedures include:

- ✔ **Notification of the concern.** Your teacher may call you or e-mail you to discuss the problem.

- ✔ **Documentation of the problem.** The instructor takes screen shots of what you may have posted and any communication surrounding the incident, along with the plagiarized source.

- ✔ **A hearing.** You have the right to a judicial hearing if you want one. This may involve a university judicial hearing officer and is most likely to be held via a telephone or Web conference for an online student. You would need to compile and present a case as to why the plagiarism occurred.

Sanctions for plagiarism range from failing an assignment to being expelled from school. The degree of plagiarism and whether this is your first offense often determine the outcome. In some cases, the instructor may keep it at the class level, give you a failing grade for the assignment, and choose not to have it become a part of your permanent academic record. In other cases, the instructor has little say in the matter and must refer it to a different administrator.

Your attitude and how you deal with the instructor and the process can play a role in what happens. Consider the difference between apologizing and taking responsibility versus blaming the instructor or the software. Also, if you are invited to schedule a hearing and fail to respond, recognize that the judicial officer has to make a decision without your input.

Chapter 14

Finishing and Submitting Your Assignments

....

In This Chapter

▶ Reading and interpreting rubrics to your advantage

▶ Writing for the best grade

▶ Understanding the variety of possible assignments

▶ Turning it all in

....

*F*rom earlier chapters in this book, you know the drill: how to log in, who's in class, and how and why you should communicate clearly with everyone else. But how do you get a grade? You're not there just to have fun and converse with strangers, are you?

Instructors have several methods of determining how you're doing in class. They may assign papers or projects, or ask you to take a quiz or test. Some determine how you're doing on a weekly basis through your participation in discussions. Hopefully, your class will utilize all these methods!

With technology, getting work to your instructor may require taking a couple extra steps or following different procedures than the traditional classroom environment. This chapter walks you through the basics of getting your assignments turned in so you can get the grade. After all, if you do the work, you deserve the score! We also review the use of rubrics and how to write different types of assignments effectively to help insure the best outcome.

Understanding the Ramifications of Rubrics

Instructors have a challenge explaining to students what they want. In online courses without live communication, it's difficult for students to ask — and for the instructor to answer — the many little questions that come up with an assignment. For that reason, instructors have a clever way of telling you what they want: They use rubrics. *Rubrics* are scoring systems instructors use to evaluate student work. This section gives you the lowdown on rubrics along with insights on how you can use them to your advantage.

Breaking down rubrics

Rubrics sometimes come in chart form, although they may be formatted as lists as well. A rubric makes giving the teacher what she wants doable by categorizing for you the important parts of an assignment that the instructor will judge and making statements about what earns full points. You may find rubrics in a couple locations:

- ✔ **On the home page:** At the start of the course, rubrics are sometimes included in the syllabus or as a separate link to a document with multiple rubrics (for example, one for discussions, one for weekly papers).

- ✔ **On the assignment page:** Sometimes instructors post a rubric within each individual assignment. This is a big hint that they want you to review your own work before submitting it!

For example, look at the rubric in Table 14-1, which describes how a paper in a course will be graded. This rubric presents three levels of quality: excellent, average, and needs improvement. Within each level are specific criteria for judging. You can see that the paper will be judged on the quality of your writing as well as the overall structure and mechanics of the document. Not to mention the fact that the assignment must be turned in on time.

Notice, for example, that if you want full credit, you need to properly cite sources in APA style (see Chapter 13 for more about citations). As for critical thinking, if you identify two problems and don't offer possible solutions, you don't get all the points. On the other hand, if you clearly show the connection between theory and practice and give at least one example, you're home free in critical thinking.

Table 14-1	An Example of a Rubric for a Paper		
Criteria	*Excellent*	*Average*	*Needs Improvement*
Development of ideas and evidence of critical thinking	Essay is well developed, and presentation is logical based on a clear thesis statement with supporting materials, such as course readings, outside research, interviews, and so forth.	Essay is developed in a logical manner; however, thesis statement and/or supporting materials require more depth.	Essay lacks logic in presentation and/or lacks a clear thesis statement with supporting materials such as course readings, outside research, interviews, and so on.
	Essay ideas/examples demonstrate the student's ability to analyze, apply, and synthesize content outside the classroom environment.	Essay ideas/examples do not directly relate to content or adequately demonstrate the student's ability to analyze, apply, and synthesize content outside the classroom environment.	Essay lacks ideas/examples that demonstrate the student's ability to analyze, apply, and synthesize content outside the classroom environment.
	(15 - 20 points)	(10 - 15 points)	(0 - 10 points)
Institution format and structure	Essay demonstrates proper use of institution format and structure by having a properly formatted title page, body, and reference page. Formatting includes proper use of spacing and page numbering.	Essay has a few errors specific to institution format and structure regarding a properly formatted title page, body, and reference page. Formatting includes proper use of spacing and page numbering.	Essay has multiple errors specific to institution format and structure regarding a properly formatted title page, body, and reference page. Formatting includes proper use of spacing and page numbering.
	(4 - 5 points)	(2 - 3 points)	(0 - 2 points)

(continued)

Table 14-1 *(continued)*

Criteria	Excellent	Average	Needs Improvement
Citations and references	Essay properly uses APA style to provide in-text citation and references.	Essay has a few errors specific to APA style regarding in-text citation and references.	Essay has multiple errors specific to APA style regarding in-text citation and references.
	(4 - 5 points)	(2 - 3 points)	(0 - 2 points)
Mechanics	Essay uses standard English mechanics and has few or no grammatical and/or spelling errors.	Essay uses standard English mechanics but has some grammatical and/or spelling errors.	Essay has multiple grammatical and/or spelling errors to the point that meaning is obscured.
	(4 - 5 points)	(2 - 3 points)	(0 - 2 points)
Timeliness	Essay is submitted via the assignment's digital drop-box on or before the scheduled deadline as stated in the course calendar.	Essay is submitted via the assignment's digital drop-box within 24 hours after the scheduled deadline as stated in the course calendar.	Essay submitted via the assignment's digital drop-box more than 24 hours after the scheduled deadline as stated in the course calendar.
	(4 - 5 points)	(1 point)	(0 points)

Using rubrics to your advantage

From your instructor's perspective, a rubric takes the guesswork out of grading. (A lot of instructors love to teach but hate to grade.) With the pre-determined categories in a rubric, the instructor simply measures your work against the ideal as stated in the criteria.

If the instructor can do this, why can't you? Here are a couple of guidelines:

- ✔ **Any time you have an assignment, first read the rubric.** Determine the major criteria and compare these to what you find in the instructions. Make a list that includes both the criteria in the rubric and the criteria given in the instructions. Sometimes instructors forget to put simple instructions like page counts in the rubric, which is why we advise double-checking and making a combined list.

  ✔ **After you write your assignment, judge it for yourself using the rubric.**
  Go through each category and ask yourself for evidence. Pretend you
  are the instructor, and be critical! By writing out the expectations in the
  rubric, your instructor has told you what she will measure and how. You
  can do the same.

Writing 101

The reality is that most online courses are 95 percent text and little audio. That
means instructors and students "talk" with their fingers. Writing skills become
the language! Online students write papers, discussion posts, e-mails, reflections . . . the list seems endless. How well you write, according to the assignment and your instructor's expectations, determines your success. To get the
best grades, you must understand the style you need and the expectations of a
specific assignment. In addition, you must show critical thinking through your
writing. We work through what each of these means in this section.

Checking out different writing styles

Think about everything you wrote today. This list may include a text message to your boyfriend, a newsy e-mail to your mom, your grocery list, some
discussion posts for school, and countless documents for work. Did they all
sound the same in terms of style and form? We hope not!

What you write for class depends on the assignment and the audience. This
section considers different types of writing you can use in an online course.

Academic or scholarly writing

You use academic or scholarly writing in assignments such as short essays,
long papers, and group projects. This kind of writing calls for a different
"voice" — a more serious tone with academic embellishments. It stands apart
from everyday writing in several ways:

  ✔ **The organization is obvious.** Whether you're writing an essay or a dissertation, academic disciplines have clear expectations for organized
  writing. At the essay or paper level, this means related paragraphs that
  begin with topic sentences and are held together with a main thesis. On
  a larger scale, this means chapters held together with a primary thesis.

  ✔ **The vocabulary changes.** When you write about your academic area of
  interest, you need to use the correct vocabulary for the context. This is
  not to say that you have to use multisyllabic words to impress the reader,
  but you do need to be precise and accurate in vocabulary use. For example, in nursing you might describe a patient as being in a supine position,
  whereas in other contexts you'd refer to the person as sitting.

✔ **You use outside references to support your ideas.** In an academic paper, simply writing your opinion isn't enough. You need to back up your ideas with legitimate sources from other authors. Anytime you quote, summarize, or refer to someone else's work, you need to properly cite the source. The format for citations depends on your discipline and your instructor's preference. We write about finding resources at length in Chapter 11 and discuss the need for citations to avoid plagiarism in Chapter 13.

Read the rubric for any assignment carefully, as we suggest earlier in this chapter. Chances are good that it will mention that you need to appropriately cite references as a condition of the assignment.

✔ **The grammar follows standard conventions.** In academic writing, punctuation, spelling, and syntax all count. What is passable in spoken English isn't always acceptable in written form.

If this is a weakness of yours, we highly recommend that you seek assistance, either through an online service available through your college or a Web site you find particularly helpful. For example, Purdue University's Online Writing Lab (OWL) is a wonderful Web-based resource at `http://owl.english.purdue.edu/`.

The following items shouldn't appear in academic writing:

✔ **Colloquialisms and exclamations:** Ya know what I mean? Gee whiz, like, you just gotta learn to write or yer gonna flunk! This kind of casualness is unacceptable in an academic paper.

✔ **Texting language:** A whole new language has been invented thanks to mobile telephones and text. Abbreviations such as LOL or IDK have almost become mainstream. (If you're really out of the loop, LOL is short for *laughing out loud* and IDK means *I don't know.*) Yet as mainstream as you may think these abbreviations are, your instructor and fellow students may have no idea what you're saying. For this reason, texting language is inappropriate in online education. Keep it on your phone.

Casual conversation

There are appropriate places within an online course for casual conversation. For example, if your instructor sets up a discussion area called "Student Lounge" or "Cafe," you can pretty much assume she doesn't expect scholarly writing in those forums. Also, some instructors allow for more casual student-to-student responses within discussion.

Here's an example. Suppose coauthor Kevin has to answer a discussion question about an educational theorist. Following the guidelines and the rubric of the instructor provided, Kevin writes three scholarly-sounding paragraphs, including references to two outside sources. He follows APA style as requested by his instructor.

In response, coauthor Susan writes, *"Wow! I just had an epiphany! You are so on target with your analysis of this theory. I was just telling my sister yesterday about how. . . ."*

Susan's style and tone is a little too casual for academic or scholarly writing, but it's appropriate as a response to Kevin's post.

Knowing what's expected in your writing

Before you plunge into a writing assignment, take a look at what's expected. You can find this information within the instructions and the rubric. Three important aspects that influence how you write are the type of assignment, the length or word count, and any formatting requirements.

Remember how we advise you to make a list of criteria based on the rubric plus the instructions in the earlier section "Using rubrics to your advantage"? If you do this, you can't help but meet the expectations.

Recognizing the type of assignment

Read your assignment instructions carefully so you know what's appropriate to include in your writing. Although all assignments require academic writing (which we describe earlier in this chapter), some of them allow more of your personality to shine through.

Think about the differences among a journal entry, a critique, and a literature review. Each of these calls for a slightly different type of writing:

- ✓ **A journal entry** is personal and written in first person, meaning it's quite appropriate to use the word "I."

- ✓ **A critique** is less personal but involves judgment. It may also refer to other resources and texts, thereby requiring proper citation.

- ✓ **A literature review** is a little more cut and dried with no judgment, just summary and reporting. It obviously requires references and citations.

Nothing is wrong with asking for an example. If you're confused from the beginning and can't get started with an assignment, ask your instructor whether she can share an example from the past.

Counting words to get the length right

How many words or pages you're allowed for a specific assignment tells you a lot about the writing. If your instructor asks you to answer a discussion question in 300 to 500 words, she's not looking for a full-blown paper on the topic! This also means that you need to write succinctly. Get to the point as quickly as possible, and then add a few examples. We recommend you restate a portion of the question in your first sentence and skip lengthy introductions or storytelling.

On the other hand, if you're assigned a ten-page paper, the instructor expects you to fully develop each idea and back it up with outside resources. You can take a little more time and space to add details and illustrations of your main ideas.

Most word-processing programs can help you determine your word count. If the count doesn't show in your bottom task bar, go to file information or properties and see whether the statistics are available there.

Formatting correctly

Check with your instructor about institutional formatting requirements. Do you need a title page? What margins are standard, and is there a preferred font? Should you number the pages? Some institutions have very specific guidelines, and you want to know what they are before you start.

If your institution or instructor has formatting requirements, this information is usually found in the syllabus and again within the instructions for each assignment. If it's an institutional guideline, the institution may even provide you with a sample document that you overwrite so you know your formatting is correct.

Demonstrating critical thinking

Coauthor Susan remembers asking a student a question once in a traditional face-to-face classroom and seeing the student visibly think through the response. He took the concept she was discussing, broke it into pieces, related it to something he had read, and then gave a well reasoned, theoretically grounded response with his own insights. His eyes squinted, he rubbed his chin, and he spoke slowly with a few pauses. This was critical thinking in action in a traditional classroom. How does this work online?

Online your instructor may not see your quizzical looks or chin-rubbing, but she can tell whether you thought critically about the question before you gave your response. She determines this through the quality of what you write. Your thoughts become transparent through your writing.

If you're not clear on the definition, *critical thinking* is the application of disciplined, thoughtful analysis to a problem. It combines what the experts say about the situation, what you know from life experience, and a dose of rational thought. You first break down the problem, and then reassemble it with your own evaluation.

There is no magical formula for giving an A+ answer in critical thinking, but here are some telltale signs that you're on the right track. Do the mental stretch and you'll be rewarded with better grades! Try to incorporate these indicators into your written work:

- ✔ **Look at the question from multiple perspectives and explain this clearly.** Some people rush to judgment, but if you can show the "other side" of an argument or perspective, you're in a better position to demonstrate critical thinking.

- ✔ **Actively ask questions.** People with strong critical thinking skills ask questions like, "What if . . ." or "How could the author have stated this differently?" Asking a lot of questions before you write may help you organize your thoughts, too!

- ✔ **Find support through literature or research.** Critical thinking requires you to look beyond your own opinion and compare what you believe or know to others' ideas. In most academic writing, this is where we expect you to weave in references to other studies, books, or literature.

- ✔ **Figure out how this relates to you and real life.** Any time you can put something into today's context, it demonstrates critical thinking. It shows you've reconstructed the idea.

Instructors know when students don't think before they type, so don't just sit down and start typing your assignment. Organize your thoughts by outlining the assignment first. In your outline, define the problem, summarize the literature, clarify your thoughts/opinions on the topic, and note examples of past experiences or possible future applications.

Completing Different Types of Assignments

Instructors measure student achievement in many different ways, all of which come in the form of assignments. You may be asked to write a paper, put together a project, participate in discussion, or take a quiz or test. In this section, we look at each type of assignment and what it means to an online student.

Mastering papers and projects

For college-level online courses, papers and projects are the most common assignments. They keep students busy throughout a portion of the course and are a good vehicle for having students comprehensively review major course concepts. If you're asked to submit a paper or project, consider the following ideas for success.

Papers

One of the most common assignments online students receive is "the paper." The following are examples of papers you may be asked to write:

- ✔ Write a ten-page essay on your philosophy of integrating technology.

- ✔ Write a five-page paper on your theories related to the causes of the Civil War.

- ✔ Compare and contrast in a three-page paper the structures and functions of animal cells versus plant cells.

Your instructor looks for several markers of quality:

- ✔ **Organized writing:** As we explain earlier in this chapter, scholarly writing requires organization. Whatever your topic, develop a clear thesis and present it from the beginning. Then write in a manner that supports the thesis.

- ✔ **Points of view other than yours:** Instructors want to see you've done the research and can summarize or quote from the experts. Citation is required!

- ✔ **Original ideas:** While your instructor expects you to research and provide sources for your background knowledge, she also expects you to develop some original ideas. Don't just tell what the experts say; add your own insights based on past experiences and intellectual speculation.

Here are a few of the most common blunders we've observed:

- ✔ **Not answering the question that was asked.** There's nothing more heart-wrenching than seeing a student submit a paper that has nothing to do with the question that was asked. As teachers, we assume that you put some work into this, and we hate to think that you wasted your time.

  Therefore, save your teacher and yourself some heartache and make sure you understand the question she asks! In fact, sending a private e-mail to double-check that you have it right before you start writing isn't a bad idea.

- ✔ **Failure to cite any outside resources.** At the college level, inclusion of research and resources is a basic expectation.

- ✔ **Confusing writing or writing that's full of nothing.** Sometimes we see writing that's poorly organized or grammatically askew, making it difficult to understand what the student wants to say. Or, the student goes on needlessly with little substance (we're being polite here!).

  There are a couple ways to check for confusing reading. First is to ask someone who knows nothing about the subject to read your paper. Clueless people are very helpful, sometimes. Absent the extra reader, eliminate all the extra phrases and make the sentences short. Get to the point. Then, see what sentences you can combine to make the piece read a little more fluidly.

Projects

Instead of papers, your instructor may assign projects. Like papers, these generally call for a comprehensive understanding of the course content, but you complete them with a variety of tools. Consider these examples:

- ✔ Develop a Web page that shows an image, a banner, and a table.
- ✔ Create a spreadsheet you could use as a general ledger for a small business.
- ✔ Design a ten-minute presentation to sell your colleagues on the idea of social networking.

Projects allow you to show a great deal of creativity. Unless you are told which tool to use, you can explore different kinds of presentational tools. For example, you could build a narrated presentation using a Web-based tool such as Jing at www.jingproject.com. Or, you could upload images and slides to a service such as SlideShare at www.slideshare.net.

Most projects come with a rubric. Especially if the activity is complex, instructors provide guidelines and rubrics to help you determine whether you are meeting all the criteria. In the same way that you need to carefully read the rubric for any written work (as we explain earlier in this chapter), you should do the same for a project in order to complete it successfully.

Participating in discussions

The heart and soul of many online courses is the discussion area. This is where students answer key questions and respond to each other by replying to each other's messages and offering multiple perspectives. We have a few ideas about how to make your participation shine in terms of quality and quantity, even without seeing your instructor's rubric. (Flip to Chapter 10 for an introduction to discussions.)

Quality

Quality always trumps quantity! Take your time to answer your question succinctly yet thoroughly. Introduce some of the literature you've been reading in class or refer to other sources you know of. Of course, add appropriate citations.

A good pattern to establish is: Restate the question, present your initial view in one sentence, point to some of the literature on the topic, and close with an interpretation of what this means in real life. If you can do that in a grammatically clean and clear fashion, you'll be submitting quality work.

Before you hit the post or submit button, proofread and double check for accuracy!

With respect to your responses to other students, the instructor looks for quality writing here, too. You may want to say, "I agree!" but your instructor expects you to add why you agree with some depth of thought. Follow up with an additional point from the literature or an example that exemplifies some data the original author proposed. Don't just post, "Me too!"

A good rule of thumb is to ask yourself whether the work you post has instructional value. Can people learn something from what you have written? If not, consider reworking the response.

Quantity

How often you post responses to other students depends somewhat on the nature of the class, the instructor's expectations, and the learning community. Typically, the instructor notes the minimum number of posts she wants to see. Be sure you know the expectations, which are typically described in a rubric handed out at the beginning of your course or within the instructions for the assignment.

Reading and following discussions can become overwhelming in an online course if students post too frequently. Plus, the conversations can get long and drawn out and break down to little more than trivial responses. And yet, your presence on the discussion board is one of the few ways the instructor knows whether you're engaged. By all means, meet the expectations, but then nudge yourself to go a little higher.

Look at your postings and see whether you're monopolizing the discussion board. If you're authoring more than 10 percent of the total posts, you're probably overactive. Pace yourself!

Taking quizzes and tests

One final method of measuring student success is the traditional quiz or test. Whether you're asked multiple-choice questions or essay questions, quizzes and tests are relatively easy for instructors to administer and, in cases where the computer does the scoring, results are immediate.

When an instructor decides that a quiz or test is an appropriate measure of student achievement, she makes several decisions concerning the administration of the test. These clearly impact the students! You may encounter these types of quizzes and tests:

- ✔ **Tests with all kinds of questions.** Most testing software allows the instructor to choose from multiple choice, true/false, short answer, and essay questions. This is nothing new to you as a student. The only thing that may be new is clicking in a box with your mouse instead of filling in a form with a pencil.

✔ **Tests that have a time limit.** You may be limited in how long you have to complete the test. Instructors commonly leave a test "open" for only a few days and then set the software so that you must answer all the questions within so many minutes. This is to discourage you from looking at other sources (like your book) for answers. You have to know the material and answer quickly.

✔ **Self-quizzes with no score.** Sometimes instructors build "self" quizzes to test your knowledge before taking a test for points. Practice makes perfect, so if you have the opportunity, test yourself!

✔ **Open book/note exams.** To be truthful, we advise faculty to assume students will use whatever resources they have available, including notes, books, and browsers. Your instructor may tell you that using your resources is permissible.

✔ **Mail-in pencil exams.** Believe it or not, in some cases an online instructor may ask you to complete a paper/pencil exam and mail it in.

When you have an independent third party monitor your exam, we say it is *proctored.* Proctors are like exam police making sure you are who you say you are and that you're not cheating. For high-stake exams, schools insist on proctors. The methods for proctoring vary. You may be required to take a test

✔ **At a center on-campus with a restricted IP range.** If you're taking the course from your local college, you may be required to come to campus and take the exam on their computers in their assessment center. This may not be the most convenient method, but it verifies identity and prevents you from using materials you may have saved on your computer.

✔ **With a professional "contractual" proctor.** Your school may allow you to find a proctor in your city and get that person authorized to monitor you. For example, coauthor Kevin proctors for a student he used to work with. When she has an exam, she takes it in front of him, he signs the exam to verify she was honest, and then he mails it to the school. If a school requires a proctor, they'll give you guidelines for types of people who are acceptable. Library staff are always favorite choices!

✔ **By using a Web-based service with enhanced technology.** There are now companies that proctor exams online with technology like Web cameras. For example, ProctorU at www.proctoru.com/ has students log in, talk to a live proctor at the other end of the technology, turn on a Web cam, scan the environment where they're taking the exam, and then take the exam. All of this is an attempt to make sure the person completing the exam is really you!

How well you do on an exam depends on old-fashioned study skills. Chapter 11 guides you through strategies such as setting aside time every day to keep up with coursework, reading effectively, and taking notes. But perhaps the most valuable tip is staying engaged and active to increase your chances of success. The more you work with the ideas, either by reading discussions, taking self-tests, or practicing problem sets, the better your retention. If you're engaged and prepared, there's no need to panic at exam time!

Submitting Assignments

Think back to middle school (if it isn't too painful to remember those days!). Did you ever complete a homework assignment and forget to take it to school and turn it in? The same thing can happen online; you do the work and forget to submit it. In this section, we review several methods for getting your homework to the instructor. These include drop-boxes, e-mail attachments, and "submit" buttons. We also provide some pointers for turning in any kind of assignment.

Drop-boxes and e-mail attachments for papers and projects

Some course management systems use a "drop-box" feature whereby students upload assignments. Different from e-mail, you can only put the document in one place and you don't need to know the instructor's address. The instructor retrieves your document, downloads it, and reads it. She may then comment on it and add a score to the grade book all within the same drop-box tool.

If there's a secret to using drop-boxes, it's knowing how to upload and hitting pthe submit button until you get a confirmation. In most systems, you look for a button that says "Add a file" or "Upload." This prompts you to browse your computer to find the file. Usually you click Open once you identify the file you want, and then hit Submit. Your next screen should be a confirmation that the file has been uploaded! Figure 14-1 shows what a drop-box looks like from the student view in Desire2Learn®.

If your instructor doesn't use the drop-box feature or doesn't have this tool available, she may ask you to attach your work to an e-mail. This process works the same as attaching photos to send to your dear cousin Ted. You find the attachment icon, usually a paper clip, browse for the file, and upload. The uploading skill seems to be universal, whether you're attaching a document to an e-mail or a discussion board posting. (Chapter 3 has the basics on fundamental e-mail skills you should have before you enroll in an online course.)

Post, Emily! Submitting discussion posts

When you have a discussion question to post or respond to, the magic words change slightly.

Figure 14-1:
A drop-box in Desire2 Learn.

✔ **Compose:** Look for this button if you need to start a new discussion, one that isn't attached to anyone else's idea.

✔ **Reply:** Use this button when you want to respond to something another person wrote. Here's a super tip: Copy and paste one or two lines from the original text (delete the rest) so you can quote the first author and focus your comments.

✔ **Post:** After you have composed or replied, you must remember to hit Post or Submit. Otherwise, your great ideas don't appear on the discussion board.

The "submit" button on quizzes and tests

Your teachers probably told you this when you were younger: Check your work before you turn in the test. Make sure you answered every question. Technology has an interesting way of forcing you to do this with online quizzes and tests. It's called the "submit" button. Look at Figure 14-2, and you'll see that in this case, you're given the option to Submit, Save without submitting, Submit page, and Submit all and finish. All of these make you think twice and check your work!

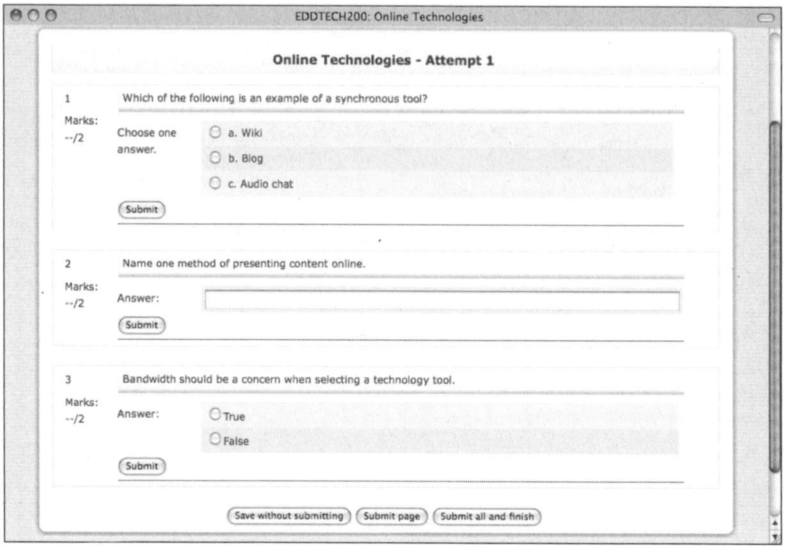

EDDTECH200: Online Technologies

Online Technologies - Attempt 1

1
Marks:
--/2

Which of the following is an example of a synchronous tool?

Choose one
answer.

○ a. Wiki

○ b. Blog

○ c. Audio chat

(Submit)

2
Marks:
--/2

Name one method of presenting content online.

Answer: [   ]

(Submit)

3
Marks:
--/2

Bandwidth should be a concern when selecting a technology tool.

Answer: ○ True

○ False

(Submit)

(Save without submitting) (Submit page) (Submit all and finish)

Figure 14-2:
A quiz page
in Moodle
shows
different
variations
on the "sub-
mit" button.

Tips for submitting any assignment

Whether you're working with papers, projects, discussion posts, quizzes, or tests, consider the following general pointers: Submit early, have a backup plan, and keep a copy. Here's why these are important:

✔ **Submit early when possible in case of problems:** What if you plan to submit your assignment at 11:56 p.m. on the night it's due by midnight, and the whole system crashes or your hard drive freezes? You don't have a lot of time to remedy that situation. A safer bet is to submit your work during normal working hours, well before you need to. That way if you encounter a problem, you're more likely to contact a real tech-support person who can assist you (see Chapter 9 for more information on technical support).

✔ **Attach to e-mail when technology fails:** Still on the 11:56 p.m. track? When all else fails, send the same assignment as an attachment to an e-mail to your instructor. Include a polite note explaining that the system wasn't cooperating and that you wanted to be sure to get the assignment turned in one way or another. This shows good problem-solving skills.

✔ **Keep a copy:** Always, always keep copies of your work for the term of the course. You never know when you might need them. It's common for the system to freeze up when you're trying to submit a great discussion post (always when you've written something worthy of a Pulitzer), so if you first compose in a word processor and then copy and paste to the discussion area, you're safe in knowing that you have the original text. Should there be any question, you can find the file and resubmit it.

Chapter 15

Transitioning after School

. . . .

. . . .

*I*n Chapter 5, we talk about finding a program and institution that meet your needs. Why are you in school? The vision of your goal should be a constant driving force throughout your academic career. Keeping your main objective in mind helps motivate you to complete courses and stay on track.

If you plan to look for the perfect job after you finish your online education, collecting a few artifacts throughout your journey can help you when it comes time to prepare for interviews. Artifacts are like souvenirs of your trip. They should demonstrate your skills and abilities within the field. This chapter introduces some ideas on how to find and prepare for that dream interview through the creation of an *ePortfolio*.

Developing an ePortfolio

A portfolio is a physical document that outlines a person's past work, both academic and professional. It demonstrates skills and abilities by providing sample work created in various work and school settings.

An ePortfolio does the same thing, but instead of sharing a physical document with prospective employers, you simply provide them with the URL to a Web site where the same information is stored digitally, either for public viewing or by private invitation only. Figure 15-1 illustrates what a public ePortfolio may look like (specifically, this figure is the public view of the Desire2Learn® ePortfolio 2.0). The illustration displays a single project a student documented on his ePortfolio site. On this particular student's site, he allows visitors to interact with him by providing the ability to leave comments specific to the information being displayed.

Courtesy of Desire2Learn Incorporated

Figure 15-1:
The public
view of
the Desire
2Learn
ePortfolio
2.0.

In this section, we explain how you can use an ePortfolio to your advantage, and we describe its components. We also help you choose a method for building an ePortfolio, provide pointers for successful design, and tell you how to include items that aren't a part of your online coursework.

Understanding how to use an ePortfolio

You can use an ePortfolio in two important ways:

✔ **To satisfy educational requirements:** Many degree programs now require students to build and maintain an ePortfolio throughout their academic career as a way of documenting growth and highlighting their academic accomplishments. In this situation, students are often asked to also reflect on the experience of creating the artifacts added to the ePortfolio as a way of assessing the student's understanding of the project overall (see the later section "Reflection statements" for more information). As a degree program requirement, graduating is dependent upon the completion of the ePortfolio. Some institutions even require a formal presentation to accompany the project.

✔ **To land a job:** ePortfolios can also be used for promoting your knowledge, skills, and abilities to prospective employers. When applying for a new job or promotion, you can share your ePortfolio's Web site address (URL) with the hiring manager. The hiring manager can visit your site and get a clearer picture of your academic and work experiences to facilitate the hiring decision.

Checking out typical components of an ePortfolio

You can choose several items from your online coursework to add to your ePortfolio. Choose the pieces carefully and organize your site in a manner that's logical and easy to navigate. This section reviews different types of items and provides some examples of specific information to include.

Attaching artifacts such as papers and projects

Artifacts are objects created by you that can be added to your ePortfolio as attachments. When adding artifacts to your ePortfolio, you want to be sure your audience understands why you included them. Therefore, for each artifact be sure to include a title, description, and the context in which the artifact was created.

When adding artifacts to your site, keep in mind that visitors will be downloading your work directly to their computer. Therefore, consider protecting files before uploading and linking them to your ePortfolio (we show you how in Chapter 3). This allows visitors to open and view your documents, but not edit them.

Here are a few examples of the different types of artifacts you may want to consider adding to your ePortfolio (Figure 15-2 shows the administration page for uploading and organizing different types of artifacts in the Desire2Learn ePortfolio 2.0):

✔ **A document:** For example, an essay on the connection between Bloom's Taxonomy and ePortfolios as it relates to education. Consider using text to briefly summarize the essay's contents with a link to click on to download the document in its entirety.

✔ **Images:** Perhaps a series of digital images that you took and modified for an online photography course. Consider using text to describe the images and the purpose for taking them.

✔ **An audio file:** For instance, an audio interview you conducted with a professional in your field. Consider adding a written transcript and general description of the assignment when attaching an audio file to your ePortfolio.

✔ **A PowerPoint presentation:** Say, a group presentation on the benefits and challenges of creating and maintaining a Web site for your Web development course. Consider describing your contributions to the project and the tools you used to collaborate with your group in a reflection statement (see the next section).

✔ **A video file:** For example, a video illustrating your ability to take, edit, and encode video for your Introduction to Video Editing course. Consider adding a written transcript and general description of the assignment when attaching a video file to your ePortfolio.

If your institution doesn't require you to use an ePortfolio system, please be sure to acquire your instructors' permission before posting graded work with their comments on it. Instructors may ask you not to display their comments or grades publically. The reason for this isn't that they treated you differently than other students; it's because it has the potential to stir up other classmates who may not have done as well as you.

Figure 15-2:
An artifact in the Desire 2Learn ePortfolio 2.0.

Creating reflection statements

Reflection statements are used in the academic world as a way of helping the instructor assess your process as well as your final product. These statements can be very helpful to both instructors and employers reviewing your ePortfolio for either academic or professional reasons. For example, by seeing your reflections on a project you completed in school, an employer can see how you organize and process information in order to obtain a goal.

The length of a reflection statement can range from one paragraph to multiple pages, depending on the context. A good rule of thumb is to briefly describe the project, the educational objectives it meets, how the project can be applied, and what you learned from completing the project. For example, following is a reflection on an assignment requiring the creation of an ePortfolio Web site:

> *"By requiring me to organize and document all of my academic, professional, and volunteer experiences, I have been able to better understand where I have been, where I am currently, and where I am going. As a part of this project, I was required to learn about the resources and services available to create an online portfolio. The design process required me to develop a site that organizes my information into manageable chunks while maintaining an easy navigation structure for my visitors. This project also forced me to reflect on each assignment and how lessons learned could be applied in my life outside of the classroom. As a living document, my ePortfolio will continue to be updated, and therefore require me to continuously reflect and grow with my field."*

Providing informal transcripts of courses

Posting transcripts on your ePortfolio Web site lets your visitors see your level of dedication and provides a general sense of the quality of your work. You can let your visitors know what grade you earned for each course or your cumulative grade point average (GPA) for a program in a couple ways:

- ✔ **You can simply provide your cumulative grade point average (for example, 4.8/5.0) on the program description page and the actual grade earned (A, B, and so on) next to the title of each course.** In this case, the reader has to believe you.

- ✔ **You can scan your official transcript, adding it to your ePortfolio as an artifact and linking to it from your program's description page.** Of course, scanning your transcript, even an official transcript, takes away its official status. Prospective employers may still require you to send them official transcripts directly from the institution in a sealed envelope.

If for any reason you had a bad semester (and many people do), consider not adding this information to your ePortfolio. Most employers don't require this information, and if they do, you can supply them with official transcripts upon request. Being consistent in presentation and supplying this information for all courses and programs is better than posting it only for those courses you did well in.

Including recommendations from faculty

There are no better people to serve as your advocates than your instructors. They know the quality of work you produce and the level of dedication you put forth to complete your assignments. Therefore, be sure to build a professional relationship with them, and don't be afraid to ask them for letters of recommendation. Here are some guidelines to follow:

- ✔ **Be selective about which instructors you ask for a recommendation.** You don't need a recommendation from every instructor. One way of filtering is to ask only those instructors who teach subjects that most resemble the type of work you're doing or hope to be doing in the future.

- ✔ **Don't wait until you've completed your program to ask for a recommendation.** Timing is everything. Think ahead and ask each instructor at the end of the course, when your participation and the quality of your work are fresh in the teacher's memory.

- ✔ **Provide instructors with an overview of your professional goals and a link to your ePortfolio.** Doing so helps them write a letter that matches your career goals. You can also send them your resume if your ePortfolio is still in progress.

- ✔ **Provide instructors with two or three weeks to complete the letter.** Extending this courtesy gives them time to turn in grades and review your information more before writing.

- ✔ **Be sure to explain to your instructors exactly what you're looking for and the fact that you would like to publicly display the recommendation on your ePortfolio Web site.** Many institutions house instructor recommendations in the student's file, but these recommendations are anonymous to the student, making them unsuitable for your purpose.

Incorporating your resume and work history

Have you ever wanted to add more details to your resume so that prospective employers see what you really do on a daily basis? The nice thing about having an ePortfolio is that it gives you the ability to expand on things you can't fit on a two-page resume.

Though this is a great feature, don't forget to spread chunks of information across multiple pages so that everything isn't on the same page — you don't want to overwhelm the reader. Arrange chunks of information by dates of service and organization. Following is a list of components to add when including work history in your ePortfolio:

- ✔ **Organization profile:** Provide the organization's name, geographic location, and mission.

- ✔ **Position title:** Include the title of the position(s) you held within the organization and a brief description of the position's overall purpose.

- ✔ **Dates of service:** Sequence your position titles within each organization by dates of services, in descending order. This puts your most recent experience at the top of the list.

- ✔ **Accomplishments:** Provide a bulleted list of the accomplishments by stating the tasks you handled, how you accomplished each task, and the end result in quantifiable terms when possible. For example, you might say: "Created a database that analyzed recoverable charges to the organization, which led to the company's recovery of 1.5 million dollars."

- ✔ **Project artifacts:** Provide artifacts for the accomplishments listed when possible. For example, you could provide an empty copy of the database that was created to recover the 1.5 million dollars noted in the preceding bullet.

Don't forget to remove private information that could violate the law or have negative repercussions. For example, in the preceding database example, you'd want to share the database with either no data or fictitious data in it, so that viewers could see what you developed without seeing the private information used by the organization, such as names, addresses, dollar amounts, and so forth.

Sharing favorite resource links

Providing your visitors with a list of resources proves that you're aware of what's going on within your field. Plus, it provides you with a single location to return to when you need to find information yourself. Resources can include links to professional blogs, podcasts, journal articles, associations, conferences, citation style resources, career help, and other academic resources.

This is not the place to link to your favorite satire blog, cartoon site, or daily word puzzle; stick to professional links.

Choosing a method for creating an ePortfolio

You can go about creating an ePortfolio in three different ways: You can use institutional resources, subscribe to a service, or create your own from scratch.

Using institutional resources

Your institution may incorporate the use of an ePortfolio system in its program curriculum, which you are subsequently required to use. This system may be either built-in or external:

✔ Some institutions build ePortfolio programs into their course management systems and tie them directly to each major assignment's rubric. This allows the student to upload the assignment and import the instructor's assessment with comments to the ePortfolio system.

✔ Some institutions alternatively use an external service in a similar fashion, but it requires the student to log in to a separate Web site using a different username and password. The system may also have the capability of allowing instructors to create rubrics to attach to artifacts. However, in this situation, the instructor is required to also log in to a separate system and copy/paste rubric elements and assessment comments to that system.

To find out whether or not your institution provides an ePortfolio system, first ask your academic advisor. If he is unable to help, you can either contact your instructor or career services staff. Some institutions provide a career-oriented ePortfolio product, which is often available after graduation for a yearly or monthly fee.

Either way, this type of ePortfolio system allows the institution to dictate some of the artifacts to be added, along with their respective grades and instructor comments. Required artifacts could include course essays, final projects, or reflection assignments. By having all this information in one place, program faculty and deans can see each student's growth throughout the program as a way of assessing student performance and program effectiveness.

One benefit to using your institution's required ePortfolio system is that you're already paying for it through program fees. Therefore, you won't have an external cost to use it while you're a student. However, the possible down side is the fact that you may be required to subscribe to that service upon graduation in order to maintain your site and its contents. In some situations, you get to continue using the service for one year after graduation before having to decide whether to subscribe to that service or re-create your site by building it yourself or subscribing to a different service.

Subscribing to a service

You can subscribe to a service if your school doesn't have a required ePortfolio system or you prefer to exercise more control over its contents. Several subscription-based services offer Web space for you to house and display your ePortfolio. These services offer templates for adding content and disk storage for uploading documents and other artifacts. Following are a few such services:

- ✔ **TaskStream:** www.taskstream.com
- ✔ **Pupil Pages:** www.os4e.com/pupilpages/pupilpages.htm
- ✔ **Live Text:** https://college.livetext.com/college/

One advantage to subscribing to a service is that it provides online templates for you to complete, requiring only Web navigation skills and your portfolio content. Another advantage is the ability to lock down your site so that only invited guests can view it.

Of course, these sites cost money, so prepare to pay for the convenience, and keep paying the bill. Imagine the embarrassment of sending a potential employer to your site and finding out that it's not available because you forgot to make a payment!

Creating your own ePortfolio from the ground up

The third method of building an ePortfolio is to create your own from scratch. The biggest advantage to creating your own ePortfolio is the ability to customize the design and navigation of the site to reflect your individuality. When you subscribe to a service, you're limited to the number of templates available from the service provider, which means your portfolio may physically look like those of other students who subscribe to the same service.

The biggest drawback to creating your own ePortfolio is that you're limited to your own programming skills. Programming your own site also requires more time because you have to create the design of the site as well as the content that will be placed within the site.

If you want to create your own site, you need the following:

- ✔ **A Web hosting service:** A service where you can store your site so that it's available to others with an Internet connection. One example is http://dreamhost.com.
- ✔ **A registered domain name:** Domain names are used as the Web site address for navigating to your site, for example, http://kevinjohn-sonresume.info. Most Web hosting services have a process that includes registering and paying for your domain.
- ✔ **Programming knowledge:** You need to be able to program using HTML or other Web programming languages, such as PHP. If your online education has focused on these languages, you're set! But if you don't

have this knowledge and want to learn, consider picking up *Creating Web Pages For Dummies,* 9th Edition, by Bud E. Smith (Wiley) to help you get started. You can also consider using an HTML editing program such as Dreamweaver, which uses a more visual approach to programming, allowing the user to enter information on the screen while it writes the code in the background. And, of course there's a resource for that too if needed: *Dreamweaver CS4 All-in-One For Dummies* by Sue Jenkins and Richard Wagner, also from Wiley.

Some students have found creative ways to use free Web 2.0 tools, such as blogs and Wikis, to create ePortfolios for free. These tools often require less programming skills and don't cost you a dime!

Designing a successful ePortfolio

Think about all the things you've accomplished as an employee, a volunteer, and/or a student. You probably have quite a list. The most helpful tip we can provide is to advise you to find a way to organize your information into chunks so that visitors can quickly access data without being overwhelmed. Here are a few more tips for designing a successful ePortfolio site:

✔ **Create a top-level navigation based on categories:** Organize information into logical sections and create a Web menu and navigation system around that structure. For example, consider organizing your information using the following categories: Home, Overview, Education, Work Experience, and Community Involvement.

✔ **Create a sub-level navigation within your top-level categories:** Arrange and sequence the information in each of the top-level categories based on dates, organizations, job titles, and so on. For example, when a visitor clicks on Education, he should see a list of institutions you've attended, the dates you attended, a brief description of the program you were enrolled in, and links that give him the option to see a list of specific courses, course syllabi, and course-specific projects. When a user clicks on Work Experience, a page should appear with a list of job titles, organizations, brief job descriptions, dates of employment, and links to specific job responsibilities and projects for each job. Figure 15-3 illustrates what sub-level navigation in an ePortfolio may look like (specifically, this figure shows sub-level navigation in the Desire2Learn ePortfolio 2.0).

✔ **Create a welcome page:** The first thing a visitor to your ePortfolio site should see is a welcoming screen with basic information such as your name, current position, contact information, and possibly a picture. Think of this page as a digital business card.

✔ **Create an overview page:** The overview page should include a brief overview of who you are academically/professionally, what you've learned from your school/work experience, and how your education has been applied in different situations. Think of this page as your digital cover letter, preparing visitors to view your digital resume.

✓ **Know your audience:** Understanding why you are creating your ePortfolio can help you design for and write to your audience. For example, you may write differently for your instructors than you would for future employers. Because your ePortfolio may be shown to multiple audiences, be sure that the description of each component reflects the intended context. For example, when writing for instructors, provide an overview of each assignment along with what you learned specific to the objectives of the course. When writing for a more general audience, again provide an overview of each assignment, along with how you scored, what you learned from the project, and how what you learned can be applied to other situations such as a work environment.

✓ **Be authentic and cite sources when necessary:** Displaying work that's authentic in nature and providing sources when you share non-original ideas are important. Remember, this site is a reflection of you, including your ethical standards.

✓ **Keep your information up-to-date:** A portfolio is always a work in progress. However, unlike your physical portfolio, viewers may have access to your ePortfolio at any time. Therefore, it's important to keep your information current.

Figure 15-3:
Sub-level
navigation
in the Desire
2Learn
ePortfolio
2.0.

Courtesy of Desire2Learn Incorporated

Transferring your existing portfolio to the Web

You may have previous work, volunteer, or education experiences from an existing portfolio that you want to include in an ePortfolio. Great! The next step is to prepare that material for the Web. Here is a list of the different artifact types and considerations to make when transferring them to the Web:

✔ **Word processing documents:** Consider converting short (one page or less) word processing documents to HTML so that visitors don't have to download them. Save longer documents as one of the more common file types so that visitors can view your work in multiple applications. Some of the more popular document types include .pdf, .rtf, and .doc. Each of these formats can be opened with either a free document viewer or a basic word-processing program that comes installed on most computers.

✔ **Images/photographs:** Unless you're in the field of marketing or photography, consider reducing image size and resolution to a Web-friendly configuration. Web files should be set at 72 dpi (dots per inch) and around 20 to 50k (kilobyte) in size. A great free program has been created for both Windows and Mac machines that can help you do this quickly: Gimp (www.gimp.org). Reducing image size and resolution allows for quick loading. Common image file types include .png, .gif, and .jpg.

Try not to place multiple images on one page when possible. The fewer the photos, the faster the page loads for your visitors.

✔ **Audio files:** Audio files are larger files and can take longer to download. Consider using a compressed audio file type such as .mp3 for adding audio to your ePortfolio. For the more advanced programmer or more up-to-date service providers, embedding streaming audio is better for longer pieces.

Streaming refers to how media such as audio and video files are delivered to a user over the Internet. Audio and video files are often large in size. If visitors are required to wait for the entire file to download to their computer before listening to or viewing the file, they may get bored and navigate to another site. Streaming audio and video files are stored on a Web server and begin to play for the visitor immediately, while slowly continuing to load in the background, so that visitors have less wait time.

✔ **Video files:** Video files are large files that can take a long time for visitors to download. Consider streaming these files as well. Common video file types include .avi and .mpg.

If large video files are needed, consider providing visitors with a clip of the video online and contact information on how to request a full-length video on CD or DVD via snail mail.

No matter what type of artifact you choose to add to your ePortfolio, we recommend that each element have some introductory content that allows your visitors to quickly look at your work and choose which elements they want to explore in greater detail.

Getting Help with Finding a Job

Once your online coursework is done and your ePortfolio site is up-to-date, you may want to find a job that puts your newfound skills to use. Several resources are available to you online to help you in the job search process.

Utilizing career services at your school

Most academic institutions have a career services department to help students who need career counseling, job-searching skills, and other career resources. Most of these services are available online so that they're accessible by both campus-based and online students. If you're not sure whether your institution offers such services, contact your academic advisor (we introduce the role of this important person in Chapter 5).

Services provided by these career centers include:

- **Career counseling:** A career counselor may meet with you one-on-one or in a group setting over the phone to help provide direction in the areas of self-assessment, goal setting, and basic job searching.

- **Job and internship listings:** Most career services departments have a private list where students can view jobs and internship possibilities posted by organizations. These listings are often organized by profession for easy searching.

- **Career and internship fairs:** The fact that you may not live in your school's locality doesn't mean you can't attend a job fair. Online institutions are beginning to offer job fairs online. Organizations are asked to provide quick presentations via synchronous tools such as Elluminate (see Chapter 12), and students are invited to join the session, ask questions, and submit resumes.

- **Career resource Webinars:** Career services staff may also offer Webinars using tools like Elluminate to provide tips, tricks, and other resources on topics such as searching for jobs, building a resume, interviewing, and following-up with prospective employers.

✔ **On-campus recruiting:** Again, just because you're not local, don't assume you can't work for the institution you're attending from a distance. Most likely, some of your instructors didn't live near the campus, right? Online institutions understand that work can be done even when co-workers aren't in the same physical location. So, don't ignore those campus ads when browsing the career service's Web site. Your institution may provide both student jobs and full-time employment upon graduation.

Perusing general job search sites

Whether your institution provides career services or not, you can still do a lot of things outside of the institution to promote yourself. Specifically, several job sites post local, national, and international job opportunities. The advantages of these sites include the number of employers that utilize them and the ability they give you to filter searches by profession and location.

Job search sites usually offer two types of services: free and paid.

✔ **Free services** provide you with general searching capabilities and give you access to several jobs available in your field.

✔ **Paid services** usually include more customized features, such as the ability to create a profile that is placed in a database that's searched by employers.

Job search sites also offer free resources such as strategies for building your resume, searching for jobs, and interviewing. Be sure to review each site's resources to get a variety of ideas, and then customize those strategies to suit your personality and needs.

Here are a few job search databases to consider when conducting your employment search:

✔ **CareerBuilder:** www.careerbuilder.com/

✔ **HotJobs:** http://hotjobs.yahoo.com/

✔ **Indeed:** www.indeed.com/

✔ **Monster:** www.monster.com/

✔ **USA Jobs:** www.usajobs.gov/

Establishing networks while studying online

As you attend your classes, be cognizant of all the networking possibilities you run into. These could lead to future project collaboration or jobs. Here are a few networking opportunities to keep an eye out for:

- ✔ **Student introductions:** Pay close attention to the introduction of your peers. You'll probably find that they come from a variety of backgrounds and experiences. Befriend those who currently work in your field of interest and/or have a lot of experience.

- ✔ **Partner and group work:** Much like the student introductions, you'll also want to network with group-work partners. Take time to introduce yourself to your partner or group, and share your goals and your current situation. (Chapter 12 has the basics on working in groups online.)

- ✔ **Volunteer and internship opportunities:** Look for opportunities to volunteer or intern within the field you're studying. By doing this, you connect with professionals in the field, demonstrate the quality of your work, and get experience to add to your resume. Many students end up working for the organization where they either volunteered or interned.

- ✔ **Guest lecturers:** If your online course has a guest lecturer come and interact with the class, be sure to document the guest's name and contact information. One way to get on that person's radar for future interactions is to send the guest a private thank-you letter with your contact information.

- ✔ **Associations:** Professional fields are often defined by their associations. Though they cost to join, most associations have a student rate. Take advantage of this while you can, and join the professional organizations associated with your profession. Doing this provides you access to professionals within the field, job bulletins, and conference discounts.

- ✔ **Conferences:** Look for and attend conferences within your field. If none are offered locally, consider traveling and asking peers within your program to split travel costs such as gas and hotel. Attending conferences is a great way to hear presentations on trends and issues within your field. Conferences are also great for networking with professionals and prospective employers.

- ✔ **Social networking Web sites:** You may want to take advantage of social networking applications available on the Web, such as Facebook (www.facebook.com), LinkedIn (www.linkedin.com), and MySpace (www.myspace.com). These sites provide networking opportunities on both social and professional levels. However, we recommend that you try to create separate profiles for your professional networking versus your social interactions. These sites often post updates from your friends on your site, and you may not want prospective employers to view that material on your site. It's best just to keep the two separate to save any possible embarrassment.

Creating a business card with your contact information and the Web address of your ePortfolio on it is a great way to be prepared for those unexpected run-ins with prospective employers. For example, a friend of coauthor Kevin attended a conference in his field at the end of his studies and was provided several opportunities to network with professionals in the field. He was able to give prospective employers his business card, which directed them to his ePortfolio site. Within two weeks of the conference ending, Kevin's friend had two interviews, one of which landed him a job.

Part IV

Special Considerations in Online Education

The 5th Wave   By Rich Tennant

@RICHTENNANT

"This online course uses a football/math program. We're tackling multiplication, going long for division, and punting fractions."

In this part . . .

One of the truisms about online education is that it offers more educational possibilities for students who don't have access to the traditional educational system. We address three special populations in this part.

First we look at younger students with a chapter on students from kindergarten to high school (whether they're homeschooled or not). We then move to international students, because the Internet makes it possible to enjoy the benefits of an education from the United States without having to travel. Finally, we address students with disabilities and how they can access services to assist them in their online experience.

Chapter 16

Educating Students from Kindergarten through High School

A popular viral video is circulating among teachers that reinforces the idea of preparing students for jobs and futures we haven't yet imagined. In other words, what kids learn today may be obsolete in the near future, but we should try our best to teach skills that transfer. What this means to average kids in the 7th grade is that their education must be relevant to their futures; they need to be taught to creatively apply what they learn today to what they'll experience tomorrow. Without critiquing the entire educational system, we can agree that in North America we are looking for alternatives to the traditional school. Perhaps this is why charter schools and homeschooling have become so popular in the last decade. Online education may be the next wave for young learners.

In Chapter 2 we briefly introduce the idea that kids are learning online. This chapter examines why younger learners of all ages are taking courses online, and how this type of online education is different from that of their adult counterparts. We walk through the various models of online learning for young students and discuss what you should know before signing up your child for an online course.

Understanding Why Kids Are Going to School Online

We could point you toward The Pew Internet and American Life Project and their reports regarding Internet usage among kids ages 12 to 17, but you probably don't need research to know that kids are online. Granted, a lot of their time is spent checking social networking accounts and playing games, but a growing amount of time is spent learning. In this section, we review some of the reasons kids of all ages are attending online classes, either because they want to be or they need to be.

Wanting to be online

Our first category includes families who voluntarily move all or part of their children's instruction online. Notice we introduce the idea of family decision-making; independent children rarely make this decision. Nevertheless, here are a couple popular reasons:

✔ **Families are homeschooling.** Online education allows families who homeschool to select curricula and programs that better meet their needs. Parents who aren't expert educators stand a better chance of introducing materials and methods that will truly help their children learn better because the online school provides a teacher who partners with the parent.

✔ **Kids can learn at their own pace.** Because most online programs are set up to allow a child to complete the work independently, a fast learner can move at a fast pace. Gifted and talented children are not held back by the pace of instruction. The same is true for children who need more time to master a subject. Because she's working independently, a child can take longer on a particular lesson if she needs to.

Needing to be online

Sometimes the decision to move instruction online comes from an external force. Here are a few such circumstances:

✔ **Health or family concerns interfere with traditional education.** Unfortunately, a child may find herself dealing with a significant health issue — for example, extreme epilepsy — that prevents her from attending a traditional school. Additionally, older children occasionally need to drop out of school to contribute to the family, either by providing child care or medical care for parents. Online education allows these kids to continue learning at home with a schedule that's more convenient.

Online opportunities allow kids to make progress toward their educational goals despite such circumstances.

✓ **The course is only available online.** Advanced and specialized classes may not be available to kids who live in rural school districts or whose local public schools have limited resources. However, these students may find these types of classes online through virtual schools. Advanced placement courses are available through many online programs, for example.

✓ **The student has had disciplinary issues.** A child may have made some bad decisions in the past that resulted in expulsion. When a child is expelled from school, families have few options other than homeschooling or extremely costly private schools. Online education may be a method whereby kids can continue learning.

✓ **The kid has a career.** Child athletes and actors lead unusual lives. It used to be common to read about a child actor and her tutor, but today with online education, tutoring may be electronic. The same is true for athletes. A rising star in the ice skating world, for instance, may complete her education online while training for major competitions.

✓ **The teacher sends the student online.** Traditional high schools may offer a portion of instruction online as a hybrid or Web-enhanced course. The teacher may ask students to complete homework assignments or quizzes online so that class time can be used for other activities. While this chapter doesn't go into details on this type of structure, we at least want to note that kids are partially online because their teachers have directed them there.

Seeing the Differences between K-12 and Adult Online Education

So what makes online education unique for younger learners? After all, it can't be the same as online education for college students, can it? In this section we consider safety issues, extra parental involvement, synchronous meetings, and the need to work offline.

Safety concerns with children

We won't kid you: There are safety concerns when it comes to having children learn online. For starters, children tend to trust anyone and may not have the same sense of boundaries that adults do. Plus, there are creeps on the Internet who prey on children. In the interest of avoiding hysteria, we want to frame some of these concerns with the positive solutions that online schools have put in place:

✓ **Online education must be supervised by adults.** In the next section, we discuss enhanced parental involvement, and one of the primary reasons for this is to monitor what children do online, where they go, and with whom they communicate.

✓ **Online programs must be password-protected with limited access.** Institutions establish protocols so that only the students and their adult supervisors can log in to the learning space. Coursework is conducted within that space so that it isn't necessary for a child to interact with anyone else online. (Chapter 3 introduces the basics of password protection.)

✓ **Educators who work with children online must pass stringent background checks.** In the same way that teachers in brick-and-mortar schools must be blemish-free, online institutions ensure that their faculty are likewise squeaky clean.

Aside from addressing adults who prey on children, anyone with children online must also be aware of cyber-bullying. *Cyber-bullying* is the act of a child embarrassing, threatening, or harassing another child through online tools such as e-mail, instant messaging, social networks, and public discussion forums. With adult learners, the same behavior is possible and disconcerting, but children need to be afforded special protection. (As soon as adults become involved, the language changes to *cyber-stalking* or *cyber-harassment*.) Schools help children understand what is acceptable communication with their classmates and encourage those who experience bullying to report it swiftly. Policies and procedures guide schools in addressing and adjudicating offenders.

If your child decides to study online, here are some pointers to keep in mind:

✓ **Beware false identities.** One form of cyber-bullying is tricking a person. A student may believe she is communicating with a friend, when in fact it's a false identity. Help your child discern when and what to disclose online. Personal information should be off-limits.

✓ **Monitor social networking.** It's natural for classmates to form interpersonal relationships online. Your student may want to communicate with her classmates through e-mail or social networking spaces such as MySpace. However, these activities should be monitored by an adult. In other words, if your kid has a MySpace account, make sure you can see what's going on.

✓ **Report inappropriate activity.** If another child posts embarrassing or harassing statements or images, report this to the school officials immediately. It may be out of the range of their ability to discipline, but noting the behavior can have a significant impact on stopping it.

Then again, online schools know the types of behaviors that should be further reported to the police. For example, consider reporting to the police if personal information is involved in a threat against your child.

You may hesitate, thinking that the incident is minor, but it's best to let the police sort it out. Don't immediately delete the offending messages. The authorities may need to see them.

Whatever you do, don't retaliate with the same kinds of threats or harmful messages. Getting involved in a verbal tit-for-tat will only result in your child being accused of being a cyber-bully. Teach your child to walk away from the computer and cool down before reporting such an incident.

✔ **Block bullies.** By all means, block communication with cyber bullies. E-mail programs and instant message software such as Yahoo Messenger allow you to do this.

For more information about cyber-bullying, consult one of these sites: Stop Cyberbullying at `www.stopcyberbullying.org` or the National Crime Prevention Council site on cyber-bullying at `www.ncpc.org/cyberbullying`.

Enhanced parental involvement

In traditional schools, parent-teacher communication may be hit or miss. For example, coauthor Susan finds out her daughter's academic progress by checking a backpack. If her daughter forgets to bring home a science test, Susan has no way of knowing her cherub's grade. (This is changing somewhat in traditional education via parental access to electronic grade books.)

Parental involvement is completely different with virtual schools. If you follow any of the virtual school links, you will quickly note that every institution requires greater parental involvement than traditional schools. Parents have access to everything: grades, feedback, and lessons. Adults who supervise at home are given various monikers by online schools — parent/guardian, home facilitator, and onsite instructional support, to name a few — but their roles are the same. The need for enhanced parental support stems from the age of the learner:

✔ **Because most information is delivered by way of text online, the only way to survive in an online course is to read.** That's impossible for the average six-year-old! Adults serve as readers.

✔ **Few children are as self-motivated and disciplined as they need to be for online learning.** Adults serve as watchdogs and taskmasters.

✔ **Because an online teacher may not see the whole family situation, routine communication becomes more important.** Teachers schedule weekly or monthly communication with parents or supervisors, depending on the age of the learner and the structure of the school.

Pennsylvania Leadership Charter School has an interesting way of communicating parental expectations in its course catalog. It tells parents how much time and effort should go into their supporting role based on the grade level of the learner. For example, home facilitators with children in 2nd grade are expected to assist the child 90 to 100 percent of the time that the child is working on material. In other words, if you have a 2nd-grader, you'll probably need to teach the material and watch your child do assigned tasks. You can't expect a 7-year-old to read the computer screen and know what to do independently. As the child progresses academically, the amount of assistance decreases. By the time a student is in 12th grade and takes more ownership of the learning process, the adult shouldn't be active more than 1 to 10 percent of the time and not at all instructionally. Instead, the adult's role shifts toward holding the student accountable while continuing to provide motivation and support.

Any decent virtual school for kids requires parental involvement! Schools tell you this through some of the main links on their Web pages, for example, a "Parents" tab or a link to parental involvement. It shouldn't be a secret! If it seems obscure, look at another school.

More real-time opportunities

The world of online education for children is more synchronous than their adult counterpart's experience (in other words, it takes place in real time more frequently). Students may be expected to participate in online meetings daily, weekly, or monthly. These synchronous meetings with instructors and other students reinforce the subject matter, build strong community bonds, and generally keep learners on task. Even schools that follow a self-paced model for curriculum usually back up their courses with regular synchronous meetings.

Synchronous meetings typically use Web-conferencing software (which we describe in Chapter 12) and call together multiple students in a class. These meetings can be a lot of fun! The teacher may present new information or reinforce what the students are studying. She can ask and answer questions about content or assignments. Perhaps the greatest value of the synchronous meetings is the feeling of interpersonal connection between the student and teacher, which is still very important in virtual education for children. Figure 16-1 shows what a synchronous interface may look like for an online K-12 course.

Don't forget that the telephone is a synchronous tool, too! Teachers often call students to monitor progress and talk about what's happening in class.

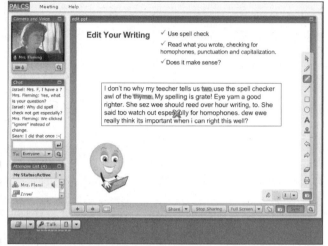

Figure 16-1: A synchronous class interface.

PA Leadership Charter School

The need to work offline

Surprisingly, not all online education happens online. Although adults can work offline (as we explain in Chapter 11), such work is especially important for younger learners. Young learners need time away from the computer to accomplish academic tasks that involve the following:

- ✔ **Textbooks and workbooks.** Can you imagine learning to print numbers without having a pencil and paper in hand? Some early academic tasks have to be done away from the computer screen. Further, at the point when children learn to read for information (around 4th grade), they begin to access materials like books and periodicals offline.

  Almost every virtual school uses textbooks. Flashy media may be available online to explain concepts, but online education for young learners also involves print materials.

- ✔ **Old fashioned, hands-on learning.** Curricula for young learners includes hands-on opportunities to experiment with concepts. For example, if a child is in an Earth science class, she may be provided rock samples to examine and evaluate. Or, she may be asked to collect leaf samples for a botany unit. Exploring one's natural curiosity is part of learning, and good online curricula requires students to go out in the world and find these key relationships.

When you're researching online schools, ask how much learning occurs online versus offline. If a program seems especially off-balance with no adequate explanation, consider looking at a different school. Kids need balance.

What? No diploma?

You may be surprised to learn that students who complete an academic program in a virtual high school may not earn a high school diploma, even though they take the same courses as their brick-and-mortar counterparts. Instead, they take the test for General Educational Development (GED) test to earn a diploma or certificate. Homeschooling families are very familiar with this process and have a long-standing practice of documenting their children's academic progress on an annual basis through portfolios that show how their child is progressing and provide examples of their work. When it comes time to apply for colleges, a homeschooled or virtual schooled student takes the same entrance exams (ACT or SAT) as any other student, and submits her portfolio along with a list of courses completed.

Checking Out Different Kinds of Virtual Schools for Kids and Teens

If online education interests you or your child, how do you go about finding a suitable program? This section sorts through the variety of programs available for families who want to learn online. A survey of existing programs reveals common structures, whether state-funded or private.

State-funded schools

Many states have state-funded online schools. In the following sections, we explain the basics on how these schools work and describe a classic example of a state-funded school. We also touch on outsourced instruction and charter schools.

Looking for a virtual school in your state? We know of two methods: use your favorite search engine and search for "virtual high schools in [your state]" or visit http://distancelearn.about.com/od/virtualhighschools/ Online_High_School.htm.

The basics on how state-funded schools work

Before we get too far into how the state-funded schools work, we need to clarify that there are two general types:

- **Schools that are publicly funded and open to all residents:** These schools may offer complete diplomas or only a few courses, and are generally accredited. These public schools are usually linked to a state's department of education, and therefore follow the state mandates as to what to teach. However, they may be outsourced and run by a major education provider, such as the K-12 company.

✔ **Charter schools:** These schools are also paid for by the government, but are a little more experimental in nature. They often target a specific subject or group of students, such as technology, math, or performing arts. Many times, charter schools are also directly linked to a public school district and enrollment may only be available to residents in that district.

In both types of state-funded schools, there are state standards that must be followed. What a child learns in 11th-grade English, for example, should be fairly consistent whether she sits in West High or her virtual campus. It's the *how* that may vary when we consider online education.

Online instruction in a publicly funded school often blends workbook/reading time with viewing and discussion online. The student accesses lessons online, completes a good deal of work offline, and then logs back in to submit assignments. Older students are often required to discuss ideas with their peers via discussion boards. There are usually opportunities for live or synchronous interaction with the teacher, too. Parents monitor progress and communicate frequently with the instructor.

So what should parents ask if they're looking at this kind of schooling for their child?

✔ If this is publicly funded, who is eligible?

✔ How closely aligned to state standards is the curriculum? What courses are available?

✔ What are the qualifications of teachers? Is the instruction provided by local teachers, or is this outsourced to a national company? The quality may be no different; you just may be curious as to where the teacher is coming from.

✔ What happens on a daily, weekly, or monthly basis? What kind of calendar would we follow? Can my child complete classes early or take more time if needed?

✔ In what ways are parents involved? What expectations should they have about communicating with teachers?

Understanding curricula and state mandates

What children learn in school is often determined at the state level according to mandated standards. For example, if you live in Montana, *Montana Content Standards and Performance Descriptors* tell you that all students will be able to "reflect upon their literary experiences and purposefully select from a range of works." The performance descriptors then break each standard down into a more meaningful explanation according to age level, so teachers understand what is expected by the end of fourth grade versus eighth grade, and so on. Teachers use this information to plan lessons and to select curricula that match the state standards. *Curricula* is a fancy term for what is taught, including the textbooks and instructional materials. For example, if you're the person in charge of getting kids to "reflect upon their literary experiences and purposefully select from a range of works," you select a textbook and materials that help you achieve that purpose.

The International Society for Technology in Education (ISTE) asks states to consider the role of technology in their state-mandated curricula. ISTE's National Educational Technology Standards (NETS) suggest that educators should get students "to demonstrate creative thinking, construct knowledge, and develop innovative products and processes using technology," for example. While the NETS technology standards are not mandated, if you put them together with the state standards, you can see how online education may be a solution. Using the previous Montana example, an online educator could get students to reflect on their literary experiences and choices through online discussion boards.

In 2006, Michigan rattled the education chains by passing legislation requiring high school students to take at least one online learning course or participate in an online learning experience prior to graduation. While not all states have followed with legislated mandates, the idea that schools should prepare students for a technologically rich future is unquestionable.

Ask about whether a computer and textbooks are part of the package with any state-funded school. In some states, students receive laptops or desktop computers along with textbooks and workbooks. Some even offer stipends to help pay for Internet service if it's deemed necessary based on financial need and if the online program meets the student's academic goals.

You may wonder about the instructors for virtual schools. Virtual instructors for accredited schools must be certified teachers. They are real educators and have the same academic credentials as Mrs. Smith at the local public school. Some teachers may also be nationally board certified, and in quality programs, all will have received significant and ongoing instruction in how to teach online. Some schools also have robust professional development programs that focus not only on specific strategies for online teaching but also on researched-based teaching methods in general.

A classic example: The Florida Virtual School

Perhaps the best-known and longest running (since 1997!) online school is the Florida Virtual School (FLVS) at `www.flvs.net/`. Any child whose parents are residents of the state of Florida can take classes through FLVS for free. This includes homeschooled kids who are registered with their school district. In 2007-08, FLVS served more than 63,000 kids online. Those students successfully completed more than 137,000 single-semester credits online.

Students at FLVS select courses from a standard curriculum that closely follows state standards. For example, the curriculum includes four levels of high school English along with two Advanced Placement English courses. Students earn the same half-credit per semester per course that students in traditional schools earn.

Students can work at varying pace options, from accelerated (fast) to extended (slow). Even within a given pace option, students can speed up or slow down as needed, depending on how well they're grasping the material. While pacing varies, students are by no means working on their own. Teachers are proactively involved in their day-to-day learning through assessment feedback, discussions, phone calls, e-mail, chats, and more. Students may also communicate with one another and with teachers through discussion boards and synchronous meetings online. The blending of asynchronous and synchronous learning works effectively for most learners.

A typical online course at FLVS includes some sort of multimedia presentation, rich in visuals. The method of presentation engages young learners who bring sophisticated expectations to learning (see Figure 16-2 for an example). It has to look good, be relevant, and contain a fun factor. As the student works through a lesson, she communicates with the instructor or her fellow students either through discussion boards or synchronous meetings like Webinars or chat sessions.

Outsourced instruction and charter schools

Other states have programs similar to FLVS's for their students, but they may outsource the instruction instead of having dedicated state schools. For example, Arizona provides free online opportunities for children registered with a school district. However, Arizona's courses are outsourced to the K^{12} company (`http://k12.com`), a proprietary group that develops and sells curricula. Like FLVS's courses, K^{12}'s courses are self-paced and include media. Here, the difference is simply in who develops the courses. The quality of instruction and expertise of their teachers is consistent.

In some states, charter schools deliver online courses to their students. A charter school is a publicly funded alternative to traditional school. Charter schools are often started by concerned parents or community groups and target a problem believed to be unaddressed through traditional means. In virtual terms, state charter schools are smaller online schools. For example, Wisconsin and Pennsylvania each operate several charter online schools.

Each of these schools is open to any resident of that state, regardless of proximity to the home office.

Because charter schools are smaller in scale, they may differ in curriculum. For example, in Wisconsin, more than one of the charter schools use K^{12}'s curricula. In contrast to using proprietary curricula, Pennsylvania's Leadership Charter School (PALCS) at www.palcs.org/ uses curricula developed by individual teachers. Drawing from resources available in traditional print and publishers of online media, instructors customize lessons according to grade and state standards. This results in a highly personalized method of instruction. Like the other programs, PALCS's program blends asynchronous and synchronous methods. The students receive a list of tasks to be completed by the end of the quarter and are also encouraged to meet routinely in synchronous sessions with the teacher.

Some virtual schools are outsourced. The state subscribes to the services of a large provider. In many cases, this works to your advantage because you're tied to a vast network of resources and personnel. However, it's worth asking about so you feel comfortable that your child's educational program matches your state's standards and expected curriculum.

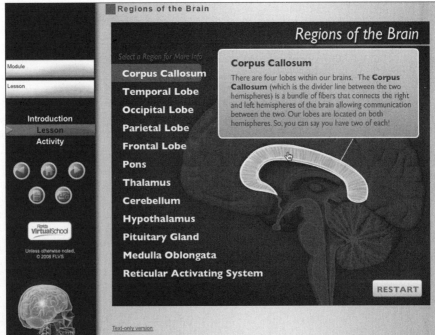

Figure 16-2: A glimpse at what an online course for K-12 looks like.

Courtesy of Florida Virtual School

Private online schools

If a state doesn't have a publicly funded virtual school, or you want to look for alternatives, private school is an option. Private virtual schools operate the same way the public schools do. With a combination of self-paced and instructor-led lessons, rich interactive media, and routine synchronous meetings, the public/private debate has little to do with qualitative difference in education and everything to do with funding bases! As long as you're willing to pay the tuition, it doesn't matter what state you live in.

A quick online search yields many online schools, but what should you consider in decision making? Following are some guidelines:

- **Make sure the program is accredited.** This should be an obvious notation on the school's Web site. Two major accrediting agencies are the Commission on Colleges of the Southern Association of Colleges and Schools (SACS) and the Commission on International and Trans-Regional Accreditation (CITA). (See Chapter 5 for more information about accreditation.)

- **Ask about the school's history and experience.** When it comes to online education and your child, you want to know the designers and teachers have done this long enough to be confident it works! The same questions we mention earlier about the quality of teachers, curriculum, and so on apply to these schools, too!

- **Recognize that sometimes size is an advantage.** One of the power-houses in private online high schools, for example, is Insight Schools at www.insightschools.net. Insight Schools is owned by the same parent company as University of Phoenix, the Apollo Group. As such, Insight can draw on the experience and resources of the behemoth university. Your child has access to research-based curriculum and best practices in instruction.

- **Ask about the school's courseware.** Was it developed in-house? If so, is it aligned to state standards? How interactive is it? Ask to see a demo. You want to see a course that is highly visual, easy to navigate, filled with interaction, and full of options as to how students can "show what they know." Also find out how often the school's courseware is updated. Online courses should be updated regularly — that's part of the beauty of being online!

- **Ask about teacher certification and training.** Choose a program that supports instruction by providing training specifically in online education.

> ✔ **Find out what the face-to-face requirements are, and be sure you can meet them.** It's okay if there are no face-to-face requirements, but you should look for a program that strives to at least offer the opportunity for such communication.
>
> ✔ **Look for a program that offers a healthy combination of synchronous and asynchronous learning opportunities.**

If you homeschool for religious reasons, you may prefer a curriculum that fits your beliefs. Online programs are available, such as that of The Morningstar Academy at www.themorningstaracademy.org/. However, as you shop around for an online school, exercise the same caution we mention in the preceding list regarding accreditation and experience.

Going through the K-12 Enrollment Process

If you decide that online education is right for your child, how do you sign up? This section details how you can find courses to meet your child's needs, confirm their credits, and be sure they transfer as you need them.

Applying for an online K-12 school isn't much different from what we describe in Chapters 4, 5, and 6 for adults. You learn about the school and program online, ask for an application packet, and have the opportunity to talk with a real person about the school before committing to anything. The school typically wants records of prior work (similar to transcripts for adults). You'll also need to provide a birth certificate and maybe immunization records (yes, even for some online schools!). Some schools, for example, the Illinois Virtual School, require that you get permission from your local school during the registration/application process before being approved to take online courses. In this same example, high school credit isn't granted by the virtual school but can be approved by the student's local high school.

What's really consistent between K-12 and adult schools is that you look at accredited programs and ask questions! If you're not getting the answers you need, move on!

Finding the right classes

How often have you heard of a student reaching the end of his senior year and being short one course for graduation? The solution is typically summer school, but if that student has access to online resources, an alternative may be to make up missing coursework through online education.

Or, how about a homeschooled student who really wants to take an elective in Chinese language, but whose parents can't find the right course material? Online education can fill this type of curriculum gap.

By searching through what's available in your state or looking at proprietary curricula (as we suggest earlier in this chapter), you may be able to identify online programs that can help your student make up missing courses to get back on track or take courses that aren't otherwise available.

Like colleges, virtual schools maintain course catalogs. These catalogs describe course offerings and the associated credit a student earns for completion. Schools make these freely available to interested consumers, but if you don't find a course catalog readily available online, be sure to call the contact number and request one.

Virtual schools are also available for children who need to complete *all* of the classes online. That's when you must read through the school's Web site to look for "full-curriculum" or "full-service" leading to a diploma. As you might expect, you want to select an accredited school. Trust us, there are a lot of opportunities for earning a diploma online.

Confirming credits before taking classes

We mention credit several times in this chapter, and perhaps we should clarify what that means. American institutions "count" credit according to the Carnegie system, a well-established and accepted system for higher education and K-12. High school credit is counted in full or half units according to how long a student is in class — literally the time the student sits in her seat!

A full unit of credit is equivalent to 120 hours of contact time with an instructor, so in a traditional school where English class meets for 50 minutes five days a week, it takes roughly a year to earn a credit. (Schools factor in vacation days.) A semester-long course such as an elective in mythology may earn half a credit.

Obviously, this credit-counting method is antiquated for online education, but it's still the system in use. Virtual schools award the same credit as their brick-and-mortar counterparts by considering how long a student is engaged in learning activities (online or offline) and the amount of time the student is expected to be in communication with faculty or other students.

Before registering for any online course, be sure to confirm how many credits that course will award upon completion. How many credits a course awards is listed in the curriculum (for example, 3rd-year English at the high school level earns one credit). The school's admissions and registration personnel can verify this information, and it should be completely transparent to you as the consumer. You want to be sure that you're signing up for a course that counts toward the academic goal!

Understanding articulation agreements

An articulation agreement is a formal plan that details what courses will be accepted at which schools and under what circumstances. Suppose your child is gifted and wants to take an Advanced Placement English course that earns dual credit for college and isn't available at your local rural high school. You find that this exact course is available for free through a charter school elsewhere in your state. It would be easy to assume your child could enroll in that charter school and have the credit count toward graduation at your local school. Don't make that assumption! Before you go any further, ask both schools about the articulation agreement so you know the credit will count. The registrar at either school is the keeper of these documents.

Checking articulation agreements is especially important for high school juniors and seniors who want to earn dual credit. Not only must you verify that the brick-and-mortar high school will accept the online credit, but you also need to make sure the future college will honor the credit, as well. We don't want to make it sound as if this is problematic, but the adage "better safe than sorry" comes to mind.

Can you go to high school as an adult?

If you didn't earn a high school diploma in a traditional fashion and now want to make up the difference, you can achieve this online. However, the virtual schools for traditional children that we discuss in this chapter, such as publicly funded charter schools, cannot accept you. Because they are state-funded, provisions are written into their charters only allowing students up to a certain age to enroll. There are, however, online schools available for adults to complete high school study. Mostly you want to obtain the background knowledge necessary to take the General Educational Diploma (GED) test. Credit is not as important as passing the test.

Start by contacting your state board of education to see whether an online program is available for residents. If not, run a quick search of online education for GED, and you'll find plenty of programs and services. Be sure to dig deep to find the kind of program that suits your needs.

Chapter 17

Connecting with International Students

· ·

In This Chapter

▶ Going to school in the United States without leaving home

▶ Getting on the Internet

▶ Enjoying your time in class

· ·

*N*ot every online student logs in from within U.S. borders, and we acknowledge that a much bigger world is out there. This chapter deals with students who live in other countries and want to study at online schools based in the United States. Some of these students are U.S. citizens who live abroad and take online classes, while others are international students who seek the advantages an online education from the United States will give them. International students experience unique issues related to language, credentials, Internet access, time zones, and more.

Taking First Steps toward Going to a U.S.-Based Online School

Following the awful events of September 11, 2001, the U.S. State Department began monitoring student visas a little more closely. Some believe this resulted in a decline in international student enrollment at schools in the United States, although the numbers may have been falling for other reasons. Nevertheless, the number of international students applying for admission to U.S. schools has been on the rise again for the past five years or so. According to the Institute of International Education, in 2007-08 more than 623,000 international students were enrolled in courses in the United States, comprising 3.9 percent of all college students. The majority of these are graduate students working on masters or doctoral degrees.

Ah, but these are students studying *in* the United States. What about those who didn't cross the border? With online education, it's possible to be an international student at a U.S. school without leaving home! In this section, we walk you through the initial steps you need to take to attend an online U.S.-based school: fully understanding the advantages of this type of education, proving English language competency, transferring credits successfully, and figuring out course costs and payments. Keep in mind that the other parts of the application process are identical to what U.S.-born students go through, as we explain in Part II of the book.

Getting a grip on the benefits of attending a U.S.-based online school

Few argue that the United States is a leader in higher education, and this fact makes studying in the United States especially attractive to international students; the degree is valued in the marketplace. However, international students who can't travel to the United States can reap many of the same benefits by studying online; in the end, the transcripts confirm that the degree is from an American institution.

Here are a few additional reasons why someone may want to stay in his home country and attend a U.S. school online rather than travel to the United States for school:

- ✔ **It's less expensive.** If you don't have to travel to the United States, find housing, and deal with the U.S. cost of living, you'll probably be better off financially. While the United States isn't the most expensive country in the world, studying online from your home country is less expensive than coming to the United States. Plus, if you have a job in your home country, you can keep it while studying, which means you won't lose income.

- ✔ **You can take a wide variety of courses.** With the exception of the United Kingdom's Open University, the United States has the broadest online catalog for courses in English. You can find almost anything you want within U.S. institutions.

- ✔ **You get the benefit of learning from different cultures.** While this isn't the same as sitting across the table from coauthor Susan and having her introduce you to her native Pennsylvania Dutch cooking, you can learn a lot about U.S. culture from participating in an online course. Via peer-to-peer communication and study groups, international students interact with U.S. counterparts in writing and through synchronous (real time) meetings. This interaction provides an opportunity to ask U.S. natives about what they think and why they behave as they do.

Proving language proficiency (if necessary)

If English isn't your first language or your previous education wasn't in English, you may need to prove English proficiency as part of the admission process to an online school based in the United States. To find out whether you need to do so, first look at the school's Web site. Most schools have a statement in their admissions section about whether they enroll international students and who to contact for further information. If you want an immediate answer while visiting the Web site, consider "chatting" in real time with a recruiter or an admissions person who can tell you what you need to know. There are two primary ways to prove English competency:

- ✔ **Do well on college entrance exams.** These may be required if you're entering college for the first time, no matter where you're from; see Chapter 6 for more about these tests.

- ✔ **Take an exam specific to the English language.** This is required if you're transferring credits from a school outside the United States; see the next section for details on this process.

If you're reading this book, you're probably proficient enough in English, but if you're struggling with the simple English in this text, imagine what academic work is like!

Schools in the United States generally accept test scores on English competency from several sources, including the Test of English as a Foreign Language (TOEFL) and a handful of other tests. Schools specify which tests they accept in their recruitment literature and on their Web sites. If you follow our advice and talk to a recruiter or admissions person, he can also verify this.

TOEFL and TSE exams

TOEFL is the best known and most widely accepted measure of English language competency. It's offered worldwide in many testing centers, and depending on where you need to go for the exam, you may take it as a paper-based test or an Internet-based test. A fee is involved, and both the format and fees vary from country to country.

TOEFL assesses your ability to read, write, and listen in English, and takes about four hours to complete. The Internet-based version of TOEFL also assesses your English speaking skills. Because the paper-based format doesn't assess speaking skills, you may be asked to submit scores from the Test of Spoken English (TSE), an exam given by the same company. However, this is more common for on-campus students who apply for graduate teaching assistantships. In the world of online education, your speaking skills become less central.

To find out more about the exams and when and where they're offered, visit the Educational Testing Service (ETS) site at www.ets.org. From there you can find information on both TOEFL and TSE.

When you take the TOEFL, you can indicate which schools you want to receive the results of your exam. Some schools use TOEFL results as a minimum requirement for acceptance, and if you don't score above a given school's set standard, you're not considered for admission. (The highest score for the paper-based test is 677, whereas the highest Internet-based test score is only 120.) In some cases, the schools require just one number — your total score — for admission. In other cases, schools specify a minimum score for each skill area (reading, writing, listening, and possibly speaking, if you're required to take the TSE). Do your homework and research the school before taking the exam! Find out their minimum accepted score and how they make decisions. Minimum acceptable scores are sometimes published in the recruitment literature and on Web sites, but a recruiter or admissions person can tell you more about how they make decisions.

TOEFL scores are only good for two years. Plan ahead, so you can use yours in a timely fashion.

Other measures of fluency

The school you want to attend may ask for other tests as proof of your English competency. Here are three alternatives:

- ✔ **Test of English for International Communication (TOEIC):** This exam has a lot in common with TOEFL, namely because it's published by the same company, ETS. However, the primary difference is that the TOEIC was developed to test the user's ability to put English into practice on an everyday level in business. In other words, it tests everyday English rather than academic English. Nevertheless, it may be an alternative for proving English language competency for admission. You can find out more about TOEIC at www.ets.org.

- ✔ **International English Language Testing System (IELTS):** A British counterpart to TOEFL, this exam is partly managed by the University of Cambridge's English as a Second or Other Language department, so it has an academic backing. The exam tests all four major skills: reading, writing, listening, and speaking. The IELTS is administered at various sites worldwide and is widely accepted as an alternative to TOEFL. See www.eilts.org for more information.

- ✔ **EIKEN:** This test is administered in Japan by the Society for Testing English Proficiency. A number of schools in North America are beginning to recognize this as proof of competency. Check out the Web site at http://stepeiken.org.

Learning English online

Years ago, the first online course coauthor Susan developed was English as a second language. You can't imagine how often she was asked, "Can you really learn English online?" Yes, you can! If you want to improve your skills in English, you have many online choices available:

✔ You can find many free sites that support language development. One Language at www.1-language.com/englishcourse/index.htm, Learn English Online at www.learn-english-online.org/ and Real English at www.real-english.com/ are examples. Just be aware that you have to wade through a lot of advertisements on these sites, and some of the free sites are not updated frequently. Kind-hearted teachers typically author and maintain these sites with little institutional support.

✔ You can pay for a number of private courses through companies like English Online Classes at www.eslonlineclasses.com/ or Englishtown at www.english-town.com/. These courses connect you with online tutors. Some include live communication and Web conferencing.

✔ You can study through an accredited college program such as the one offered by Rio Salado College at www.riosalado.edu/programs/eslonline/Pages/default.aspx. These online courses are a little more challenging to find because if you search for "online English," you may be directed to English degree programs — that's not what you want. Also, you have to pay for these courses, but the advantage is that you'll have the personal attention of the faculty.

If you really want to learn a language, pay attention to all the major skills areas: reading, writing, speaking, and listening. Look for opportunities to speak and write so you can put your skills to the test. Be wary of studying only grammar because that's only part of the language. Unless you have identified a deficiency in one area, look for a balanced program for learning.

Further, look for a site that includes asynchronous and synchronous communication. You need live communication to strengthen listening and responding skills. Real-life communication is never as rigid as the textbooks say, and you need to interact with real native speakers who will teach you new phrases and enrich your cultural understanding.

Finally, you may wonder about the difference between American and British English. The languages' vocabulary, spelling, and pronunciation are different. One isn't better than the other — just different. However, if you're planning to enroll in a U.S.-based school and first want to improve your English through an online program, you'll want to choose American English.

Most of the Web sites we reference in the preceding list offer free tutorials and sample practice materials. Be sure to check them out to see what you can learn for free!

Transferring credits from schools abroad

Whether you want to start a new academic degree at a U.S.-based online school or complete a degree you started earlier, you have to meet the academic requirements for admission. This includes having completed high school or college, depending on the degree you want to pursue online.

To begin with, the transcripts or documentation required by an online school depend on the program you apply to. Therefore, the first place to check is the school's catalog. This is usually downloadable from the Web site, and the departmental requirements are specified in that document. You typically need a copy of your diploma and a transcript, no matter the program.

In addition to a copy of your original diploma and course transcript in your native language, you need to provide a word-for-word version translated into English. While some online schools say they accept "informal" translation, we advise you to have these documents professionally translated. In fact, some schools maintain a list of preferred translators or certified foreign credential evaluators, so they know the accuracy of the translation. You can find out who the preferred translators are by calling or e-mailing the admissions office.

The academic transcript lists the courses you completed and the grades you earned. Along with listing the courses and grades, most colleges also want an explanation of the grading scale. In other words, what did it take to earn a "B" in your country? This is so they can better compare you to U.S. applicants.

After you provide the transcripts, the institution evaluates each course to see how closely it matches the one they expect an American applicant to have taken. Listing the courses you took and the grades you earned isn't enough; each and every course must also be described to the prospective school. This is typically done in a separate document prepared by the preferred translator or evaluator.

For example, if you're a teacher in Mexico applying to an online school for a Masters in Education, the U.S. school would expect you to have completed a bachelors degree, including a course equivalent to "Foundations of Education." In the United States, the foundations course looks at historical and contemporary issues in education and puts these in a context of education in a democracy. To appropriately examine these issues, American students are typically asked to read classic educational text as well as more current writings. See where this gets tricky? The translation of your coursework must adequately explain how your class in Mexico meets the same criteria as a U.S. course. This is why you need a certified academic document translator to help you.

We're not suggesting that this review process is demeaning or nitpicky, but a different level of evaluation is associated with international documents. After all, you're going to earn the new degree from a U.S.-based school, so you should expect to be held to the same standards as the other students.

Handling costs and payments

You already know this because you live outside of the United States: Sometimes the U.S. dollar is strong and other times it's weak, and this phenomenon directly impacts the exchange rate and how expensive products and services are. When you figure the cost for courses, carefully consider the strength of the U.S. dollar. Is it relatively weak or strong, and how does that determine the cost of a course? No one can predict the economy, but if you're considering an entire degree that spans several years, you must plan ahead to be sure you have sufficient financial reserves. You figure your costs the same way a U.S.-born student does: Calculate the number of credits you need multiplied by credit hour costs and fees (don't forget textbooks!). We discuss costs in more detail in Chapter 6.

Also, be sure to ask your recruiter or the admissions person working with you about how you need to pay. Does the school accept Visa or Mastercard? Must you request a bank transfer or money order? The more established schools have the process clearly worked out; less sophisticated schools may need you to help them understand how you can make payments. A Canadian friend had to explain to a small school in the United States that Canadians do, in fact, have Visa credit cards and that they work the same way the U.S. cards work!

Don't forget your books!

As you're figuring costs, don't forget the cost of buying textbooks and having them shipped to you. First, see whether they're available as electronic books that you read from your computer. If you prefer a hard copy, can you purchase them from a retailer within your country? If you can, you'll save money in shipping costs. In Chapter 7 we discuss the textbook-buying process and the alternatives that may be available to you in detail.

Accessing the Internet around the World

Like any student, you need a reliable Internet connection to succeed in online education. Where and how you find these connections may present challenges most people don't have in the United States, so we discuss these in the following sections.

Considering residential expenses

How much does Internet service cost where you live? In the United States, a basic residential high-speed connection (cable or DSL) can range from $30 to $50 per month. Compared to Americans' incomes and other expenses, this is relatively little money.

However, depending on where you live, Internet service may be much more expensive than in the United States. In western Africa, for instance, the same service costs well over $100 U.S. per month. In India, the costs are comparable to U.S. prices if you live in a metropolitan area. International students must determine the relative cost of a reliable residential high-speed Internet connection in figuring the overall cost of an online education from a U.S.-based school.

If residential high-speed connection costs are a little pricey in your corner of the world, investigate the following home alternatives before registering for an online course or program. The best person to ask these questions of is the course instructor, but a recruiter may be able to give you answers, too:

- ✔ **Ask whether you can use a dial-up connection.** Assuming you have reliable phone service, this may be an option. If the course requires high speed because of video or audio, ask whether alternatives are available, such as transcripts you can read.

- ✔ **Ask about how much work can be done offline and how much synchronous time you should expect.** Can you download assignments, work on them offline and then connect for less time to upload? Will you be required to be online at specific times?

Getting connected outside your home

If you can't afford residential Internet service, what are your options in terms of connecting? For students living abroad, you may find that you can connect where you work or in more public areas such as Internet cafés or community centers. This section looks at some of the advantages and disadvantages of these locations.

Connecting at work

If you work in a business that has a high-speed connection, ask your employer whether he can allow you to complete your coursework using company computers after working hours. This is a common solution for U.S.

online students whose future degrees directly relate to their professional lives. Here are some of the advantages to connecting via your workplace:

- ✔ **You are focused on the coursework and not distracted by family or friends.** Not that you want to rush, but you aren't as likely to multitask because you want to finish your schoolwork and go home.

- ✔ **Applying what you're learning to your professional situation is easier when you're sitting at work.** Not only is your mind on business, but if you need to reference a policy or procedure, you have the resources at your fingertips.

Of course, connecting at work has a couple disadvantages, too.

- ✔ **You may be expected to repay your company's generosity through continued employment.** In other words, don't start looking for another job!

- ✔ **You open yourself to privacy concerns and criticism.** Whatever you do on the company's computers is traceable. In theory, your boss could read what you write. As long as you're happy with your employer and honest in your communication, this shouldn't be a problem.

Connecting at Internet cafés, community centers, and universities

In developed countries, people who don't have residential service at home often connect through Internet cafés. If you live near an Internet café and can afford to pay for the service, this may be an option for completing your coursework.

Of course, you need to compare prices and determine whether this is affordable. You also need to consider whether you have your own laptop computer or need to use the café's hardware. If you're using their computer, it may not have the software you need for certain course aspects.

In developing countries, you may find a community center sponsored by a nonprofit organization where Internet skills are taught primarily to children. Although their services may target younger students, these organizations may allow you to access the Internet through their satellite connections if they understand that education is the purpose. Again, you need to consider whether you have your own equipment or need to use theirs, and to what extent you can do some work off-line to save connection time.

Finally, if you live near a major university in your country, you may want to ask about the possibility of connecting via their services. Of course, you need to explain why you're taking a course from a U.S.-based school and not from their institution, but they may say yes if you can adequately explain how you and the community will benefit. A U.S.-based school on foreign soil, such as American University of Beirut, may be more likely to understand your situation.

Contact the U.S. Embassy in your country and ask what outreach programs or services they're working on with Non-Governmental Organizations (NGOs) that serve the public. They may have programs or services available to you.

Being aware of restrictions

Because of political and sociocultural differences, some Web-based resources may be restricted by your government. For example, coauthor Susan once shared a link to a video posted on YouTube with her graduate students in an education course. The student in an Arab country could not see the video because his Internet Service Provider had restricted access.

You must understand any restrictions prior to starting an online course so you can tell the instructor if you can't access certain course materials; he can then provide alternative information. You'll know you're blocked when you can't access the site or program and receive an error message. If you want a thorough explanation as to why you're restricted, ask your Internet Service Provider, who can then interpret your government's policies.

Making the Most of Your Class Time

Once you get accepted by a school and find the Internet access you need, you still have a few details to work out. This section introduces you to a little information about how the U.S. system of education works, tips for navigating time differences, and pointers for joining study groups.

Understanding what's different about classes in the United States

The U.S. online education system may offer some surprises to folks who live elsewhere. Here are some differences you can expect from online education based in the United States:

> ✓ **You may address your instructor by her first name.** Americans tend to be a little more casual about relationships in higher education, and your instructor may ask you to call her by her first name (Susan), rather than her title (Dr. Manning). When your classes begin, ask your instructors how they prefer to be addressed.

✔ **Given the nature of online education, your instructor may not be highly active in class discussions.** He may opt to say less and ask the students to think for themselves. This is a very deliberate educational strategy and not because the teacher is lazy.

✔ **Students are expected to speak up and to ask questions.** If you don't understand something, the instructor expects you to ask. Saying that instructions are confusing is not considered impolite. We recommend asking privately (see Chapter 10 for information on private communication methods), but be sure to follow through until you understand.

✔ **American instructors expect students to deconstruct the ideas of experts.** In other words, finding fault with a theory or piece of work from another scholar, your professor, or a famous author is not only permissible, it's also how we believe students develop critical thinking. As long as you provide your reasoning, we appreciate dissent. (Remember, this country was founded by dissenters!)

✔ **The definition of plagiarism is very strict in the United States.** This is so important to the integrity of higher education that a portion of Chapter 13 is all about avoiding plagiarism. The U.S. system of education insists that other authors and works that help form your ideas must be acknowledged and cited.

✔ **Americans are extraordinarily punctual.** If a virtual meeting is scheduled for 7:00, the teacher will start talking at 7:00, not 7:10 or 7:20. Be prepared, and log in early!

✔ **When working in student groups, U.S. students may have a different timeline for establishing trust and credibility.** Because our educational system is fairly competitive, U.S. students may be less skillful at collaborating in small groups and find it difficult to trust other members.

✔ **Not every U.S. student is comfortable with interpersonal conflict.** In fact, when working with study groups, you may find students who ignore conflict or don't handle it well. Don't take it personally.

Adjusting for differences in time zones

What time is it? What day is it? It all depends on where you are! Getting a handle on date and time are critical so you're not late with meetings and assignments.

Handling synchronous class meetings

Instructors may call virtual class meetings using synchronous (real time) communication or Web conferencing tools. These meetings usually give students the opportunity to interact in text and voice.

To ensure that you make all meetings on time, you first need to determine what time it is where you are compared to your instructor's location. You probably already know about the World Clock Web site at www.timeand date.com/worldclock/. From this site you can enter the Meeting Planner, where you state your country and city and the location of the instructor. For example, if you live in Vietnam and the instructor is in Chicago and calls a 7 p.m. meeting on Wednesday, you need to be ready at 7 a.m. Thursday!

American culture is a very punctual culture. Plan to log in five minutes before the scheduled time so you're not late to synchronous meetings.

Of course, synchronous class meetings may not be very convenient if you're called to a meeting in the middle of the night. Politely explain the time difference to the instructor or your fellow students. We're confident they will tell you to sleep through the meeting.

If you're concerned about language and afraid you'll be asked to speak in English, don't be! In general, Americans are pretty forgiving when they hear accents and grammatical errors from speakers of other languages. If you're more comfortable talking through text, let the instructor know in advance and make provisions to type in chat.

Figuring out assignment due dates

Your assignment is due by midnight on Thursday. What does that mean if you live on the other side of the world? It probably means either the next day or a day ahead! Don't be caught on the wrong day. Use the same world clock tool we suggest in the previous section to synchronize due dates.

Joining study groups

One of the advantages of having a global economy is the richness of diversity, and the same can be said of study groups with students from around the world. Don't be shy! Online education thrives on dialogue, and your unique perspective enriches everyone. If you're presented with this opportunity, go for it!

Study groups may form for a specific task, as we discuss in Chapter 12. Or, they can be informal groups of students who agree to share notes and additional resources. In fact, the group may choose to maintain its own wiki or a separate group space in FaceBook. This provides another avenue for discussing what's happening in the class without the instructor present.

You'll find when you interact with your U.S. classmates that some seem more open to international students than others. The others aren't necessarily snobby or deliberately racist; instead, they're probably intimidated by their own lack of knowledge about the world. The United States is a geographically large, ethnically diverse country, but there are still many homogeneous communities where students grow up interacting only with people like themselves. Consequently, they're not sure whether asking about your country, culture, or habits is polite, and as a result, they appear aloof.

There's no magic potion to make others like you, regardless of where you come from. However, here are a few reminders about the American culture that you may find helpful:

- ✔ We're fairly informal with communication. Of course, you need to follow the protocol of the academic class, but typically you can address your classmates by their first names.

- ✔ It's fine to ask questions like, "Are you married?" and "Do you have a family?" but it's not okay to express disagreement with someone if their lifestyle doesn't match your beliefs.

- ✔ We pepper our language with many idiomatic expressions. If you don't know what something means, don't be afraid to ask! For instance, to say someone runs a tight ship may not make sense in an education course, until you understand that it means the principal is strict.

- ✔ Generally speaking, we are punctual, so if a meeting is set to begin at 8 a.m., we really start at 8 a.m.

- ✔ Get to know us, and you'll be surprised at the diversity! It really is hard to stereotype an American when you recognize our many ethnic and religious groups.

- ✔ We love jokes! Good, clean puns always catch our fancy.

If you have the chance to work in groups and are asked to select members, think about the students who display a natural curiosity and interest in your country. That welcoming behavior can make group work very pleasant as you exchange ideas. Have some fun together by sharing cultural information and being open with each other. Chapters 9 and 10 provide pointers on introducing yourself to your classmates and communicating clearly with them.

Chapter 18

Accessibility in Online Education

*W*hen it comes to accessibility for people with disabilities, we're being brutally honest in saying that the field of online education is still working on getting it right. Even the most committed institutions rely on individual instructors and outside vendors who aren't always familiar with the design and development strategies best suited for persons with disabilities. However, we can honestly say that this is a hot topic within the field, and more state and federal laws are forcing institutions to be more cognizant of the subject.

Does this mean you shouldn't attempt to take an online course if you have a disability? Absolutely not. The benefits of online education, as we explain in Chapter 2, definitely extend to people with disabilities. Federal laws prohibit any school that receives federal funding, whether private or public, from discriminating based on disability. These same institutions are also required to provide reasonable and appropriate accommodations to insure equal access to all students. Plus, there are a lot of assistive technologies that can help when needed.

We believe this topic is extremely important, and that's why we include this chapter. Here, we explain how to figure out the accessibility of courses you want to take and how to let your selected school know about your disability. We also describe assistive technology options to help you during class. However, a single chapter isn't enough to cover all that there is to say about this subject. Therefore, following are a few additional resources that can help you better understand your rights and responsibilities in an academic setting:

✓ **The Americans with Disabilities Act of 1990, as Amended (ADA):** The ADA (www.ada.gov/) prohibits discrimination on the basis of disability by public entities and has additional standards for public organizations. (We talk more about the ADA in the later sidebar, "Defining 'disability' according to the Americans with Disabilities Act.")

- ✔ **Section 504 of the Rehabilitation Act of 1973:** Section 504 (`www.section508.gov/index.cfm?FuseAction=Content&ID=15`) prohibits discrimination on the basis of disability by schools receiving federal funds.

- ✔ **Family Education Rights and Privacy Act (FERPA):** FERPA (`www.ed.gov/policy/gen/guid/fpco/ferpa/index.html`) protects your privacy. This law allows information specific to your disability to be shared only with faculty and staff that are involved in the development and implementation of an accommodation plan.

- ✔ **The Individuals with Disabilities Education Act (IDEA):** The rules and regulations of IDEA (`http://idea.ed.gov/`) require public schools to provide all eligible children with disabilities a free, appropriate education in the least restrictive environment. IDEA does not apply to postsecondary education.

Determining Whether the Courses You Want to Take Are Accessible

As promoters of self advocacy, we provide you with a list of questions specific to accessibility and accommodations that you can ask online schools you want to apply to. By asking the questions in the following sections up front, you can find out very quickly how well-equipped an institution is to accommodate a variety of learners' needs. Unfortunately, what you find may not please you, but figuring this out before enrolling in courses can save you a lot of headaches.

Note that when you ask these questions, your academic advisor may not know the answer. Though we hope that the instructional design and technical staff are providing some level of information to those marketing the program and answering student questions, that may not be the case. Therefore, be patient if your advisor needs to find out the information and get back to you. On the other hand, if the advisor doesn't respond in a timely manner, you've received good information that will allow you to consider eliminating that school from your list of schools to which you may apply. (See Chapter 5 for additional questions to ask your advisor as you research online schools.)

Do the courses follow any accessibility standards?

This question is a tell-all question. Institutions that are committed to making content accessible to all students are able to easily answer this question. The guidelines and standards for creating accessible Web sites and course content are so specific that any instructional designer responsible for developing content will be able to provide you with specific examples of how the content meets those standards. It's easy for a school to claim accessibility. The level of detail they're able to give you in terms of the standards to which they adhere is telling.

Commonly used guidelines

Schools are required to follow federal guidelines when developing Web content. A few organizations in particular are heading the pack when it comes to creating standards for Web accessibility. Here is a list of those organizations:

- ✔ **Section 508 Information Technology Accessibility Standards:** A federal law that mandates federally funded organizations to provide employees and members of the public with information that is comparable to the information provided to employees and members of the public without disabilities (`www.access-board.gov/sec508/standards.htm`).

- ✔ **World Wide Web Consortium (W3C):** An international consortium where contributors work together in the development of standards and guidelines for the Web. The organization has an initiative specific to developing Web accessibility standards and guidelines (`www.w3.org/wai`).

- ✔ **Web Content Accessibility Guidelines (WCAG):** Recommended guidelines for creating Web content that is more accessible for persons with a wide range of disabilities, including blindness and low vision, deafness and hearing loss, learning disabilities, cognitive limitations, limited movement, speech disabilities, photosensitivity, and combinations of these (`www.w3.org/TR/WCAG/`).

Defining "disability" according to the Americans with Disabilities Act

The Americans with Disabilities Act (ADA) defines disability in respect to an individual as "a physical or mental impairment that substantially limits one or more of the major life activities of such individual." The act provides good examples for determining whether a person's inability to do something is due to a disability or due to other reasons. For example, a person's inability to participate in a program due to a lack of financial resources isn't considered a disability. However, a person who's unable to participate in a program because of a documented physical or mental condition such as dyslexia is considered a person with a disability by law. Find out more about the act at `www.ada.gov`.

The preceding standards are geared towards Web-based content only. However, your online class may include links to external content such as word-processing documents, PowerPoint Presentations, and multimedia clips. Some states already have guidelines covering these types of content. For instance, all Illinois agencies and universities are required to implement the Illinois Information Technology Accessibility Act (IITAA) Web Accessibility Standards in order to ensure that all Web content, documents, videos, and other resources are accessible to persons with disabilities (`www.dhs.state.il.us/page.aspx?item=32765`). Be sure to ask the institutions you're interested in whether *all* their content is created in an accessible manner, especially if you want to attend a school based in a state that doesn't have guidelines similar to Illinois's. For further information as to the guidelines every state is required to follow, visit the ADA's Accessibility of State and Local Government Websites to People with Disabilities page at `www.ada.gov/websites2.htm`.

Examples of accessibility

Here are a few examples of how institutions should be making content accessible to all students (these are the sorts of answers you should look for when you ask this question of academic advisors; see the later section "Using Assistive Technology Online" for more information about these options):

✔ **Using heading styles inside documents:** Heading styles are text formats that tag important text. Headings are used to organize a Web site by importance. Each Web page should have one Heading 1, which serves as the title for that page. Heading Style 2 is used for topics within the page, and Heading Style 3 is used for subtopic information. Heading styles help screen readers quickly navigate from topic to topic without having to read an entire page. This is extremely helpful, especially when you have to reread the same document multiple times. For example, a person who needs to check a course policy within the syllabus doesn't want to listen to the entire document via a screen reader. She wants to scan for headings and subheadings to find the respective policy quickly.

✔ **Providing transcripts for audio files:** Audio files bring a nice touch to a class and often reduce the psychological distance between the learners and the speaker. They can be especially helpful to students who learn better by listening. However, they're not helpful to students who are deaf or have hearing loss, so instructors should provide a transcript of every audio file used in class. Transcripts can also be helpful to students whose first language is not English.

✔ **Providing captions, auditory descriptions, and transcripts for videos:** Videos are another alternative way to deliver content to students that stimulates visual learners. However, students who are blind or have vision loss and those who are deaf or have hearing loss don't benefit from these delivery methods. Captioning videos (displaying text on the screen as a subtitle in real-time with the video) and providing an accessible transcript is an easy way to make the same content accessible to a lot more learners. Auditory descriptions are interspersed narrations of what is happening on the screen. This helps a person listening to the video to understand the context in which the dialogue is being used.

You probably noticed as you were reading this list that accessible design benefits not only students with disabilities but also students with a variety of learning preferences, by providing multiple ways to access the same information. For example, someone who prefers to read information rather than hear it may choose to subscribe to a captioner during a live session rather than pay attention to the instructor's voice. This is the goal of universal design.

Are the courses tested for accessibility?

Institutions that have a centralized process for course design usually have established standards for designing and testing new courses. In an ideal world, every institution would have a variety of users with a variety of learning styles and needs to test every course before it goes live. However, we don't live in an ideal world, and many institutions don't have a centralized process for testing. Courses are often developed by individual instructors with little to no understanding of accessible design. As accreditation becomes more prevalent specific to online courses (see Chapter 5 for more information), these types of courses are becoming less common.

Asking whether the institution's courses are tested for accessibility will help you understand the school's design and testing process. If your academic advisor doesn't know, ask her to help you contact someone who does. If course design isn't centralized, it's important that you work with your academic advisor to develop a schedule of all the courses you want to take. That schedule needs to be provided to someone who's responsible for coordinating your accommodations. That person should research your course list to determine what the challenges will be and what accommodations will be made to overcome those challenges. If you're unable to get this type of information from the institution, and staff haven't convinced you that accessibility is a forethought, consider looking at other institutions.

If you find that the courses you're enrolled in aren't as accessible as you thought they'd be, contact your instructor, academic advisor, and accommodation team leader as soon as possible (see the later section "Understanding why and when you need to disclose" for more about accommodation teams). Provide a detailed description of the information that is inaccessible to you and explain why. In this situation, you may want to offer to help test changes to the content and/or course. Even though it isn't your responsibility to help the institution test the course, you'd be doing future students a favor by helping the institution create more accessible content.

How will the school help me if I'm unable to access information in the courses?

Depending on your specific needs, institutions can provide a variety of assistance types to accommodate your learning needs. Determined strategies are based on a comprehensive review of your disability, documentation, and discussions between you and your accommodation plan team (see the later sections "Understanding why and when you need to disclose" and "Figuring out what information to disclose" for more information about this process). During these sessions, it's important for you to share any experiences that you've had in the past and what has worked best for you and why.

Here are a few examples of some accommodations that can be made for students taking online courses:

- ✓ **Extended time on assignments and quizzes/tests:** For students who need more time to access and absorb information due to their disability, institutions may arrange for assignment deadlines and testing times to be extended.

- ✓ **Access to tutoring services:** Several institutions subscribe to online tutoring services that provide academic assistance in a variety of areas. Tutors can be accessed 24/7 via the Internet.

- ✓ **Content in text form and large print if needed:** For content that isn't in text form or isn't scalable, printed and large-print documents can be mailed to students needing these accommodations.

- ✓ **Content in Braille:** For students who are blind or have low vision, Braille versions of content can be printed and mailed when deemed necessary.

- ✓ **Early access to online courses and course materials:** Early access to the virtual classroom provides students with access to course materials such as the syllabus and calendar. By accessing this information early, students can begin to organize and better determine what additional accommodations may be needed.

- ✓ **Oral examinations or assignments:** Institutions can request that instructors meet with students via the phone or another audio device to conduct interviews as a way of completing assignments and exams orally. During these sessions, the instructor can ask the student to answer questions about the assignment to determine whether the student truly understands the material. Again, exam dates and assignment due dates can be altered on a case-by-case basis for students whose disabilities warrant that accommodation.

Disclosing a Disability to Your Chosen Online School

In any academic setting, including an online course, students want to feel independent and be known for their contributions to the class. Therefore, we understand the desire to avoid disclosing a disability to peers, instructors, or even the administrative staff. However, sometimes accommodations that are needed can only be provided if requested. This section provides some general information about disclosing a disability and devising a plan to create and implement appropriate and reasonable accommodations in a respectful and private manner.

By the way, people with temporary impairments don't qualify for disability services under the law. For example, a student who breaks her arm and requires a cast over the hand she types and writes with isn't considered to have a physical disability. In this situation, you should work with your instructor directly to see whether temporary accommodations can be made, such as oral exams or recorded presentations.

Understanding why and when you need to disclose

Simply put, institutions can't provide services if they don't know that the services are needed. Also, accommodations are not retroactive. So, if you receive an assignment or course grade that reflects negatively on you because your accommodations were not in place, the institution doesn't have to change that grade, even if you document the presence of a disability at a later time. Therefore, disclosure is in your best interest if you need special accommodations. For example, for the most part, a person who is deaf could easily participate in an online course without disclosing and without needing accommodations. But what happens when the instructor wants to use a synchronous (real-time) audio tool for meeting with students throughout the semester? Many synchronous technology tools have captioning capabilities; however, these tools don't automatically transcribe voice to text. They require a person with captioning skills to log in and type using a dictation device similar to what you see in courtrooms. These people are often hired out-of-house and need time to gain access to your virtual course, test the technology, and meet with you to discuss logistics. (We describe captioning videos in more detail later in this chapter.)

So when do you need to disclose your disability? Institutions should include a statement either on the application or acceptance letter that provides information on disclosing a disability and requesting accommodations. If you can't find the statement or it's unclear who to contact, ask your academic advisor for direction. She can provide you with the proper forms and submission policy.

If you know you'll need accommodations from the start, it's best to disclose as soon as appropriately possible. Institutions need time to confirm documentation and meet with experts who can review your specific situation and develop an accommodation plan to match (see the next section). This process can take a couple weeks, depending on the staff and resources available. (For example, if you need a captioner for synchronous sessions, it may take two weeks to find a person available on the dates and times of your sessions.) If you wait until classes begin to request services, you risk not receiving the service in a timely manner and falling behind in your academic progress.

If the question is a part of the application process, and you feel uncomfortable disclosing at that time, that's okay. Waiting until you are formally accepted is understandable. However, waiting could delay accommodations and possibly your start date, as well.

In most cases, discussing your situation with your academic advisor first is perfectly acceptable. This person will be able to help you complete the proper documentation or point you in the right direction regarding how to get additional help. And don't worry: Anyone you disclose to is obligated by law to only share this information with staff directly involved with creating and implementing the accommodations necessary for you to be successful. (See the later section "Keeping privacy in mind" for more about this topic.)

Most institutions require you to request accommodations every term or at least once a year. This allows the accommodation team to reevaluate the accommodation plan and see whether anything needs to be modified.

Figuring out what information to disclose

In most cases, when completing the disclosure information, you're asked to provide formal documentation regarding your disability. Formal means that the information is provided by a licensed professional who is familiar with you and your respective disability. Your academic institution will have specific requirements for documenting a disability (disclosed on the institution's Web site or outlined in a Request for Accommodations form provided by your academic advisor), but documentation may include the following requirements:

✔ **Diagnostic description of the disability:** This helps your academic institution understand your specific situation and provides them with the proper documentation to justify making the requested accommodations.

✓ **History of diagnosis:** When you provide the history of your diagnosis, staff are better able to understand specific challenges you may face. For example, a person who recently lost her sight as an adult may need more assistance than a person who has been blind since birth.

✓ **Functional implications of your diagnosed disability:** This information is extremely important and must be as detailed as possible. Knowing how your disability impacts your daily life, staff can develop a more successful accommodation plan specific to your needs.

If you're blind or deaf, you may not have needed to provide this documentation in the past due to the obvious nature of the impairment. However, online institutions aren't able to make such visual judgments and usually require all students requesting accommodations to submit formal documentation by a licensed clinician.

Keeping privacy in mind

Specific to health issues and education, the Family Education Rights and Privacy Act (FERPA) protects your privacy (see the reference to this resource in the introduction to this chapter). Assuming your institution adheres to FERPA requirements and properly trains faculty on how to implement an accommodation plan privately, your information will be only between you and the professionals charged with helping you succeed. As a matter of fact, your instructor should know only the accommodation plan to implement and very few details about your medical record, unless you choose to share.

It may also help to know that your information isn't shared with other staff or students. Therefore, you may come across times where you feel the need to disclose because the services you're receiving don't meet your needs. For example, your in-class resources may be accessible, but research materials found when conducting library research may not. Therefore, you may be required to ask a librarian for help in getting your necessary information in a more accessible format. This may require you to disclose your situation and provide staff with proper documentation.

On another note, at times you may choose to disclose to other students in your class. For example, say you're a person who is deaf, and you've been assigned to work in a group. Your group members post that they would like to meet synchronously using the phone. You can consider a couple of options:

✓ Try to inconspicuously persuade your group to meet in a chat room.

✓ Disclose to your peers that you're a person who is deaf, and suggest using a telephone interpreting service.

Working in a group with someone who has a disability

If you're in a class where a person has disclosed publically or privately to you that they are a person with a disability, there are a few things you can do to help create a successful environment:

✔ **Maintain the person's privacy:** Whether your classmate discloses publically or privately, that is her right. Maintaining your classmate's privacy is important. Don't share any information about the disability or medical history with anyone else — inside or out of the virtual classroom.

✔ **Focus on the work at hand:** As curious as you may be, which is completely natural, keep focused on your coursework and refrain from asking personal questions about your classmate's impairment.

✔ **Don't make assumptions about your group member's abilities:** Remember that the qualifications to participate in your program are the same for every student. You will only embarrass yourself if you make assumptions about your group member's abilities to complete the assigned work based on stereotypical conjecture. If the person is not completing the work, then address the issue privately and respectfully first with that person, and include the instructor when appropriate.

✔ **Be flexible and comply with special requests when possible:** If you're asked to communicate with your classmates using alternative methods, be flexible and positive about complying with this request. For example, if you've requested to meet synchronously as a group over the phone without knowing that a group member is a person who is deaf, be willing to conduct the meeting using text chat or an interpreting service. It may take a little longer, but it's necessary.

When attending a synchronous session where an interpreter or captioner is present, use the following netiquette guidelines:

✔ Speak at a "normal" pace and articulate.

✔ Restate your name each time before speaking.

✔ If you reference something that was asked in the text messaging box, repeat the question and the name of the individual asking the question before answering.

✔ If applicable, when working in groups, use text-only chat upon request. (The captioner can't be everywhere!)

The decision is up to you. Some may interpret this as a teachable moment, whereas others may want to focus solely on the task at hand. Meeting with your accommodation team and discussing your preferences in these types of situations may help. If your instructor knows your preferences ahead of time, she can assign groups and dictate the technologies to be used without singling anyone out.

Using Assistive Technology Online

Assistive technology is a term used to describe tools that help people complete daily tasks. For example, the spell check on your word-processing program is considered an assistive technology. It helps people write faster by automatically correcting most misspelled words and highlighting those it doesn't know. This helps speed up the writing and editing process.

People with disabilities can benefit from assistive technology when they take online courses. The following sections describe a few assistive technology tools that institutions should provide and/or design coursework for.

 Depending on what accommodations you need, your institution may be able to supply some or all of the assistive technology to you for free. This doesn't mean the institution will buy your computer for you, but other resources may be available for free or reduced costs if needed. This is another reason why it's important to communicate openly with the staff member in charge of your accommodations plan.

Reading Web pages with screen readers

People who are blind or have other visual impairments often navigate the Web via sound. An application that runs in the background, called a screen reader, reads the information on the Web page using a digitized voice. Screen readers rely on good site organization and design to allow the visitor to quickly scan each site and navigate more efficiently. This technology is also helpful to students with dyslexia.

Think about how sighted people navigate a Web site. They go to the site, look to see what links are on the page, and quickly click on what interests them. The links they use may be the first thing on the page or on a navigation bar on the left of the screen. A screen reader goes to that same page and starts reading every word on the site from top to bottom. If the site is designed appropriately, the user can ask the screen reader to announce all the navigation links and headings on the page (see heading style information in the "Examples of accessibility" section earlier in the chapter). This allows the person to more efficiently browse the page and navigate to desired links.

Screen readers are software applications that either come with your computer or have to be purchased and installed separately. For example, Mac computers have a built-in screen reader, so there's no additional charge for the application and it works out of the box. Windows machines also have built-in accessibility tools including a screen reader. However, the robustness of these tools is sometimes questioned, requiring users to purchase and download an external program. For example, Windows users can purchase and download a screen reader called Jaws for Windows from Freedom Scientific (www.freedomscientific.com). It's not cheap ($895), but if your accommodations require you to use a screen reader, you may be able to get a copy of the program from your institution at a discounted price or for free. Contact the person in charge of your accommodation plan for more information.

Transcribing and captioning audio and video files

A transcript is a text-based document that provides a word-by-word account of what was said in a separate audio or video file. Providing a transcript for audio and video files is a must for making content more accessible to students with a variety of learning styles and special needs.

Another option for video files is captioning, which provides synchronized text that matches the video in real time. This allows viewers to read what is happening while seeing an image that coincides with the text. This is helpful to students who are unable to hear the audio correctly or prefer to learn by reading versus listening. Figure 18-1 illustrates a video with closed captioning.

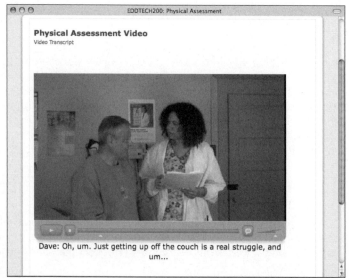

Figure 18-1:
An example of a captioned video.

Courtesy of University of Illinois Global Campus

Courses that are designed with accessibility in mind caption videos and add transcript links directly within the course where everyone can easily access them. For example, you may click on a link that has a video pop-up on it. In an ideal situation, the video would be captioned and a link to the video transcript would be directly under it. If this isn't the case, the institution may hire an internal or external resource to add captions to video or transcribe the audio on the spot. Once complete, the video is reposted and/or the transcript is provided by the instructor.

Considering accommodation options for synchronous sessions

A person with a disability can attend a synchronous (real-time) session using any of the following assistive technology tools:

- ✔ **Closed captioning:** Programs that require synchronous sessions should either provide a captioner for those events or a live video of a sign language interpreter; these options benefit students with hearing impairments.

    Videos occupy a lot of bandwidth and are often very small, making it difficult to see the interpreter's hand signs.

- ✔ **Archive links and transcripts:** In case a student misses a synchronous session or needs to review the session to better understand a topic discussed during the session, each session should be recorded and an archive link provided to all students in the course. When necessary, a written transcript of the event should also be provided by the instructor.

- ✔ **A telephone bridge:** A telephone bridge allows a person to connect to an Internet meeting by calling a phone number instead of logging on to a computer. For example, if you're a person who is blind or has other visual impairments, the screen display may not matter to you. A phone bridge allows you to call in and listen to everything that is going on without having to log in using the computer.

Part V
The Part of Tens

"It's been like this ever since Hogwarts started offering courses online."

In this part . . .

*E*very *For Dummies* book concludes with the Part of Tens, which features bite-sized pieces of key information and tips. We begin with a list of ten myths about online education. Get these straight, and you're on your way to succeeding as an online student! We conclude with a list of ten nationally recognized online schools you may want to consider researching when looking to take courses online.

Chapter 19

Ten Myths about Online Education

Despite the growing popularity of online courses, a number of myths related to online learning persist. People don't know what to make of studying and learning online. In this chapter, we bust ten of the most common myths about online education.

Online Education Is Anytime/Anywhere

Asynchronous courses have no set meeting times, and you should be able to complete your assignments whenever it's convenient for you. In theory, as long as you have a decent Internet connection, you can access course materials and submit assignments at any time.

That said, students sometimes fall into a trap with this statement because they fail to recognize that even an asynchronous course maintains a schedule. Your instructor expects you to turn in work by the stated deadlines. For example, you may be required to respond to a question on Wednesday, and then read and respond to posts submitted by your peers by Sunday. Though you can decide what time of day to submit your posts, if you don't follow the class schedule, you'll probably find yourself losing ground in the grading scheme.

The other area in which this statement becomes problematic is the "anywhere" part. In theory, you should be able to travel and do your work as long as you have a decent Internet connection. However, our experience is that online education and vacation do not mix! If you must take a two-week vacation in the midst of an eight-week course, consider rescheduling one or the other. Even if your hotel has free Internet, do you really want to stop playing on the beach to come inside and do homework? The reality is that you probably won't.

Online courses come in two flavors: synchronous and asynchronous. In a synchronous (real-time) course, you meet at a prescribed time using Web conferencing software. In an asynchronous course, you don't have a set time to meet, but you do have deadlines. Make sure you know what kind of course you're taking before you run into problems; see Chapters 2 and 4 for more about the distinction between synchronous and asynchronous classes.

Only Kids Take Online Courses

Check the statistics for some of the larger online programs, and you'll find the average online learner is middle-aged. The convenience of studying while balancing work and family attracts slightly older students to online courses. Younger, traditional-age college students are also online, but they're more likely to be blending Web-based and traditional courses at a land-based college.

The notion that young kids know how to use computers to their advantage and slightly older students do not is an erroneous assumption. Don't overlook the computer skills of working professionals. Few of us get through our workday without e-mail, shared projects, and collaboration. These are the same skills needed in online education! Chapter 2 describes groups of all ages who can benefit from online courses.

An Online Course Is a Great Way to Learn How to Use Your Computer

This statement may be true if you're enrolled in a personal development course on using a computer. However, for the kinds of courses that we discuss in this book, taking an online course to learn how to use your computer is a very bad idea. People who do this spend so much time focusing on learning to use their computer that they waste money by not learning anything about the content area of the course. Why pay $300 for a geology course and not learn about rocks?

Additionally, the instructor may not have the time or patience to walk you through every little course-related task. Even if you have 24/7 technical support, their job is to help you with software related to your course, not tell you how to use your computer.

In fairness to the other students and your instructor, learn how to use your computer well before you enroll in an online course. Chapter 3 describes the technology and technological skills you need to succeed.

Contact your local two-year college or continuing education department and see what kinds of basic computer courses they offer. Chances are very good that they have an introductory course that would be perfect for you!

You Must Be a Computer Geek to Take an Online Course

You do need to understand the basics of how your computer works and how to find files (see the preceding section), but you don't need to be a full-fledged geek to survive in an online course! Here is a short list of skills that you should have before you enroll. You should be able to

- ✔ Turn on your computer and start a Web browser (the software that connects to the Internet).
- ✔ Navigate the Web including opening links in new tabs or windows.
- ✔ Create a folder on your hard drive to store course-related information and know how to locate that information for later access.
- ✔ Open and answer e-mail with and without attachments.
- ✔ Download and install applications and application plug-ins.

Flip to Chapter 3 for more details on basic skills you need for online courses.

Online Education Is Easier Than Traditional Education

Some people assume that online education is easier than traditional education, but we don't know what "easier" means. To some people, easier means less work, but guess what? In an accredited educational program, the amount of work expected of a student is the same whether the course is delivered in a traditional classroom or online.

Here's an example: If you attend a course offered once a week in a regular classroom, the instructor may lecture or guide activities for three hours and expect you to work on your own completing readings or assignments for another six hours, resulting in a total of nine hours of active involvement in learning. The same course transferred online may deliver the lecture or activities by way of technology tools, but the assignments and the outcomes are the same. And, most importantly, you're expected to be engaged for approximately nine hours total.

Many online programs are accelerated, which has the potential of doubling your workload per course. For example, an on-campus course might take 16 weeks, whereas online, the same course covering the same amount of material may be only 8 to 12 weeks. We can't see how that's any easier. (Chapter 4 has more details on accelerated courses and programs.)

We will allow, however, that online education can be much more convenient in that you can do the work when it suits your lifestyle and schedule as long as you still meet required deadlines set forth by the instructor. (We explain this in the earlier section "Online Learning Is Anytime/Anywhere.")

Online Education Is Lower in Quality Than Traditional Education

In the early days of online education, some courses were little more than technology-enhanced correspondence courses with hardly any accountability as to how well the students learned. We've come a long way since then, and today's online courses offer the same standards and outcomes as traditional courses. Not only does research fail to reveal a statistically significant difference between online and traditional delivery methods, but it also fails to show that online courses are of lower quality. In fact, reputable institutions routinely review their courses using accepted standards of quality. Online programs are also beginning to participate in separate accreditation processes from agencies such as the United States Distance Learning Association.

Look for an accredited program or institution. Chapter 5 reviews how to determine accreditation.

Online Education Is Always Independent

While you may do a considerable amount of work independently, such as reading or writing assignments, most online courses require students to interact with each other in a manner that is far from independent. Following are two examples:

- **Discussion forums:** In discussion forums, students read one another's submissions and comment on or reply to them. This becomes a rich exchange of ideas and extends everyone's understanding of the concepts. This manner of learning is hardly independent! In fact, it can't happen without participation from multiple voices, including the instructor's. (We cover discussions in Chapters 8 and 14.)

✔ **Group projects:** Group projects are carried out online, too. Often students collaborate with peers to create a final product. These situations may require even more time and commitment specific to communicating with others than traditional classroom projects. (Flip to Chapter 12 for more information on group work.)

Taken directly from how people work in the twenty-first century (across distances and with others), teamwork rather than independence seems to rule in online courses.

Online Education Is Less Personal Than Traditional Education

An amusing video on the Internet shows a professor refusing to accept a late exam from a student. The student asks, "Do you know who I am?" to which the professor replies that he doesn't. The student jams his paper into the middle of the stack of exams, smirks, and walks away. That's impersonal!

You can't hide in an online course. Your instructor will get to know you and your ideas possibly better than he would have had you sat in a traditional classroom and said nothing. This is because the majority of online classes require participation; you can't log in and lurk and not do the work. In fact, if you try to approach your course that way, at the very least you're going to have a few intimate conversations with your instructor!

There's another explanation as to why online education is not impersonal. Have you ever noticed that some people feel free to disclose information about themselves to strangers? Some instructors report similar occurrences with online students, indicating that students are freer to share insights and personal details that support course concepts than they would if they had to face a classroom full of live people.

You Need a Webcam for an Online Class

No one needs to see you sitting in your pajamas at the computer. While Webcams have real advantages for communication, they're rarely required in online courses. For starters, you only use a Webcam if you have a synchronous component that accommodates video; for example, an office hour in a Web-conferencing tool. Even then, because Webcams require greater bandwidth, instructors may ask you to turn them off. However, it doesn't hurt to go ahead and purchase a headset with a microphone for those occasional synchronous sessions.

Most of the communication in an online course occurs on the discussion boards or via e-mail. These are not communication tools that require a real-time connection or video. If classmates are curious about what you look like, a photo works just as well. Chapter 10 introduces the basics of online communication methods.

Everyone Cheats Online

There is no evidence of greater cheating online than in a traditional classroom. Unfortunately, there's too much cheating everywhere! However, smart online instructors now design their courses to minimize the possibility of cheating and use tools to help them detect plagiarism. Cheating online simply doesn't pay because the technology is on the instructor's side. For example:

- Instructors ask for major projects to be submitted in pieces, showing prior drafts and revisions. Or, they ask for projects that are based on personal or professional circumstances knowing that no one else could possibly write about your life the way you can.

- Some institutions use very sophisticated software that checks written submissions for plagiarism.

- Finally, some instructors actually have one-on-one conversations with students where they ask questions to see whether students are able to properly articulate course materials.

A working definition of plagiarism is taking someone else's ideas and presenting them as your own without giving proper citation. In Chapter 13 we give you lots of ideas for how to avoid plagiarism, along with excellent Web links so you can find out more about how to write correctly.

Chapter 20

Ten Nationally Recognized Online Schools

*W*hile it seems almost every college in North America offers some form of online education, a handful do it exceedingly well. In this chapter, we give you contact information and notes on ten of the most widely recognized online schools, listed in alphabetical order.

These institutions have been chosen based on our personal interactions with faculty and staff, as well as our own experiences as students at a few of them. We also conducted our own research, much like the research we suggest you do, browsing each institution's Web site and calling staff to confirm information such as accreditation, the application process, program structure, and the like. However, just because we're familiar with these institutions and list them here doesn't mean there aren't other institutions out there that are just as good. As you talk to friends, family, and acquaintances who have taken online courses, you can begin to build your own list of favorites. Word-of-mouth is often the best recommendation you can get.

California State University, Chico

Center for Regional & Continuing Education
400 W. First St.
Chico, CA 95929-0250
Phone 530-898-6105
Web site http://rce.csuchico.edu/online/

Here are some of CSU-Chico's noteworthy traits:

- ✔ It offers certificates, bachelors and masters degrees, and extensive professional and personal development courses completely online.
- ✔ It's accredited by the Western Association of Schools and Colleges (WASC).
- ✔ It's considered a leader in terms of student support services and faculty development.

The California State University system is huge, and many of its campuses have been in the online education business for a long time. To see what each of its 20 campuses offers in distance and online courses, visit `www.gateway.calstate.edu/extension/Online/ol_campuses.cfm`.

Capella University

225 S. Sixth St., 9th Floor
Minneapolis, MN 55402
Phone 888-CAPELLA (227-3552)
Web site `www.capella.edu/`

What makes Capella University stand out? Take a look at a few reasons:

- ✔ It offers certificates as well as bachelors, masters, specialist, and doctoral degrees completely online.
- ✔ It's accredited by The Higher Learning Commission and is a member of the North Central Association of Colleges and Schools (NCA).
- ✔ It has a large enrollment — more than 28,000 adults.

Florida State University Online

600 W. College Ave.
Tallahassee, FL 32306
Phone 850-644-8004
Web site `http://learningforlife.fsu.edu/online/`

Here are a few reasons why Florida State University Online makes the grade:

- ✔ Undergraduate and graduate degrees and certificates are available completely online.

✔ As the school's Web site says, when you complete a degree from FSU online, there's no distinction between that degree and one you may have earned in a traditional campus-based program.

✔ All degree programs available online are regionally accredited, and some have national accreditation.

Florida Virtual School

Suite 200
2145 MetroCenter Blvd.
Orlando, FL 32835
Phone 407-513-3587
Web site www.flvs.net

The Florida Virtual School (FLVS), which caters to students from kindergarten to high school, has many impressive credentials, such as the following:

✔ Founded in 1997, FLVS is unquestionably the leader in K-12 education in the United States in terms of longevity, size, and quality. Other states' charter schools and some parochial schools use FLVS's curriculum.

✔ Florida state legislation ties funding to student performance. This regulates academic standards for curriculum and instructor qualifications, which contributes to student success.

✔ FLVU offers many programs, including summer school for Florida residents as well as out-of-state students through its Global School. A fee applies to out-of-state residents.

Kaplan University

Online Programs and Admissions
6301 Kaplan University Ave.
Fort Lauderdale, FL 33309
Phone 866-971-TIME (8463)
Web site www.kaplan.edu

Here are a few traits that make Kaplan University stand out:

✔ It offers certificates and bachelors and masters degrees completely online. It also includes Concord Law School, making Kaplan the first university in the nation to offer a law degree completely online.

✔ It's accredited by The Higher Learning Commission and is a member of the North Central Association of Colleges and Schools (NCA).

✔ Kaplan offers a variety of federal grants and other financial aid options to help you pay for school.

Nova Southeastern University

3301 College Ave.
Fort Lauderdale-Davie, FL 33314-7796
Phone 800-541-6682
Web site www.nova.edu

Nova Southeastern University offers the following advantages:

✔ Nova Southeastern has a traditional campus based in Ft. Lauderdale, but also supports a sizeable online program with undergraduate and graduate degrees.

✔ It's accredited by the Commission on Colleges of the Southern Association of Colleges. Most disciplines and programs have additional professional accreditations as well.

✔ Some of the best known names in the field of instructional technology and distance education teach in Nova's Fischler School of Education and Human Services — just ask Kevin. This is where he earned his doctorate degree.

Penn State Online

Penn State World Campus
The Pennsylvania State University
128 Outreach Building
University Park, PA 16802
Phone 800-252-3592
Web site www.worldcampus.psu.edu/

Wondering about Penn State Online? Here are a few benefits to consider:

✔ Penn State is accredited by the Middle States Association of Colleges and Schools. Many of the academic programs hold additional accreditations and endorsements from professional associations and agencies.

✔ It offers undergraduate and graduate degrees, including postgraduate and undergraduate certificates.

✔ Penn State has been a pioneer in the field of distance education for over 100 years. Penn offered its first correspondence course in 1892.

University of Phoenix

4615 East Elwood St.
Phoenix, AZ 85040
Phone 866-766-0766
Web site www.phoenix.edu/

The University of Phoenix is a leader in online education for the following reasons, among others:

- ✔ It's unquestionably the giant in the higher education market as the largest private institution. The University of Phoenix enrolls over 420,000 students.

- ✔ It's accredited by The Higher Learning Commission and is a member of the North Central Association, and offers more than 100 degree programs ranging from the bachelor to the doctorate levels, along with certificates.

- ✔ The university maintains numerous campus sites throughout the United States and Canada for students who prefer some face-to-face instruction.

Walden University

155 Fifth Ave. South
Suite 100
Minneapolis, MN 55401
Phone 866-492-5336
Web site www.waldenu.edu

Walden University offers many advantages, such as the following:

- ✔ It's accredited by The Higher Learning Commission and is a member of the North Central Association.

- ✔ It offers degree programs from the bachelor to the doctorate levels, along with endorsement and certificate programs.

- ✔ Walden is part of the Laureate International Universities network, a for-profit organization that coordinates educational opportunities around the world in 20 countries.

Western Governors University

4001 South 700 East, Suite 700
Salt Lake City, UT 84107-2533
Phone 866-225-5948
Web site www.wgu.edu

Western Governors University (which serves all 50 states, despite its name) is tops for the following reasons, among others:

- ✔ The university takes a unique approach with competency-based courses. You complete a course when you prove mastery of the competencies, however long (or however little time) that takes.

- ✔ Programs include bachelors and masters degrees with specialized endorsements.

- ✔ It's nationally accredited by the Distance Education and Training Council (DETC) and regionally accredited by the Northwest Commission on Colleges and Universities.

Index

• *B* •

• *F* •

• R •

Business/Accounting & Bookkeeping

Bookkeeping For Dummies
978-0-7645-9848-7

eBay Business
All-in-One For Dummies,
2nd Edition
978-0-470-38536-4

Job Interviews
For Dummies,
3rd Edition
978-0-470-17748-8

Resumes For Dummies,
5th Edition
978-0-470-08037-5

Stock Investing
For Dummies,
3rd Edition
978-0-470-40114-9

Successful Time
Management
For Dummies
978-0-470-29034-7

Computer Hardware

BlackBerry For Dummies,
3rd Edition
978-0-470-45762-7

Computers For Seniors
For Dummies
978-0-470-24055-7

iPhone For Dummies,
2nd Edition
978-0-470-42342-4

Laptops For Dummies,
3rd Edition
978-0-470-27759-1

Macs For Dummies,
10th Edition
978-0-470-27817-8

Cooking & Entertaining

Cooking Basics
For Dummies,
3rd Edition
978-0-7645-7206-7

Wine For Dummies,
4th Edition
978-0-470-04579-4

Diet & Nutrition

Dieting For Dummies,
2nd Edition
978-0-7645-4149-0

Nutrition For Dummies,
4th Edition
978-0-471-79868-2

Weight Training
For Dummies,
3rd Edition
978-0-471-76845-6

Digital Photography

Digital Photography
For Dummies,
6th Edition
978-0-470-25074-7

Photoshop Elements 7
For Dummies
978-0-470-39700-8

Gardening

Gardening Basics
For Dummies
978-0-470-03749-2

Organic Gardening
For Dummies,
2nd Edition
978-0-470-43067-5

Green/Sustainable

Green Building
& Remodeling
For Dummies
978-0-470-17559-0

Green Cleaning
For Dummies
978-0-470-39106-8

Green IT For Dummies
978-0-470-38688-0

Health

Diabetes For Dummies,
3rd Edition
978-0-470-27086-8

Food Allergies
For Dummies
978-0-470-09584-3

Living Gluten-Free
For Dummies
978-0-471-77383-2

Hobbies/General

Chess For Dummies,
2nd Edition
978-0-7645-8404-6

Drawing For Dummies
978-0-7645-5476-6

Knitting For Dummies,
2nd Edition
978-0-470-28747-7

Organizing For Dummies
978-0-7645-5300-4

SuDoku For Dummies
978-0-470-01892-7

Home Improvement

Energy Efficient Homes
For Dummies
978-0-470-37602-7

Home Theater
For Dummies,
3rd Edition
978-0-470-41189-6

Living the Country Lifestyle
All-in-One For Dummies
978-0-470-43061-3

Solar Power Your Home
For Dummies
978-0-470-17569-9

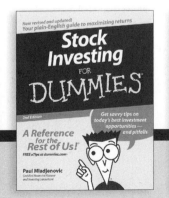

Available wherever books are sold. For more information or to order direct: U.S. customers visit www.dummies.com or call 1-877-762-297
U.K. customers visit www.wileyeurope.com or call (0) 1243 843291. Canadian customers visit www.wiley.ca or call 1-800-567-4797.

Internet

Blogging For Dummies,
2nd Edition
978-0-470-23017-6

eBay For Dummies,
6th Edition
978-0-470-49741-8

Facebook For Dummies
978-0-470-26273-3

Google Blogger
For Dummies
978-0-470-40742-4

Web Marketing
For Dummies,
2nd Edition
978-0-470-37181-7

WordPress For Dummies,
2nd Edition
978-0-470-40296-2

Language & Foreign Language

French For Dummies
978-0-7645-5193-2

Italian Phrases
For Dummies
978-0-7645-7203-6

Spanish For Dummies
978-0-7645-5194-9

Spanish For Dummies,
Audio Set
978-0-470-09585-0

Macintosh

Mac OS X Snow Leopard
For Dummies
978-0-470-43543-4

Math & Science

Algebra I For Dummies
978-0-7645-5325-7

Biology For Dummies
978-0-7645-5326-4

Calculus For Dummies
978-0-7645-2498-1

Chemistry For Dummies
978-0-7645-5430-8

Microsoft Office

Excel 2007 For Dummies
978-0-470-03737-9

Office 2007 All-in-One
Desk Reference
For Dummies
978-0-471-78279-7

Music

Guitar For Dummies,
2nd Edition
978-0-7645-9904-0

iPod & iTunes
For Dummies,
6th Edition
978-0-470-39062-7

Piano Exercises
For Dummies
978-0-470-38765-8

Parenting & Education

Parenting For Dummies,
2nd Edition
978-0-7645-5418-6

Type 1 Diabetes
For Dummies
978-0-470-17811-9

Pets

Cats For Dummies,
2nd Edition
978-0-7645-5275-5

Dog Training For Dummies,
2nd Edition
978-0-7645-8418-3

Puppies For Dummies,
2nd Edition
978-0-470-03717-1

Religion & Inspiration

The Bible For Dummies
978-0-7645-5296-0

Catholicism For Dummies
978-0-7645-5391-2

Women in the Bible
For Dummies
978-0-7645-8475-6

Self-Help & Relationship

Anger Management
For Dummies
978-0-470-03715-7

Overcoming Anxiety
For Dummies
978-0-7645-5447-6

Sports

Baseball For Dummies,
3rd Edition
978-0-7645-7537-2

Basketball For Dummies,
2nd Edition
978-0-7645-5248-9

Golf For Dummies,
3rd Edition
978-0-471-76871-5

Web Development

Web Design All-in-One
For Dummies
978-0-470-41796-6

Windows Vista

Windows Vista
For Dummies
978-0-471-75421-3

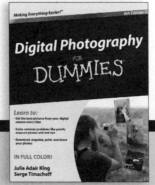